P9-AFW-628

# A CHRONOLOGICAL HISTORY OF THE EUROPEAN UNION 1946-2001

# A Chronological History of the European Union 1946-2001

Wim F.V. Vanthoor

Assistant Manager of the Research Department and head of the Historical Section, De Nederlandsche Bank, the Netherlands

Edward Elgar

Cheltenham, UK • Northhampton, MA, USA

Published by
Edward Elgar Publishing Limited
Glensanda House
Montpellier Parade
Cheltenham
Glos GL50 1UA
UK

Edward Elgar Publishing, Inc.
136 West Street
Suite 202
Northampton
Massachusetts 01060
USA

A catalogue record for this book
is available from the British Library

**Library of Congress Cataloguing in Publication Data**
Vanthoor, W.F.V. (Willem Frans Victor)
  A chronological history of the European Union, 1946-2001 / Wim F.V. Vanthoor.
      p. cm
  Includes index.
    1. European Union countries—Economic conditions—Chronology. 2. Monetary policy—European Union countries—History—Chronology 3. Europe—Economic integration—History—Chronology. I. Title

HC240. V258 2002
330.94'055—dc21                                                    200202170


ISBN 1 84376 101 7

Printed and bound in Great Britain by
Biddles Ltd, Guildford and King's Lynn

# Contents

# List of abbreviations

| | |
|---|---|
| BIS | Bank for International Settlements |
| BLEU | Belgo-Luxembourg Economic Union |
| CAP | Common Agricultural Policy |
| CEEC | Committee for European Economic Co-operation |
| CEPS | Centre for European Policy Studies |
| CFA | Coopération Française en Afrique |
| COMECON, CMEA | Council for Mutual Economic Assistance |
| CSCE | Conference on Security and Co-operation in Europe |
| DIW | Deutsches Institut für Wirtschaftsforschung |
| DM | Deutsche Mark |
| EAGGF | European Agricultural Guidance and Guarantee Fund |
| EBRD | European Bank for Reconstruction and Development |
| EC | European Community |
| ECB | European Central Bank |
| Ecofin Council | Council of Economic and Finance Ministers |
| ECSC | European Coal and Steel Community |
| ECU | European Currency Unit |
| EDC | European Defence Community |
| EEA | European Economic Area |
| EEC | European Economic Community |
| EFTA | European Free Trade Association |
| EIB | European Investment Bank |
| EMA | European Monetary Agreement |
| EMCF | European Monetary Co-operation Fund |
| EMF | European Monetary Fund |
| EMI | European Monetary Institute |
| EMS | European Monetary System |
| EMU | Economic and Monetary Union |
| EPC | European Political Community |
| EPU | European Payments Union |
| EPU | European Political Union (1962 on) |
| ERDF | European Regional Development Fund |
| ERM | Exchange Rate Mechanism |
| ERP | European Recovery Programme |

| | |
|---|---|
| ESCB | European System of Central Banks |
| ESFRC | European Shadow Financial Regulatory Committee |
| EU | European Union |
| EUA | European Unit of Account |
| Euratom | European Atomic Energy Community |
| Eurostat | European Statistical Office |
| FRG | Federal Republic of Germany |
| GAB | General Arrangements to Borrow |
| GDP | Gross Domestic Product |
| GDR | German Democratic Republic |
| IMF | International Monetary Fund |
| LMI | Luxembourg Monetary Institute |
| MCA | Monetary Compensatory Amount |
| NAFTA | North American Free Trade Association |
| NATO | North Atlantic Treaty Organisation |
| NCI | New Community Instrument |
| OECD | Organisation for Economic Co-operation and Development |
| OEEC | Organisation for European Economic Co-operation |
| OPEC | Organisation of Petroleum Exporting Countries |
| SDR | Special Drawing Right |
| SEA | Single European Act |
| WEU | Western European Union |

# Preface

This edition is a revised and enlarged version of the book *A Chronological History of the European Union 1946-1998* published in 1999. It contains an additional report of relevant items within the European Union in the period from 1999-2001. For that reason the series of recorded events, begun in 1946, ends now on 31 December 2001, at the eve of the physical introduction of the euro in the twelve countries forming the Economic and Monetary Union (EMU).

EMU is the outcome of a long and complicated process. It started immediately after World War II – the start of this chronology – and suffered many ups and downs before the Treaty of Maastricht was signed in 1993. With the birth of the euro on 31 December 1998, followed by the launch of euro notes and coins on January 1, 2002, monetary integration can be regarded as accomplished in Western Europe. For that reason this compendium logically ends at this date. However, this does not mean that the process of rapprochement has ended. At the European Summit in Laeken, Belgium, in December 2001, the heads of state agreed on a declaration on "The Future of the European Union". As this book makes clear, this item has been a question of ongoing deliberations in the past fifty years. Commission President Prodi predicts that the euro will force countries to intensify policy co-ordination. From that point of view, one can say that the European Union (EU) is getting ready for the next stage: political unification. Looking back at the history of European integration, we see that the effort to achieve closer political integration is a difficult process. With the creation of EMU the European Union has reached a kind of interim phase.

Regarding the period 1999-2001, the development of the euro's exchange rate against the dollar runs as a leitmotiv through the events reviewed. Notable are, on the one hand, the interest rate decisions made by the European Central Bank (ECB) Governing Council and, on the other hand, the comments and statements made by the ECB President, the individual Council members, presidents of the National Central Banks (NCB's) of the EMU-area and ECB watchers.

A comment to the previous Chronology is that since the beginning of the 1990s the information has become much more detailed than in the years before. The reason for this, what may seem, a rather unbalanced approach is that European integration really gained momentum with the fall of communism and the unification of Germany making the EU Treaty possible within a very short time. In this edition, the introduction of the euro and the working of the ECB in the previous three years justifies, in the author's view, a continuation of the high degree of detailed information.

In Appendix I the relevant articles of the EC Treaties referred to in the Chronology are mentioned. Appendix II shows the redistribution of voting weights within the Council of Ministers as decided at the Nice Summit meeting in December 2000.

This chronology is interspersed with quotations of relevant addresses, orations and comments by politicians and persons closely involved in that process during the period under consideration. It goes without saying that these people are of different nationalities. For that reason the author considered it useful to present their words not in the original language but to translate them into English. Although he knows that by doing so it cannot be guaranteed that these quotations have exactly the same connotation as in the original documents, he justifies that method for the purpose he wants to use them: to get insight into the views of the main actors on the European integration process over the past fifty years.

I am particularly grateful to Professor Dr. Martin Fase, Professor Dr. Lex Hoogduin and Dr. Joke Mooij for their valuable comments. My appreciation is expressed to Rob Vet for his technical assistance. It goes without saying that the responsibility for the views expressed in this Chronology and for possible errors in the quotations used remain fully with the author.

Wim F.V. Vanthoor

# Introduction

The *tableau historique* presented in this Chronology reveals that, in the post-war drive for monetary co-operation between West European countries, the attainment of political union – referred to by Winston Churchill in 1946 as the United States of Europe – was on the one hand a perpetual bone of contention in the struggle for integration while on the other it was always kept in view as its ultimate objective. Quite soon after the war it had already become apparent that political integration was not a practicable policy objective owing to conflicting national interests of the countries which had been involved in the war. Nevertheless they were all definite about one thing: never again should there be a war between Germany and France on European soil. For that reason – partly as a result of American pressure – a plan was developed in the early 1950s for achieving political rapprochement in Western Europe by a circuitous route, namely through the way of economic integration. This idea took shape with the establishment of the European Coal and Steel Community (ECSC) between the Benelux countries, France, Germany and Italy. In his declaration on 9 May 1950 the French Minister for Foreign Affairs Robert Schuman announced that there was no doubt about the underlying motives for this plan: the ultimate aim of the ECSC was to form a European federation, though the word "federation" was not given any strict legal significance. The ECSC was followed by the Treaty of Rome in 1957 which established the European Economic Community (EEC) and the Atomic Energy Community between the six ECSC countries. The Preamble of the EEC treaty speaks of "an ever closer union among the European peoples", expressing their mutual political links. Those links were equally clearly expressed by the "Action committee for the United States of Europe" set up a short time before by one of the founding fathers of the Treaty, the Frenchman Jean Monnet. This committee comprised representatives of political parties and trade unions from the six EEC countries.

The idea of political integration divided Europe from the outset. On one side were those countries which favoured the supranational approach (Germany, supported by the Benelux countries plus Italy) while on the other side some countries did not want to go further than a European organisation of and between national states. For this intergovernmental approach France was an outspoken advocate. At the first meeting of heads of state and government held in Bonn in July 1961, the Six were still united in their determination "to give shape to the will for political union". This was to be achieved by creating the "Union of Peoples" in a statutory form. In that same year the French Fouchet Committee even drafted a treaty on European Political Union (EPU) in which the "Union of States" as it was called would operate alongside the existing Economic Community in such fields as foreign policy, defence and culture. When, however, this committee extended the intergovernmental character of its proposals in its second draft, negotiations had to be postponed, after which they were never resumed. It was the French President General Charles De Gaulle who, in May 1962, called a united Europe a "myth". In his opinion it could never be more than a confederation, or to use his own words, a "Europe of states". All the same, in *Initiative 1964* the European Commission still referred with some optimism to the interim phase of the existing Communities on the road to political union. It said that this phase should comprise two elements: expansion of European union to include areas other than economic policy and improvement of the European institutional structure. The first element meant achieving a common defence, foreign and cultural policy. The second aspect concerned merger of the executive bodies of the Communities and the Communities themselves. This meant a better apportionment of democratic responsibility, especially participation by the European Parliament in the legislative and above all the budgetary procedure of the Community.

In its intergovernmental approach to European integration France was largely alone among the group of Six. French rejection of the principle of supranationality as enshrined in the Treaty of Rome came to a head in June 1965 when French delegates walked out of the EEC intergovernmental conference ("empty chair" crisis) and refused to return unless majority voting was dropped. According to the principles of the EEC Treaty, this system of decision-making was to become much more widespread in the final phase of transition to a Common Market commencing on 1 January 1966. At the beginning of 1966 the five agreed to this French demand in the famous "Luxembourg Compromise", which caused the Frenchman Robert Marjolin, another founding father of the Community, to make the forlorn remark that with this "strange legal construction the idea of a federal Europe made its last appearance". For that reason the indirect method was accorded even greater prominence than before by giving maximum priority to economic and monetary integration. This was done at the December 1969 summit in The Hague, where the heads of state and government of the six EEC member states decided on a plan to be implemented in stages with the aim of achieving EMU within ten years. The Luxembourg Prime Minister Pierre Werner was in charge of developing this plan.

The Werner Report which was published in October 1970 highlighted the sensitive issue and thus gave a new impetus to the aim of European integration. In the Report's view, the essential feature of the future EMU was to be the transfer of national sovereign powers in the field of monetary and economic policy. With the establishment of a "Community system of central banks" and a "centre for making decisions on economic policy", there could be no turning back on the road to political integration. EMU was therefore seen as the key interim phase on the road to political union in Europe. "In the last analysis, the development which has started aims at political unification of Europe. It is true that we need not achieve a European confederation or federation tomorrow. But to arrive at the ultimate goal we must first take the step of creating an economic and currency union," said Werner, commenting on the report in an interview on the same day. The plan was welcomed in Germany but encountered obdurate resistance in France because of the supranational approach. In the end, little of the stated aim was achieved. Owing to the turmoil in the international exchange rate system – the Bretton Woods System came to an end in March 1973 – and France's reluctance to commit itself by precisely defining the successive stages, EMU remained stuck in the first stage.

With the failure of the Werner-style EMU, Western Europe languished in a vacuum during the 1970s. A great deal was said, written and discussed but nothing was actually achieved. Though the Community was strengthened by the accession of Denmark, the United Kingdom and Ireland, this was not enough to liberate it from the atmosphere of "sclerosis" on Europe where many people were keen to pay lip service to political co-operation. "European Union" became the buzz word, a vague term which was launched at the Paris summit in 1972 – where political ideas were absent – as an arrangement which would transform all relations between Member States. Equally vague was the declaration about the "European identity" adopted at the Copenhagen Summit in December 1973, though there was also pressure for a more precise definition of European Union which would include a future EMU. In April 1974 a study group was formed on this subject, led by Robert Marjolin, which came to the conclusion that "Europe is no nearer than in 1969".

Whenever the subject of EMU arose, the question of supranationality proved to be the hot potato. In Paris at the end of 1974, the heads of state and government – hoping to improve the efficiency of the European Council of

Ministers – pressed for abandonment of the Luxembourg Compromise and hence the current practice of deciding unanimously on all matters. On the twenty-fifth anniversary of the Schuman declaration on 9 May 1975, Valéry Giscard d'Estaing, who had now succeeded Georges Pompidou as the French head of state, said that the task of bringing about a real union was still far from complete. On that same occasion the Federal German President Walter Scheel referred to the now traditional idea that political union would be bound to result from the progress of economic integration, which he believed had all too often been used to postpone political decisions. In June 1975 the European Commission produced a report which said that creating EMU was an essential element of European Union. While the need for a common economic and monetary policy was emphasised it also admitted that there was currently no real political consensus on the matter because there was insufficient mutual trust to assign to the Community executive institutions the powers which they must necessarily be granted. In his introduction the Belgian Prime Minister Leo Tindemans after whom the report was to be named said that he had deliberately refrained from offering a blueprint for the ideal Europe. He therefore confined himself to what was realistic and feasible by submitting proposals whereby the Community exchange rate arrangement (the snake), as a zone of monetary stability, was to serve as the basis for a new approach. At the end of December 1976 the European Council in The Hague adopted a resolution which regarded the creation of EMU as vital to the consolidation of Community solidarity and the establishment of the European Union.

The meaning the Tindemans-approach was soon to become apparent. Since EMU had been chosen as an intermediate stage on the road to EPU. However, no progress could be achieved. Because of the underlying "threat" of a supranational economic policy, the focus of the debate shifted, after the mid 1970s, from economic to monetary integration. Nevertheless, it was the then President of the Commission, Roy Jenkins, who at the first Jean Monnet lecture in Florence on 27 October 1977 managed to make the connection between monetary union and political integration by referring to the comment made by Jaques Rueff in 1949: *"L'Europe se fera par la monnaie ou ne se fera pas."* [Europe will be created by means of a single currency or not at all.] The Jenkins speech ushered in the plan launched in July 1978 by the French President Giscard d'Estaing and the German Chancellor Helmut Schmidt in Bremen for establishing the European Monetary System (EMS), which was to lead to a "zone of monetary stability in Europe". On 13 March 1979 the system came into operation with all EEC countries, except the United Kingdom, taking part. The EMS created a new currency – the ECU (European Currency Unit) as a weighted average of all EMS currencies.

In the ensuing years the EC Member States were to learn a great deal from the EMS. Insufficient co-ordination of monetary policy was the reason why the plan for consolidation of the system within two years of its launch came to nothing. Nevertheless, in political terms, the system certainly did achieve what Chancellor Schmidt had intended, namely to anchor West Germany more firmly in Western Europe, although the way it happened was different from what he might have expected in 1979. It was the German *Bundesbank* that, by its consistent stability policy, made the German mark the yardstick of the system so that Germany took the leading role in the EMS. France was more or less forced to submit to Germany's monetary discipline which actually happened in 1983 at the insistence of the newly appointed French Minister for Finance Jacques Delors. Looking back over ten years of the EMS the EC Council of Ministers concluded at the end of the 1980s that the system had resulted in lower inflation and more stable exchange rates, though it did press for greater convergence, especially in the field of budgetary policy.

The drift away from the concept of political union towards the EMU approach and from there to the EMS was far removed from what the founding fathers had intended in Rome in the mid 1950s. At the Congress of Europe which was held in Paris on 9 May 1980, to commemorate the thirtieth anniversary of the Schuman declaration, it was confirmed that the intergovernmental approach to political union in Europe had failed, prompting urgent calls on the Community institutions and national governments to take the necessary measures so that the Community could develop into a federal structure. That idea was refined a year later in the Genscher-Colombo Plan in which Germany and Italy proposed a European Act which would transform relations between the Member States Greece included) into a European Union in which economic integration was to be paralleled by political co-operation. In June 1983 the ten heads of state and government signed the Solemn Declaration on European Union in Stuttgart. However, in so doing the Member States merely promised to give a general political impetus to European integration. In June 1984 the European Council in Fontainebleau decided to set up an ad hoc committee to suggest ways of improving European co-operation in both the economic and political fields. In the spring of 1985, the majority of that committee came out in favour of majority voting, strengthening the powers of the Commission and the European Parliament – in short: greater integration. They referred to a common political will which should take the form of the establishment of a genuine political entity between European countries, i.e. a European Union (EU). In that same year the acts of accession were signed whereby Portugal and Spain joined the European Community.

The determination to deepen the process of political integration more or less automatically focused attention on economic union, which was making insufficient progress despite the disciplinary effect of the EMS. It was Jacques Delors who, in 1985, launched the plan for the creation of an internal market in goods, services, capital and labour. This plan was embodied in the White Paper on the completion of the internal market, published by the European Commission. In Milan it was decided that the internal market should be completed by no later than 1992. The linking of economic and political integration was expressed in the Single European Act which came into effect on 1 July 1987. The Act amended and expanded the EEC Treaty by extending the scope of qualified majority voting and laid down new procedures for foreign policy co-operation. But Delors, who had now been appointed as President of the European Commission, went a step further by arguing that the advantages of such an internal market could only be achieved by introducing a single currency which would eliminate exchange rate risks and high transaction costs. At the European Council meeting in Hanover it was decided to set up a committee headed by Delors to produce a blueprint for EMU. The Delors Report which was published in 1989 proposed achieving EMU in three stages. In July of that same year the European Council in Madrid decided to start the first stage of EMU on 1 July 1990. Strong commitment on the part of the leading European politicians that went hand in hand with the collapse of the communist system in Eastern Europe in the autumn of the same year brought the Delors Plan to a successful conclusion. In December 1991 the *Treaty on European Union* was concluded in Maastricht: it contained the final blueprint for EMU, including a timetable for the introduction of the euro in 1999. It also contained vague provisions on the European Political Union (EPU) as part of the EU. On the occasion of the fortieth anniversary of the Schuman declaration on 9 May 1990 the chairman of the European Parliament, Baron Crespi, referred to EMU and EPU as the final aims which Schuman had in mind in 1950. He stressed that the political union would create a new dimension for Europe. Mr. Crespi firmly believed that Schuman would have said now: "let it be realised as soon as possible". In 1995 Austria, Finland and Sweden joined the EU which now comprised fifteen Member States, of which twelve take part in the EMU.

One of the primary reasons for realising EMU so quickly was that after 1989 monetary integration came under political pressure whereby France and Germany played the leading roles. History shows that in the past fifty years the views of both countries on European integration did not run parallel. Although France as well as Germany wanted a broadening and simultaneous deepening of the European Union, this desire concealed differing national interests. For Germany, many years crippled by war-guilt, a European federation was the only way to obtain political influence. For France, integration was first and foremost the way not only to safeguard French influence, but also to remain the main power on the European continent. And the best way to realise that was political co-operation on an intergovernmental basis leaving national power unaffected. These different and perhaps conflicting views determined not only the quality of monetary integration but also its pace and speed. It was the unification of Germany in 1989 that created for both countries a new point of departure. Germany needed the support of France for its unification. France was prepared to agree, not only on political grounds – the continuance of Germany's orientation on Western Europe had a high priority – but also for monetary reasons: by the creation of a European Central Bank and a European single currency France would be freed from the monetary power of the *Bundesbank* and would get a stronger grip on the monetary policy decision making process in Europe. Germany accepted this on the condition that price-stability and the independence of the ECB were secured.

With the birth of the euro European integration has entered a new phase. Twelve EMU countries have transferred their monetary powers to the ECB in Frankfurt. Its primary objective is to achieve and maintain price-stability. Against this background, most ECB watchers will also find little cause for complaint about the bank's steering of interest rates in the past three years. In the newspapers, the way in which the ECB communicates has been mentioned sometimes as a weak spot. It indicates that the bank still has a brief tradition and is going through a learning process.

In its brief history, the euro has already dealt successfully with some external shocks and crises. There was the Asian crisis in 1997-1999, and an oil-price shock in 1999-2000. The low level of turbulence within the euro area contrasts with much sharper reactions to similar events in the period before EMU existed. The euro withstood the worst-case scenario when it kept financial markets in Europe stable following the horrible terror attacks in the United States on September 11, 2001. Had such an event occurred in the old times of the EMS, European exchange markets would certainly have come under heavy pressures leading to realignments within the ERM with negative consequences for economic growth. That this did not happen may be regarded as one of the (greatest) achievements of the euro.

European policy makers have created a monetary union that is designed to last. But institutional features alone do not guarantee EMU's success. Commitment to the union is called for. One of the ways this commitment can be ensured is the political union the Maastricht Treaty has in prospect. The question is whether political unification will prove helpful in preserving the stability of EMU. There are two different points of view on this matter.

The first view favours the historical approach. After all, the history of the 19th century monetary unions in Europe shows that political unification has rarely, if ever, been preceded by economic and monetary integration. In this respect EMU is unique, not only because national central banks have transferred their sovereignty to a supranational central bank, but also because never before national currencies have been replaced by a common currency. However, monetary union cannot, in this view, stand alone. Will it be successful, then the stage of intergovernmental co-operation should be overcome in the other policy areas in order to move on to truly common European policies. Within this framework, some historians wonder whether Europe, with the introduction of the euro, will begin to liberate itself from what they call a political standstill. In other words will the euro bring about the "ever closing union" as promised in the EEC Treaty of 1957? The answer is not unambiguous. In order to fulfil the role of driving force behind political integration, the Stability and Growth Pact is seen as a commitment which bears a risk for future instability in the longer term. There is little doubt that the Pact will stand, but there is room to fudge: the decision to impose a fine which exceeds the deficit limit is not automatic; it is subject to a lengthy political approval process involving the European Commission and the member states which may accept a non-commitment for political reasons. According to this view, the only way to guarantee ongoing fiscal discipline would be a budget for the euro-zone as a whole. This would call for a European Ministry of Finance which can issue directives on budgetary policy. Subsequently a political union would be realised.

The other view thinks in terms of the existing unique mixture of supranational characteristics and the insistence on national sovereignty Europe has embraced from the inception of the ECSC to the present day. Consequently EMU does not require a full-fledged political union. It was *The Economist* which, in 1999, pointed out that the old arguments against an EU dominated by national governments have ceased largely to apply. One argument was that these governments would always be too preoccupied with national interests to pursue a true European course.[1] But over forty years the realities of EU membership have reshaped governments and political leaders. Acting together, they show themselves finer and bolder judges of European

---

[1] "Europe's future", *The Economist*, 23 October 1999, pp. 16-17.

policies than is the European Commission that has lost much of its political authority in recent years. This development has set a new intergovernmental tone as seems from the fact that governments have for instance reserved to themselves and not to the Commission, the early development of a common foreign and security policy. On the question, where all this is to be going, the answer might be towards a confederate model. A Europe built along these lines would never be a strong political actor. It would, however, continue as a formidable economic entity allowing the euro to become an international currency in its own right.

The foregoing makes clear that thinking about European integration is strongly influenced by the way in which integration has already taken shape. From this point of view, ECB President Duisenberg's remark that in the past three years the monetary union has worked quite well without a political union is understandable.[2] It is not denied that the path chosen is not the usual "one political entity-one currency" route but that does  not exclude a European Union which is moving slowly but steadily towards more convergence in the other policy areas. This view is also shared by Commision President Prodi who calls the euro a symbol of European unity which will be more so in the future. Describing the common currency  as "a little piece of Europe in our hands" he predicts "an increase in European identity" and, in the long term, a euro "synonymous with the EU in the same way that people associate the dollar with the USA".[3] His remarks underscore how the euro has always been more a political than an economic project.

It is, however, this political dimension of the euro which creates a dilemma. Within the EU members agree that EMU has to be a part of a wider process of European integration, but they do not yet agree either on its substance or form. The EU Summit in Laeken has clearly illustrated that figuring out what type of union to form and how much power to give it, remains a serious problem for the future. Two camps have argued bitterly over this question for already more than fifty years. One of those camps, which includes Germany, wants to give Brussels more decision making authority and make the EU into a federal state, with more powers over its individual members. The other camp, including France, prefers the EU remaining an alliance of powerful nation states. Consensus must be found between the German concept of the "United States of Europe" and  the French concept of the

---

[2] M. Kurm-Engels, R. Nahrendorf, "Die währungsunion funktioniert auch ohne Politische Union" [The monetary Union works without Political Union], *Handelsblatt*, 14 December, 2001.
[3] P. Norman, "Prodi hails 'symbol of European unity' ", *Financial Times*, 2 January, 2002.

"United Europe of the States." Today's politicians are aware that political integration will not easily go beyond the minimum required for economic integration. With this in his mind, ECB chief economist Issing does not regret that, as far as economic and monetary affairs are concerned, the Maastricht Treaty did not initially go further in terms of political integration. Nevertheless he agrees that it remains indispensable for the success of EMU that congruent institutional arrangements and appropriate behavioural patterns can now develop.

But even then, we must realise that if the euro does boost European political union, it will be in a different manner than before. As the British journalist Peter Norman recently noted, the Maastricht Treaty marked the zenith of "top down" EU policy-making in which leaders exemplified by the former German Chancellor Helmut Kohl and the French ex-president François Mitterand prescribed far-reaching changes for their citizens which barely attempted to explain and still less to consult.[4] The weaknesses of this approach were clearly shown in 1992 when a Danish referendum rejected the Treaty. The convention to which the Laeken Summit concluded will be an attempt to institute a "bottom up" approach to EU reform.

The foregoing remarks do not, however, damage the conclusion that the introduction of the euro implies a big leap forward in the European integration process which nobody could have foreseen twenty years ago. It also shows that the way to further integration will be a gradual but an irreversible one. In this respect the Belgian economist Paul de Grauwe[5] may be right in predicting that political union will be realised within the next twenty years.

[4] See note 3.
[5] R. Vahl, " 'Maak van de euro geen machomunt'. Econoom De Grauwe: monetare unie slaagt alleen met politiek unie" [Don't let be the euro a "power currency". Economist De Grauwe: monetary union will only succeed in a political union], De Nederlandsche Bank, *DNB Magazine* 6, 2001, Amsterdam.

# CHRONOLOGY 1946-2001

## 1946

19 September
At the University of Zurich the British politician, Sir Winston Churchill,[1] advocates setting up a sort of *United States of Europe* with France and the defeated Germany playing the leading role: "We must set up a sort of United States of Europe ... We all need to put the horrors of the past behind us and turn to the future ... There can be no revival of Europe without a spiritually great France and a spiritually great Germany. The structure of the United States of Europe, if well and truly built, will be such as to make the material strength of a single state less important ... If at first all the states of Europe are not willing or able to join the Union, we must nevertheless proceed to assemble and combine those who will and those who can." And he goes on: "In this undertaking which is so urgently necessary, France and Germany together must take the lead. The United Kingdom, the British Commonwealth, mighty America and I hope the Soviet Union, too, ... Must be the friends and protectors of the new Europe and defend its right to live and prosper".[2] Churchill does not see Britain's place as being in Europe but "in its national grouping", the Commonwealth.

## 1947

1 January
In Germany the American and British occupation zones are merged (Bizonia). December 1948 sees the start of negotiations between France, Britain and the United States on merger with the French zone and an occupation statute which will apply pending a *peace treaty with Germany*. In April 1949 the allied powers reach agreement on the conditions for the merger and the text of the statute.

---

[1] Winston Churchill (1874-1965) is regarded as one of the pioneers of post-war European integration.
[2] "Winston Churchill – In Memoriam", *Bulletin of the European Economic Community*, 1965, no. 2, p. 5.

| | |
|---|---|
| 5 June | In a speech at the University of Harvard the American Secretary of State G. Marshall talks about *financial aid for Europe*. He asks for a programme to be set up that "should be a joint one, agreed to by a number, if not all, European nations".[3] Led by France (R. Marjolin, J. Monnet, G. Bidault) and Britain (E. Bevin), a programme is designed which will go down in history as the *European Recovery Programme (ERP)*. |
| 27 June-2 July | The Soviet Union walks out of the *tripartite conference* in Paris. The Russians only want to accept American aid if there are no strings attached. As a result, the Soviet Union and its satellite states are left out permanently. |
| 12 July | Paris sees the start of a conference by the *Committee for European Economic Co-operation (CEEC)* with sixteen European countries taking part plus Canada and the United States as observers. The participants agree with the American view that reintegration of the German economy in Europe is essential for raising the prosperity of Europe. The western occupied zones in Germany have to be included in the European Recovery Programme. |
| 20 August | The United Kingdom decides to abandon the *convertibility of sterling*. |
| 28 August | France imposes *restrictions on imports* which must be paid for in dollars. Imports of cereals, coal and some other essential goods are excluded. |

1948

| | |
|---|---|
| 1 January | The common customs tariff is introduced between Belgium, Luxembourg and the Netherlands putting |

[3] T. Bainbridge with A. Teasdale, 1995, *The Penguin Companion to European Union*, Harmondsworth, p. 322.

the *Benelux customs union* into effect.[4] This is based on the Customs Agreement of 5 September 1944 providing for a common customs tariff between the three countries.

17 March — Signing of the Treaty on Economic Social and Cultural Co-operation and Collective Self-Defence by France, the United Kingdom and the Benelux countries. This is known as the *Treaty of Brussels* in which the countries named undertake to help one another in the case of renewed German aggression. The treaty is concluded for fifty years and subsequently forms the basis for the Western European Union (WEU) which comes into being on 20 October 1954.

3 April — President H. Truman of the United States signs the *Foreign Assistance Act 1948* whereby the American Congress decides to grant financial aid to Europe from 1948 to mid 1952 on condition that the aid is granted for one year at a time and a permanent European organisation is set up "to guide Europe on the road to recovery".[5]

4 April — Signing of the *North Atlantic Treaty Organisation (NATO)*.

16 April — The *Organisation for European Economic Co-operation (OEEC)* is set up in Paris with seventeen member countries (Spain joins in 1959). Its aim is to promote the balanced expansion of the European economy by allocating the American money. During the preparatory talks, the United Kingdom presses for an intergovernmental structure with a council of

[4] Benelux incorporates the BLEU (Belgo-Luxembourg Economic Union) set up in 1921 for a period of fifty years commencing on 1 May 1922. Between 1940 and 1945 it was disbanded. Since 1971 the BLEU has been tacitly renewed for ten years at a time. The two countries hold joint gold and currency reserves, the Belgian franc and the Luxembourg franc have a 1:1 exchange rate and are legal tender in both countries.
[5] Under the Economic *Cooperation Act* of 1948, the United States granted Europe straight economic aid worth around fifteen billion dollars. *The Mutual Security Acts* of 1951 to 1957 provided mainly for military aid (defence support).

ministers deciding unanimously and the Secretary General to be appointed without any powers of his own. France is in favour of a partly supranational organisation, e.g. by letting the Secretary General himself take certain decisions. The United States want to expand the supranational element still further, but do not do so for fear of giving the impression of wanting to dictate what Europe should do. In the end, Britain wins. The OEEC becomes a totally *intergovernmental organisation*, i.e. the decision-making body is the Council of Ministers which can only pass decisions if the voting is unanimous. Day-to-day activities are run by an Executive Committee in which the Ministers are represented by their officials. There is also a Secretary General (the first one being the Frenchman, R. Marjolin[6]) who is subordinate to the Council and the Executive Committee and is responsible for supervising the implementation of decisions passed by the two bodies.[7]

20 June

In the three western occupied zones of Germany the *Erste Gesetz zur Neuordnung des Geldwesens (Währungsgesetz)* [First Law on the Reorganisation of the Currency System (Currency Act)] comes into force. This introduces the *Deutsche Mark* (DM) to replace the *Reichsmark*, in circulation since 1924 (the exchange rate with the dollar is set at DM 3.33).

20 July

In the Russian zone of Germany the *"Deutsche Mark der Deutschen Notenbank"* [German Mark of the German Bank of Issue] is introduced.

[6] R. Marjolin (1911-1986) had played an important role in the French *Résistance* where he met J. Monnet with whom he worked closely on the reconstruction of France and of Europe via the ERP or Marshall Plan. From 1948 to 1955 he was the Secretary General of the OEEC. When the EEC was set up in 1957, he became Vice-President of the first European Commission, a post which he held until 1967.

[7] As the counterpart to economic co-operation in Western Europe, the communist countries of Central and Eastern Europe set up Comecon or the CMEA (Council for Mutual Economic Assistance) in January 1949. The countries involved were Bulgaria, Czechoslovakia, Hungary, Poland, Romania and the Soviet Union. They were later joined by Albania (1949-1961), the GDR (1950), and some non-European countries: Mongolia (1962), Cuba (1972), and Vietnam (1978). After the collapse of the Soviet Union, Comecon was disbanded in September 1991.

## 1949

| | |
|---|---|
| 4 April | In Washington, twelve countries sign the treaties forming the *North Atlantic Treaty Organisation*. The members are Belgium, Canada, Denmark, France, Iceland, Italy, Luxembourg, the Netherlands, Norway, Portugal, the United Kingdom and the United States. The treaty enters into force on 24 August 1949.[8] |
| 5 May | Establishment of the *Council of Europe* by ten countries (Belgium, Denmark, France, Ireland, Italy, Luxembourg, The Netherlands, Norway, Sweden and the United Kingdom) joined by Greece and Turkey in August 1949. The Council's aim is to establish closer co-operation between the members and stimulate their economic and social development. This institution now has 40 member countries plus five candidates for membership. The Council of Europe is a compromise between the advocates of supranational integration and those favouring intergovernmental co-operation. It is in this Council that Churchill first launches the idea of a European army.[9] |
| 8 May | In the West German occupied zones, the *Grundgesetz* [Basic Law] is passed by the Parliamentary Council. On 12 May the military governors approve the Basic Law and proclaim the Occupation Statute. |
| 24 May | Establishment of the *Federal Republic of Germany (FRG)*. |

[8] Greece and Turkey joined in 1952, followed by West Germany in 1955 and Spain in 1982 (endorsed by a referendum on 12 March 1986).
[9] The other member countries are: Iceland and Germany (1950), Austria (1956), Cyprus (1961), Switzerland (1963), Malta (1965), Portugal (1976), Spain (1972), Liechtenstein (1978), San Marino (1988), Finland (1989), Hungary (1990), Poland (1991), Bulgaria (1992), Estonia, Lithuania, Slovenia, the Czech Republic, Romania (1993), Andorra (1994), Albania, Latvia, Moldavia, Ukraine, the former Yugoslav Republic of Macedonia (1995), Russia and Croatia (1996). Armenia, Azerbaijan, Belarus, Bosnia/Herzegovina and Georgia are the candidates for membership. Since 1989 the Council of Europe has operated primarily as a consultative body for the countries of Central and Eastern Europe.

| | |
|---|---|
| 28 September | *Devaluation* of the DM ($1 = DM 4.20). |
| 7 October | Establishment of the *German Democratic Republic (GDR)*. |

### 1950

9 May

Official announcement of the *Schuman Plan* ("Schuman Declaration") for establishment of a common market in coal and steel. The plan is devised by J. Monnet, head of the French "Commissariat du Plan".

20 June

Paris Conference on the Schuman Plan with six countries taking part: the Benelux countries, the Federal Republic of Germany, France and Italy. Belgium and the Netherlands object to the *supranational character* of the Plan which they do not wish to support until the full political, economic and social implications are set down in writing.

25 June

North Korea's invasion of South Korea signals the start of the *Korean War*.

1 July

The *European Payments Union (EPU)* enters into effect, with the members of the OEEC taking part. The aim of the agreement is to promote free trade in goods in Europe and free financial traffic by introducing a multilateral payment system.

24 October

The French Prime Minister R. Pléven proposes a European Defence Community (EDC) for countries involved in the Schuman Plan. The *Pléven Plan* provides for establishment of a European army which will be responsible for the defence of Western Europe jointly with American and British divisions in NATO.

### 1951

18 April

The Treaty establishing the *European Coal and Steel Community (ECSC)* is signed in Paris by the Benelux countries, the Federal Republic of Germany, France and Italy. The institutions comprise a High Authority with *supranational powers*, a Council of Ministers with co-ordinating functions, a Common Assembly to which the High Authority will report and a Court of Justice to settle legal disputes. According to Schuman, this is just the first step on the road to a wider objective: "In this way there will be realised, simply and speedily, that fusion of interests which is indispensable to the establishment of an economic community; that will be the leaven from which may grow a wider and deeper community between countries long opposed to one another by bloody conflicts ... This proposal will build the first concrete foundation of a European federation which is indispensable to the preservation of peace."[10] In his *Memoirs 1945-1953* the German Chancellor K. Adenauer makes the following comment on the Schuman Plan: "I was in full agreement with the French Government that the significance of the Schuman proposal was first and foremost political and not economic. This Plan was to be the beginning of a federal structure of Europe."[11]

9 June

The *state of war* between Germany and the four Allies (France, Britain, the Soviet Union and the United States) is formally ended.

9 October

Minister Schuman[12] declares in Ottawa that France wants a *European Defence Community* and a *European Political Community* alongside the existing ECSC.

10 November

Signing of the "Convention on relations between the West Allies (France, the United Kingdom, the United States) and the Federal Republic" in Paris.

---

[10] R. Pryce, 1973, "Historical development (of the EC)" in P.M. Hommes, 1980, *Nederland en de Europese eenwording* [The Netherlands and European unification], The Hague, p. 35.
[11] T. Bainbridge with A. Teasdale, 1995, *The Penguin Companion to European Union*, Harmondsworth, p. 7.
[12] R. Schuman (1888-1963) was the French Minister for Foreign Affairs from 1948 to 1953. Owing to the Schuman Plan he is regarded as one of the founders of European Union.

Under this *Dachvertrag* [umbrella treaty] the three powers recognise that the Occupation Statute is not compatible with the reintegration of the Federal Republic of Germany into Europe. On the other hand, in the light of the special international situation of the Federal Republic, they agree to maintain only those rights which are in the mutual interest of the four signatories. The text is not published pending the conclusion of negotiations on a number of other questions.[13]

### 1952

26 May

Signing of the treaty governing relations between the three West Allies and the Federal Republic and all other associated conventions. These are called the "Bonn Conventions", known in Germany as the *Generalvertrag* or *Deutschlandvertrag*.

27 May

Signing in Paris of the treaty establishing the *European Defence Community* with the six ECSC countries as members. The treaty provides for situations in which the Council of Ministers can decide by a simple or qualified majority. The institutional set-up is more or less the same as that of the ECSC though the Council of Ministers has a stronger position in relation to the Commission – which replaces the European Defence Ministry proposed by Pléven. The Council is responsible for co-ordinating the Commission's policy and that of the member states, and can issue directives to the Commission. Commission directives must be adopted unanimously. The Commission has nine members and is responsible for forming the European army and arranging recruitment. The parliamentary assembly of the EDC is the same as that of the ECSC. For EDC meetings it is joined by nine extra representatives, three from the Federal

---

[13] See: R.H. Lieshout, 1997, *De organisatie van de West-Europese samenwerking. Een voortdurende strijd om de macht* [The organisation of West European co-operation. An on-going battle for power], Bussum, pp. 167-168.

Republic, three from France and three from Italy. The Court of Justice of the ECSC will also function as the Court of Justice of the EDC.

27 July                      The *ECSC Treaty* takes effect.

## 1953

14 February                  The Dutch Minister for Foreign Affairs J. Beyen[14] proposes expanding economic co-operation between the six ECSC countries by adding a *customs community* with no internal tariff borders or trade restrictions and a common external tariff. This supranational community would have to have its own powers.

24 July                      The three *Benelux* countries sign a protocol on the co-ordination of their economic and social policy.

27 July                      End of the *Korean War*.

## 1954

24 March                     In Brussels the Foreign Affairs Ministers of the six ECSC countries decide, on France's proposal, to postpone devising a *European Political Community (EPC)*.

30 August                    The French Assembly decides by 319 votes to 264 not to discuss the *EDC Treaty*, which is tantamount to rejecting it. Prior to this, the new Mendès-France administration, which came to power in July, imposed extremely strict requirements for approval, adding yet more conditions in August, in order to undermine the supranational aspects of the EDC Treaty and give France maximum room for manoeuvre.

---

[14] J.W. Beyen (1897-1976) abandoned the principle adopted by his predecessor, D.U. Stikker, whereby European unity was subordinate to the Atlantic alliance. He considered that European unity could be an independent objective. He was against sectoral integration because of the disruption it would cause.

3 September

Talks between Monnet, President of the High Authority of the ECSC, and the Belgian Foreign Affairs Minister P.H. Spaak[15] on how to rescue the European integration process from the doldrums. Monnet stresses that he is in favour of further *sectoral integration* by expanding the ECSC to include transport and energy, and setting up a new community for the peaceful use of nuclear energy.

30 December

Signing of the *Paris Agreements* whereby the Federal Republic of Germany is to participate as a full partner in the common defence of Western Europe. The *Dachvertrag* is revised, ceasing to be a convention between the three West Allies and the Federal Republic and becoming a treaty between the four powers. In Article 2 the Allies state that they "will terminate the Occupation Regime in the Federal Republic, revoke the Occupation Statute and abolish the High Commission".[16]

1955

4 April

The Dutch Minister Beyen rejects further sectoral integration. In his opinion, the ultimate objective should be a community for the general economic integration of Western Europe. The *Beyen Plan* advocates a customs union which is to lead the way to a common market. The Beyen Plan sees the economic integration of Western Europe as the stock answer to the dangers created by the Cold War. It talks of the threat to Europe both from within "where fascist or communist powers try to destroy the democratic character of the political structure of the Western European countries" and from outside where

---

[15] P.H. Spaak (1899-1972) was a prominent figure in Belgian politics already before the Second World War. Afterwards he became one of the best known advocates of European integration and on that account an outspoken supporter of British membership of the EEC. Spaak was the first President of the ECSC Common Assembly and was also the inspiration behind a new drive for integration leading to the signing of the Treaties of Rome.

[16] M. van Ooijen, I.F. Dekker, R.H. Lieshout and J.M. van der Vleuten (eds.), 1996, *Bouwen aan Europa. Het Europese integratieproces in documenten* [Building Europe. The process of European integration in documents], Nijmegen, pp. 38-41.

"the Soviet Union and its satellites try to annex the territories of these countries".[17]

23-24 April      The Belgian, Luxembourg and Dutch Foreign Affairs Ministers (Spaak, J. Bech and Beyen) meet to discuss a common European initiative by the Benelux countries. Early in May a compromise is reached, contained in the *Benelux Memorandum* whereby the objective will be both sectoral integration and general economic integration.

5 May            The Federal Republic of Germany becomes a *sovereign state*. This means that the allied powers only retain certain rights relating to the whole of the German territory and Berlin.

6 May            Establishment of the WEU. The treaty provides for economic, social and cultural co-operation between the Benelux countries, the Federal Republic of Germany, France, Italy and the United Kingdom and Italy. The idea was mooted by the British Foreign Secretary, A. Eden. In the Paris Agreements the Federal Republic agreed to the French demand that it first become a member of the WEU before joining NATO.[18]

9 May            The Federal Republic of Germany joins *NATO*.

14 May           Establishment of the *Warsaw Pact* between Albania, Bulgaria, Czechoslovakia, the GDR, Hungary, Poland, Romania and the Soviet Union.

18 May           The *Benelux Memorandum* is sent to the governments of the other three ECSC countries

---

[17] J. Beyen, 1957, *Grondslagen voor het Nederlandse standpunt met betrekking tot het vraagstuk der Europese integratie* [Basis for the Dutch View on the Question of European Integration]. Archives of the *Nederlandsche Bank*, European Economic Community, History 1951-1957.

[18] The WEU was later extended to include Greece, Portugal and Spain. Austria, Denmark, Finland, Ireland and Sweden act as observers. Nine Central and East European countries have the status of "associate partner".

(Federal Republic of Germany, France and Italy) with a view to the conference in Messina (Italy).

1955

**1-2 June**

Conference of Messina where the six ECSC countries discuss a common market and the common development of the peaceful use of nuclear energy. The conference is dominated by the problem of reviving the concept of European integration. Following the failure of the EDC, the road to economic integration, to be achieved initially by a customs union, seems the best way of creating a united Europe. The *Rélance Européenne* [Relaunch of Europe] thus becomes reality. The German Economic Affairs Minister L. Erhard[19] is sceptical at first because he fears that a Europe of Six will soon become protectionist, and that is contrary to his liberal idea of free world trade. Via the Messina Resolution it is decided to set up a Committee of Government Representatives, headed by a "political figure", to begin preparing for the conference on the proposals made by the Benelux countries. As a member of the WEU and an associate member of the ECSC, Britain is invited to take part in the Committee's work. A few days later, Spaak is appointed as the "political figure".

**20 June**

The inaugural meeting of the *Spaak Committee* is held in Brussels. It is decided to set up eight technical committees which will pursue their work under the control of a *"Comité Directeur"* chaired by Spaak with the heads of the delegations as members.

**5 August**

Signing of the *European Monetary Agreement (EMA)* by members of the EPU. The agreement, which will take effect after abolition of the EPU provides for the establishment of a European Fund and a multilateral clearing system. The purpose of

[19] L. Erhard (1897-1977), as the German Minister for Economic Affairs (1949-1963) was the father of the *Soziale Marktwirtschaft* [social market economy] which formed the basis for what later became known as the German *Wirtschaftswunder* [Economic Miracle]. From 1963 to 1966 he was Chancellor of the Federal Republic of Germany.

the Fund will be to grant short-term loans for a maximum of two years for countries belonging to the EPU. Initial loans totalling a maximum of 20 to 25% of the Fund's available resources may also be granted to countries with only small gold or dollar reserves.

7 November    Meeting of the *"Comité Directeur"* at which Spaak states that only delegations agreeing to the idea of a *customs union* can take part in further talks.

11 November    The United Kingdom decides to withdraw its delegation from the *"Comité Directeur"*.

## 1956

18 January    First meeting of the *"Action Committee for the United States of Europe"* set up by Monnet with representatives of all political parties and trade unions in the Six countries except for the communists (and Italian socialists). Monnet rejects the attempt to achieve both sectoral and general economic integration. A resolution is unanimously adopted urging the earliest possible establishment of a community for the peaceful use of nuclear energy.

15 February    The conference of the Foreign Affairs Ministers of the Six, provided for in the *Messina Resolution*, takes place with Spaak in the chair. The earlier discord between the Federal Republic of Germany and France is now out in the open. Germany favours the common market but objects to Euratom (see 1957). Conversely, France is in favour of Euratom but sees nothing but problems where the common market is concerned. It is clear from the conference that one project will not go ahead if the other fails.

29 May    The *Spaak Report* is approved. This report formulates the creation of the Common Market (free movement of goods, services, persons and capital) as the general objective. In practice, the plan is to set up a customs union, to be achieved in three stages of four to five years each. The member states retain

power over general economic policy. The Council of Ministers is the only decision-making body; the Commission submits proposals which can only be amended by the Council acting unanimously. Supranationally, it is stipulated that the Council shall decide by a qualified majority of the votes in certain cases; however, in the case of important issues, this rule will not apply until the third stage of the customs union, scheduled to begin on 1 January 1966. The European Commission, whose president and members are appointed by the governments of the Member States and which decides by a simple majority of the votes, is responsible for the implementation of the treaty. The Court of Justice is the same as that of the ECSC. The Commission is accountable to the Common Assembly of the ECSC, where the number of members is expanded considerably and the ratio of seats is changed in favour of the three largest Member States. The functions for which Euratom is responsible are executed by the Council of Ministers, the Court of Justice and the Assembly which were provided for the Common Market. There is also a separate Atomic Energy Commission which operates on principles similar to those of the European Commission. The first President of the Commission is W. Hallstein[20] who will perform this role for nine years. In his book *United Europe: Challenge and Opportunity*, published in 1962, he remarks: "The logic of economic integration not only leads towards political unity by way of the fusion of interests; it also involves political action in itself."[21]

3 October

The United Kingdom proposes establishing a *free trade area* for the whole of Western Europe. The member countries would exempt their mutual trade

1955/56

---

[20] W. Hallstein (1901-1982), in his capacity as Foreign Affairs Minister for the Federal Republic of Germany in the early 1950s, developed the "Hallstein doctrine" which ruled out diplomatic relations with countries recognising East Germany as a state.
[21] T. Bainbridge with A. Teasdale, 1995, *The Penguin Companion to European Union*, Harmondsworth, p. 271.

from import duties but would retain their own customs tariff for trade with other countries.

## 1957

7 February

The British government explains why it rejects a customs union and spells out its willingness to negotiate on a *free trade area.*

25 March

In the Capitol in Rome, the *Treaties of Rome* are signed, establishing the European Economic Community (EEC), and the European Atomic Energy Community (Euratom). The EEC Treaty provides for the establishment of a common market within a twelve year period divided into three stages of four years each.[22]

1 July

The *EPU* is renewed for one year with the proviso that the EMA may take effect at any time. 1957 brings record levels of imbalance in inter-European payments.

1 August

Establishment of the *Deutsche Bundesbank* which begins work in Frankfurt as the successor to the *Bank deutscher Länder.*

14 August

The American President D. Eisenhower signs the *Mutual Security Act 1957*, whereby the United States continue their military and economic aid for the period from 1 July 1957 to 1 July 1958. On expiry of this agreement, American aid to Europe comes to an end.

---

[22] When Saarland was handed back to the Federal Republic on 1 January 1957, this ended the political tension between France and West Germany, facilitating real progress in trade relations between the two countries.

## 1958

| | |
|---|---|
| 1 January | The *EEC and Euratom Treaties* take effect. |
| 3 February | The Treaty on the *Benelux Economic Union* is signed in The Hague. The treaty is concluded for fifty years and provides for the free movement of goods, services, persons and capital between the three Member States. It takes effect in 1960. |
| 18 March | Establishment of the *Monetary Committee* (article 105 EEC Treaty) whose rules are approved by the EEC Council of Ministers on 25 February. The Committee's task is to promote the co-ordination of the monetary policy of EEC Member States. |
| 19 March | First session of the *European Parliament* which will from now on deal with the affairs of the ECSC, EEC and Euratom. |
| 1 April | The *European Court of Justice* begins its work for the three European Communities. |
| 3-11 July | Conference in Stresa, Italy, where the Vice President of the Commission S. Mansholt[23] lays the foundations for the *Common Agricultural Policy (CAP)*. It is agreed to support agriculture via a system of guaranteed prices instead of direct income subsidies. |
| 14 November | Negotiations in Paris on the *European Free Trade Association (EFTA)*. France declares that, in its opinion, it is not possible to set up such a free trade area under the current circumstances. |

---

[23] S. Mansholt (1908-1995) became Vice President of the European Commission on 1 January 1958. As a supporter of supranationalism he directly opposed the French President De Gaulle. In December 1968 he presented the Mansholt Plan for the structural improvement of European agriculture, which was approved by the Community in 1972. He ended his career in European politics as President of the Commission (1972-1973).

| | |
|---|---|
| 27 December | Ten European countries announce the restoration of the *external convertibility* of their currencies. The countries are: Belgium, Denmark, the Federal Republic of Germany, France, Italy, Luxembourg, the Netherlands, Norway, Sweden and the United Kingdom. |
| 29 December | The EPU is replaced by the *EMA* whereby the EPU countries decide to make their currencies convertible. The EPU is liquidated on 27 December according to the procedure laid down in the treaty. The liquid resources left over after the transfer of the EPU capital to the European Fund are divided among the creditors to reduce their claims. Under the EMA, the sums put into the monthly clearing by the former EPU Member States are no longer settled at parity but at the buying or selling rate of the currency concerned against the dollar (the actual fluctuation margin is ± ¾ % ). Before the end of the third year a decision will be taken on the conditions under which the agreement will continue. |
| | *Devaluation* of the French franc by 14.8% against the dollar. |

1959

| | |
|---|---|
| 1 January | First reduction in intra-Community *customs tariffs* on manufactured goods by 10%. |
| 1 June | In the six Member States of the EEC the *common market* becomes reality for energy products. |
| 8 June | Greece applies for *association with the EEC.* |
| 30 August | The German Minister Erhard proposes an *association* between the Six and the seven countries which will join the free trade organisation. |

## 1960

4 January

Signing of the Stockholm Convention which provides for the establishment of the *EFTA* by Austria, Denmark, Norway, Portugal, Sweden, Switzerland and the United Kingdom. Iceland joins in March 1970; Finland becomes an associate member in 1961 and accedes to the Convention at the beginning of 1986.[24]

12-13 January

*Atlantic Economic Conference* in Paris attended by eleven European countries plus the United States and Canada, with the EEC Commission also represented. In principle, it is decided to re-organise the *OEEC*, enabling the United States and Canada to become full members of the organisation. The conference is held after the unsuccessful attempt to form a large European free trade area, prompting doubt in various quarters about the benefits of the OEEC.[25] The EMA will be preserved in full within the new organisation.

9 March

Resolution by the EEC Council of Ministers[26] agreeing to the establishment of a *Economic Policy Committee* in accordance with Article 3 of the EEC Treaty. The Committee will be a forum for the consultations provided for by that article and will also advise the Commission on all issues relating to the co-ordination of the Member States' economic policy.

3 May

*EFTA* comes into effect.

11 May

The *European Community (EC)* Council of Ministers adopts the first directive for the implementation

---

[24] Following the accession of Denmark, Portugal and the United Kingdom to the European Community in 1973 and Austria, Finland and Sweden to the European Union in 1995, EFTA now comprises only Iceland, Norway and Switzerland (plus Liechtenstein).

[25] The OEEC's work in liberalising trade and payments within Europe had largely been brought to a successful conclusion at about that time.

[26] Unless otherwise stated, the EEC/EC Council of Ministers (the EU Council of Ministers since 1992) means the Council of Economic and Finance Ministers (Ecofin).

of Article 67 of the EEC Treaty regarding the liberalisation of *capital movements.*

12 May

Taking advantage of the favourable economic situation in the Community, the EC Council of Ministers decides to accelerate the pace at which the customs union will be created among the members. The aim will be to speed up the mutual *tariff reductions* in the industrial sector so that the overall reduction by the end of the first four-year period of the integration process (31 December 1961) will be 30% instead of 50%.

31 May

In a radio broadcast the French President De Gaulle states that the path to be followed must be that of organised co-operation between States, while waiting to achieve, perhaps, an imposing confederation. In the ensuing months France produces a number of proposals for intensifying *political co-operation* in Europe.

1 June

Second 10% reduction in intra-Community *customs tariffs* in the industrial sector.

5 September

At a press conference, the French President De Gaulle speaks of a plan for anchoring the *institutional structure* of the Community on an intergovernmental basis by opting for a form of political co-operation which is to make Europe independent of the Atlantic Alliance and of the United States.

10 November

The *Treaty of the Benelux Economic Union* takes effect.

14 December

Representatives of the OEEC countries and Canada and the United States sign the convention establishing the *Organisation for Economic Co-operation and Development (OECD).*[27]

---

[27] Later the OECD will be enlarged to include Japan (1964), Finland (1969), Australia (1971) and New Zealand (1973).

| | |
|---|---|
| 19-20 December | The EEC Council of Ministers approves the proposals submitted by the Commission in June concerning the CAP. During their meeting the Ministers agree that for the period 1962-1964 Community expenditure on agriculture will be financed by a system of national contributions. After that, a new scheme will be devised which will apply until the end of the transitional stage leading to the creation of a common market,[28] i.e. 1 January 1970. The new scheme must be ready by no later than 1 July 1965. |

## 1961

| | |
|---|---|
| 1 January | First additional 10% reduction in the intra-Community *customs tariffs* for manufactured goods. |
| 10-11 February | At a meeting of heads of state and government of the six EEC Member States a *special committee* is appointed, at De Gaulle's insistence, to examine the possibility of amending the Treaty of Rome.[29] The intention is to attach a particular form of political co-operation to the existing structure of the treaty. The committee is chaired by C. Fouchet. A second summit is deemed necessary because the five other Member States, including the Netherlands, do not like the French plans, fearing that they may affect the existing co-operation in NATO. |
| 4 March | *Revaluation* of the DM by 5% against the dollar ($1 = DM 4.00). |

---

[28] The Treaty of Rome defines the Common Market as freedom of movement for persons, goods, services and capital. This market should be established progressively during a transitional period of twelve years pursuant to Article 8. The Common Market in manufactured products (customs union) and agricultural products was in practice created during that period.

[29] This is the first meeting of heads of state and government which will later become known as the European Council (European Summit), not mentioned in the EEC Treaty. At first the meetings are held at irregular intervals: in Bonn (July 1961), Rome (May 1967), The Hague (December 1969), Paris (October 1972) and Copenhagen (December 1973). In December 1974 the French head of state, Giscard d'Estaing, proposed holding Council meetings three times a year with the option of additional meetings. Until 1985 a European Summit therefore took place three times a year. In the Single European Act entering into force in 1987, Article 2 of this Act establishes the Council as one of the Community institutions.

6 March                    *Revaluation* of the guilder by 5% against the dollar.

12 March                   *Basle Arrangement* whereby the governors of the
                           central banks of a number of West European
                           countries declare that they will not make any further
                           exchange rate changes and will co-operate closely on
                           the foreign exchange markets. A short time later they
                           announce that their policy is aimed at discouraging
                           currency speculation. Co-operation takes the form of
                           holding larger amounts of one another's currencies
                           than before, and short-term lending in the currencies
                           required.

27 March                   Finland becomes an associate member of *EFTA*.

6 June                     France agrees to the *second stage* of the transition to
                           a common market (in manufactured products)
                           commencing on 1 January 1962, but only on
                           condition that agreement is first reached on the
                           common agricultural policy.

18 July                    Summit meeting in Bonn where the heads of state and
                           government of the six EEC countries reach a
                           compromise on the French proposals regarding
                           political co-operation. Having resolved "to give
                           shape to the will for political union", they agree to
                           hold regular meetings to compare ideas and arrive at
                           a common outlook. The co-operation between the
                           Foreign Affairs Ministers is also to be maintained and
                           extended, particularly in the cultural sphere "where it
                           will be ensured by periodical meetings of the
                           Ministers concerned". The *"union of their peoples"*
                           will also be made statutory in character.[30]

31 July                    Denmark, Ireland and the United Kingdom request
                           negotiations on *accession to the EEC*.

---

[30] F.A.M. Alting von Geusau, "The case of European political unification", in P.M. Hommes,
1980, *Nederland en de Europese eenwording* [The Netherlands and European unity], The
Hague, p. 229.

| | |
|---|---|
| 30 August | The *OECD Treaty* takes effect. Apart from the eighteen OEEC countries, the new organisation also comprises Canada and the United States. The objectives are very different from those of the OEEC. They can be summarised as: 1) aiming for maximum economic growth and employment while maintaining the financial stability of the Member States; 2) promoting the expansion of developing countries; and 3) contributing to the growth of world trade on a multilateral, non-discriminatory basis. |
| 1 September | The first regulation on the *free movement of workers* in the Community enters into force. |
| 29 November | The French Fouchet Committee publishes a draft treaty on *European Political Union* (EPU). This "Fouchet Plan" refers to a "Union of States" which will function alongside the existing Community in such spheres as foreign policy, defence and culture. The new institution is to be run by a council of heads of state and government (or their Foreign Affairs Ministers) deciding unanimously and accountable to an assembly comprising members of the national parliaments. The plan is resisted by the Benelux countries which want to stick to the European Commission, which in their opinion takes greater care of the interests of the small members. When Fouchet further extends the intergovernmental aspect in his second draft, the negotiations are postponed until 17 April 1962, but they are never resumed, so that the Fouchet Plan is dropped. |
| 18 December | The Board of Governors of the International Monetary Fund (IMF) ratifies the *General Arrangements to Borrow* (GAB), a lending arrangement in which Belgium, the Federal Republic of Germany, France, Italy and the Netherlands (which are members of the EEC) take part. Together with the United Kingdom, Canada, Japan, the United |

States and Sweden they form the Group of Ten (with Switzerland as the eleventh associate member).[31]

### 1962

| | |
|---|---|
| 1 January | *Stage Two* of the transitional period leading towards a Common Market starts now that agreement has been reached on a common agricultural policy. |
| | Third 10% reduction in intra-Community *customs tariffs* on manufactured products. |
| 14 January | The CAP is created for the establishment of a single market for agricultural products and for financial solidarity through a *European Agricultural Guidance and Guarantee Fund (EAGGF)* |
| 1 February | France's five partners put forward an alternative plan for *political union*. |
| 5 February | De Gaulle advocates a *European confederation*. He does not want France to accept closer ties in the process of European integration. |
| 9 February | Spain requests negotiations on *accession to the EEC*. |
| 10 April | *Benelux trade agreement* with Japan followed by an agreement with Hungary on 15 December. |
| 17 April | The negotiations on *EPU* are interrupted because Belgium and the Netherlands request a decision on accession by the United Kingdom. |
| 30 April | Norway requests negotiations on *accession to the EEC*. |
| 15 May | De Gaulle rejects the "myth" of a united Europe. He opts for a *l'Europe des États*. The six EEC countries |

---

[31] From September 1973 onwards a more intimate group emerged as the G-5, comprising France, the Federal Republic of Germany, Japan, the United Kingdom and the United States. Subsequently, from 1985, Italy and Canada were added, making it the G-7.

decide to speed up the creation of the common market.

28 May

Portugal requests negotiations on *accession to the EEC*.

1 July

Further additional 10% reduction in intra-Community *customs tariffs* on manufactured goods.

29 October

The Commission submits an action programme to the EEC Council of Ministers for *stage 2* of the Common Market. This proposes that monetary union should be the objective of stage 3, entailing a revision of the EEC Treaty after 1965. The third stage relates to the period from 1966 to 1969. The proposal envisages fixed exchange rates at the end of stage 2 (1962-1965) and prior consultation on the application of the discount and cash reserve policy. For matters which are the responsibility of the Ministers for Economic or Financial Affairs and the governors of the central banks, the Commission proposes setting up a Community institution whose meetings will be prepared by the Monetary Committee. The action programme meets resistance from several Member States. *Bundesbank* Governor O. Emminger objects to prior consultation. He considers that it is sufficient for now to have closer co-operation in the Monetary Committee and the meetings of central bank governors.

1 November

The *association agreement* between Greece and the EEC takes effect.

31 December

The French President De Gaulle states that the United Kingdom must finally and unconditionally join Western Europe.

## 1963

1 January

Fourth scheduled reduction in intra-Community *customs tariffs* on manufactured products by 10%, bringing the total reduction to 60%.

| | |
|---|---|
| 14 January | At a press conference the French President De Gaulle declares that the United Kingdom is not yet ready to join the *EEC*. |
| 23 January | The French President De Gaulle and the German Chancellor Adenauer[32] sign *the Franco-German Treaty*. In 1989 the German politician and subsequent Chancellor W. Brandt remarked that the new relationship between the two countries, a friendship firmly established in the hearts of the rising generation, became a cornerstone of peace in Europe.[33] British accession to the European Communities was a problem according to Monnet: "Just before the signing, Monnet had a long talk with Adenauer and Hallstein at the German embassy. At this point he was still doing all he could to revive the talks on British entry. He told Adenauer, in no uncertain terms (which shocked Hallstein), that he could not possibly sign the treaty without reopening the negotiations. 'The efforts you have made and the glory that will be yours are in danger of being tarnished and destroyed.' Adenauer did not take offence– or the advice."[34] |
| 26 January | The Italian Prime Minister A. Fanfani criticises the *Franco-German Treaty*. |
| 29 January | Negotiations with the United Kingdom on *accession to the EEC* are broken off. As a result, the negotiations with the other countries applying for accession or association are also shelved. |

---

[32] K. Adenauer (1876-1967) was the first Chancellor of the post-war Federal Republic of Germany. In that position which he held from 1949 to 1963 he played a key role in the re-integration of the Federal Republic into Western Europe and the Atlantic Alliance (*Westintegration*). In March 1950 he proposed total union between France and Germany but it came to nothing. On 11 October 1963 he left the political arena at the age of 87.

[33] W. Brandt, 1989, *Willy Brandt Erinnerungen*, Frankfurt am Main, p. 256.

[34] F. Duchêne, 1994, Jean Monnet. The First Statesman of Interdependence, New York/London, p. 330.

| | |
|---|---|
| 1 February | The *Nordic Council*[35] (Denmark, Finland, Iceland, Norway and Sweden) decides on closer co-operation within EFTA following failure of the attempts to create a Nordic Economic Union. EFTA achieves customs union in 1960. |
| 23 March | France refuses to take part in the *WEU* meeting of Ministers because relations with the United Kingdom are on the agenda. |
| 9 May | The EC Council of Ministers agrees to the extension of the CAP and reaches agreement on the EEC's position on mutual tariff reductions. |
| 16 May | The German *Bundestag* approves the *Franco-German Treaty* declaring that it should promote unity in Europe in accordance with the objective of the European Communities. |
| 13 June | The French *Assemblée* approves the *Franco-German Treaty* without any declaration. |
| 1 July | The *Franco-German Treaty* takes effect. |
| 15 August | *Benelux trade agreement* with Paraguay, followed by an agreement with Poland on 11 September and one with Czechoslovakia on 8 November. |
| 15-16 October | The German Chancellor Adenauer resigns and is succeeded by the Minister for Economic Affairs Erhard ... "who felt closer to the British than to the French and who, for example, had been an ardent advocate of the *free trade area*".[36] |
| 1 December | A *bilateral trade agreement* between the EEC and Iran takes effect. This is the first trade agreement to |

1963

[35] The Nordic Council dates from the end of 1952 when the parliaments of Denmark, Iceland, Norway and Sweden approved a treaty on mutual co-operation (legal, cultural and social affairs and the movement of persons). Finland joined in 1955. The Council acquired more formal status in 1962 with the signing of the Treaty of Helsinki. When the treaty was revised in 1971, a Nordic Council of Ministers was set up, based in Copenhagen.
[36] R. Marjolin, 1989, *Architect of European Unity, Memoirs 1911-1986*, London, p. 339.

be concluded under the common commercial policy provided for by the Treaty of Rome. An association agreement is concluded with Turkey, providing for customs union to be achieved in three stages.

31 December     An OECD Council resolution extends the *EMA* by one year to the end of 1964. The EMA Board of Management is joined by a Spanish expert, bringing the number of members to eight.

## 1964

13 April        Decision by the EC Council of Ministers on the establishment of a *Committee of Governors of the Central Banks* of EEC Member States.

15 April        On a proposal by the Commission the EEC Council of Ministers decides to establish a *Committee on medium-term economic policy*.

8 May           Decision by the EEC Council of Ministers to establish the *Budgetary Policy Committee* which aims to increase the co-ordination of the Member States' budgetary policy.

25 May          The *Benelux Treaty* on taxes on frontier-zone trade is signed in Brussels.

1 July          The regulation on the establishment of the first common organisation of the market in agricultural products and the *EAGGF* takes effect.

3-4 July        Franco-German meeting on the possible re-opening of discussions regarding *political union* in Europe.

1 October       In *"Initiative 1964"* the Commission sets out a timetable for accelerating the completion of the customs union. The document in question also discusses in detail the intermediate phase of the Communities on the road to political union: "By the resolute European policy of the six Member States of our Community and also by the work of the

European institutions, the Communities can pride themselves on an achievement whose effects will be felt throughout the world and they have become the focus of the forces leading to political unity in Europe. However, we must not forget that this is still only the partial realisation of what is now commonly known as European 'political union' ... Nevertheless, we can also generally state that the 'economic' Communities – which have succeeded in amalgamating their economic and social policy which, without the Communities, would have remained among the political powers of the Member States – represent not only a preparation but already the first step towards 'political union'; they already form a 'political union in the economic and social sphere'. No-one can doubt that the road to the European federation leads via the existing Communities."[37] According to this document, political union comprises two elements: (1) extension of European unification to areas other than economic and social policy, and (2) improvement in the European institutional structure. The first element amounts to achieving a common policy on defence, foreign affairs and culture. The second element concerns merging the executive bodies of the communities and merging the Communities themselves. This is meant to ensure a better allocation of democratic responsibility, particularly regarding the European Parliament's involvement in the Community's legislative procedure and especially in its budgetary procedure.

4 November

The Federal Republic of Germany submits proposals to the EEC Council of Ministers for continuing European integration in the spheres of defence and cultural policy and in the economic and social sphere. With regard to *political co-operation*, it proposes adopting a phased approach. The initiative aimed at closer political co-operation in Europe must

[37] "Initiative 1964", *Bulletin of the European Economic Community*, 1964, no. 11, p.5.

be a multilateral effort which should initially be undertaken by the six countries. According to the German proposals it would be wrong to regard the work of the European Communities as a purely technical function, with "political tasks" taking second place. The common economic policy adopted by the Community means that a start has already been made on achieving political union via the Communities.

24 November            *Benelux trade agreement* with Bulgaria.

26 November            The Italian government submits proposals to the EC Council of Ministers and to the governments of the Member States on European *political unification*. The memorandum contains a draft "Declaration" which includes the following text: "The six governments whose ultimate objective is the political and economic union of a democratic Europe, confirm that the time has come to make a start on a gradual process of political unification, as the essential complement to the economic integration which is fully attainable. Such a policy will make a vital contribution towards reducing international tension, solving the issue of the developing countries and establishing equality in relations between Europe and America."[38]

2-3 December           The Council of the OECD decides to extend the *EMA* for one year to the end of 1965.

11 December            First meeting of the *EEC Committee on medium-term economic policy* which is to co-ordinate the general economic policy of the Member States. This includes drawing up a programme for medium-term economic policy over a five-year period. The first programme will cover the period from 1966 to 1970.

---

[38] "The Italian proposals on European political unification", *Bulletin of the European Economic Community*, 1965, no. 1, p. 13.

## 1965

1 January

Fifth scheduled reduction in intra-Community *customs tariffs* on manufactured products by 10%, bringing the total reduction to 70%.

31 March

The Commission submits its proposals to the EC Council of Ministers regarding the financing of the *CAP*. It also puts forward proposals for replacing the financial contributions of the Member States to the Community budget by the Community's own resources and consolidating the budgetary powers of the European Parliament.

8 April

The six EEC Member States sign the treaty on the merger of the executive bodies of the ECSC, the EEC and Euratom, establishing a single Council and a single Commission common to all the European Communities (*merger of the Executives*).

30 June

France withdraws from the intergovernmental EC talks on account of problems concerning the financing of the CAP. This conflict veils a fundamental disagreement over whether or not the Community should be supranational. France's rejection of the principle of *supranationality* as embodied in the Treaty of Rome is expressed in the French demand that no decisions shall be passed by a majority of the votes. This method of taking decisions is to become far more important in the third and final stage of the transitional period leading up to the Common Market (in manufactured products), due to start on 1 January 1966. The other five Member States want to adhere strictly to the letter and spirit of the Treaty of Rome.

1 July

The French government officially announces that the EC is in *crisis*.

6 July

The French government informs the other Member States that France's *permanent representative* to the European Communities has been recalled to the French capital Paris. Also, the French delegation will no longer attend the meetings of the EC Council of Ministers.

9 September

At a press conference the French President De Gaulle sets out the conditions on which France is prepared to continue co-operating in Brussels. All decisions must be unanimous. This brings him into serious conflict with Hallstein, the President of the European Commission, leading to the *empty chair crisis* in which the Commission simply fails to attend meetings.

26 October

In a declaration by the EC Council of Ministers France's five partners proclaim their allegiance to the EC Treaties and ask France to resume its place in the *Community institutions*.

31 December

A resolution by the Council of the OECD extends the *EMA* by three years to the end of 1968.

1966

1 January

The third and final stage of the transitional period leading up to the Common Market begins with the eighth reduction (including two additional reductions) in intra-Community *customs tariffs* on manufactured products by 10%, bringing the total reduction to 80%.

28-29 January

*Compromise of Luxembourg.* The Benelux countries, the Federal Republic of Germany and Italy agree to the French demand that in future – in deviation from the EEC Treaty – decisions of the EEC Council of Ministers will not be passed by a majority of the votes. As regards cases where the Council of Ministers was to be able to pass decisions by a majority of the votes with effect from 1966, it is agreed that these decisions will be postponed until unanimity has been achieved. This in fact creates the possibility of a national veto: "With this strange legal construct the idea of a federal Europe made its last appearance", commented R. Marjolin.[39] France resumes its place in the Community institutions.

11 May      The EEC Council of Ministers reaches agreement on the financing of the CAP up to the end of the transitional period leading towards the Common Market. It is also decided that the customs union which, according to the EEC Treaty, is to be completed by the end of the transitional period, should commence eighteen months earlier, i.e. on 1 July 1968.

15 May      *Benelux trade agreement* with the Philippines.

## 1967

17 March      *Benelux trade agreement* with Hungary, followed by new agreements with Czechoslovakia (11 April), Romania (27 October) and Bulgaria (15 December).

17-18 April      The meeting of the EEC Council of Ministers in the Munich approves a *report by the Monetary Committee* on the reform of the international monetary system. The Committee advocates the creation of Special Drawing Rights (SDRs) subject to certain conditions.

10 May      Official request from the United Kingdom to join the EEC, followed by requests for *accession* from Denmark, Ireland and Norway.

11 May      The United Kingdom re-applies to join the Community. General De Gaulle[40] is still reluctant to accept *British accession*.

---

[39] R. Marjolin, 1989, *Architect of European Unity, Memoirs 1911-1986*, London, p. 350. In his opinion the agreement was an impediment in important spheres of policy for the next fifteen to twenty years.

[40] De Gaulle retired from political life in April 1969 and died suddenly on 9 November 1970 in the French village of Colombey-les-deux-eglises.

1 July

*The Treaty on the merger of the executive bodies* of the European Communities takes effect. Reduction in intra-Community *customs tariffs* on manufactured products by 10 to 15% depending on the product.

18 November

*Devaluation* of sterling by 14.3%.

1968

12 June

The *balance of payments crisis in France* forces the country to resort to a number of safeguard measures such as import quotas, export subsidies and foreign exchange restrictions. The measures which take effect on 1 July are adopted unilaterally by France and subsequently approved by the European Commission (under the Article 108 procedure laid down by the EEC Treaty).

1 July

The EEC reaches the stage of *the Common Market (customs union)* for manufactured products. That means that the Common Customs Tariff replaces national customs duties in trade with the rest of the world.

3 October

Belgium suggests closer co-operation within the *WEU* in the field of foreign policy. France rejects this suggestion.

12 November

Acute *currency crisis* involving the French franc and the German mark in particular. Doubts over the French government's determination to defend the parity and persistent rumours of the apparently inevitable revaluation of the German mark dominate the market. The foreign exchange markets in the Federal Republic of Germany, France and the United Kingdom are closed for several days. The *Banque de France* announces a number of credit restrictions which will remain in force until the end of January 1969.

20 November

The Finance Ministers and Governors of the central banks of the Group of Ten countries agree on a *support arrangement* providing 2 billion dollars for the *Banque de France*. The French government decides not to devalue but defends the parity of the franc with stringent foreign exchange measures.

1969

13-14 January

EC Council of Ministers meeting in the Garmisch-Partenkirchen attended by the governors of the central banks of the six EEC Member States. They urge better *co-ordination* of economic development and greater co-ordination of the national objectives and policies, considered important for international monetary stability.

28 January

France abolishes the *safeguard measures* introduced in June 1968 with the proviso that the tighter restrictions introduced in the November 1968 crisis will be maintained temporarily (with the Commission's retrospective approval).

12 February

Commission memorandum containing an action programme for achieving more effective *policy co-ordination*, both by better co-ordination of the main policy objectives in the medium term (growth, employment, prices and balance of payments) and by closer co-ordination of short-term policy, particularly budgetary and monetary policy. The Commission argues that a country in difficulties should be able to obtain credit from its partners when desired in order to overcome its problems without endangering the operation of the Community. In that connection it proposes a system of monetary co-operation which is to ensure short-term monetary support and facilitate medium-term financial assistance.

1 March

In a lecture in Edinburgh, Marjolin – former Vice President of the Commission – expresses his disillusionment with Europe. He attributes this to the serious problems concerning the financing of the CAP, the failure to resolve the issue of Community enlargement and not least the fact that the

Community has remained primarily economic and technical. There has been no *break-through* to a political Community.

14 July

The Dutch Foreign Affairs Minister J. Luns[41] stresses that countries wishing to join the EEC have to accept the objectives of *political union* for Europe.

15-16 July

Resolution and joint declaration by the Action Committee for the United States of Europe. The Committee puts forward proposals addressed to the six EEC Member States for entering into negotiations with the United Kingdom and expressing the desire to move towards *political union* as soon as possible.

17 July

The EC Council of Ministers accepts the proposal of *prior consultation* on all important decisions or measures by a Member State relating to monetary policy.

8 August

*Devaluation* of the French franc by 11.1% against the dollar.

5 September

At the 40th anniversary celebrations of the Pan European Movement[42] its founder Count R. Coudenhove-Kalergi advocates an alliance between the Federal Republic of Germany, France, Italy and the United Kingdom as the first step towards a *European confederation.*

15 September

The Foreign Affairs Ministers of the six EEC Member States decide to hold a *Summit* of their heads of state and government in The Hague on 17 and18 Novem-

---

[41] J. Luns (1911- ) was the Dutch Minister for Foreign Affairs during the period 1952-1971 and Secretary-General of NATO from 1971 to 1983. With regard to European integration he was in favour of enlargement of the Community (by accession of the United Kingdom) and of extension of powers of the European Parliament.

[42] The Pan European Movement is sometimes seen as the forerunner to the idea of European Union. The Movement was founded in October 1923 by the Austrian-born Count Richard Coudenhove-Kalergi; its objective was to create a European federal union. His ideas were ardently defended by leading politicians such as A. Briand of France and G. Stresemann of Germany, but they faded into the background in the early 1930s with the rise of German Nazism. Count Coudenhove-Kalergi died on 27 July 1972 in Schruns (Austria) at the age of 77.

ber (the date is later postponed to 1 and 2 December). The Commission is invited to attend the debates relating to Community issues.

1969

19 September

In the American journal *Foreign Affairs* the leader of the British Conservative Party E. Heath[43] wonders whether the European countries can reach agreement on a system to replace American dominance in the *international monetary system*. From the political angle, he feels that a system which harmonises external policy in the EC Council of Ministers should be the first step.

29 September

The German government decides to cease intervening to maintain the *DM exchange rate* within the prescribed margins either side of the parity.

2 October

In an article published by various newspapers the Belgian politician P.H. Spaak states that the French devaluation, the crisis over the agricultural policy and the continuing monetary tension indicate the need for a *political authority*, not just to secure the Community's progress but also to safeguard what has been achieved.

13 October

Celebration of the 25$^{th}$ anniversary of the *Benelux agreement* in Brussels.

24 October

*Revaluation* of the DM by 9.3% against the dollar ($1 = DM 3.66).

28 October

The French newspaper *Le Monde* publishes extracts from the book *Pour une monnaie européenne* [For a European currency] by the Swiss writer, F. Garelli. Taking the example of the situation in Switzerland, the writer wishes to demonstrate that a single

---

[43] E. Heath (1916- ) conducted the 1961 negotiations when the United Kingdom first attempted to join the European Communities: "Government documents suggest that Heath has been misled into thinking that the talks were going well, and that the ill-feeling caused by De Gaulle's veto was compounded by French accusations that the United Kingdom had signed 'secret agreements' with Washington" (*The Times*, 1 January 1994). Heath signed the Treaties of Rome in 1972 on behalf of the United Kingdom.

currency for the six EC Member States is totally compatible with divergent financial and fiscal policies. Until the last war, customs duties and a few insignificant taxes were the sole source of all the funds for the federal budget in Switzerland. Essentially, the cantons were responsible for managing their finances and they each decided on their own budgetary policy.

1 November

The Italian Foreign Affairs Minister A. Moro says in *Le Monde* that the conference in The Hague was instigated by France, which is concerned about the development of the Community: "We expect the summit conference to provide a stimulus not only for the economic construction of Europe, but also for its *political construction.* My country has always supported this work in the belief that it is the essential complement to the integration for which the foundations were laid in the Treaties of Rome. In our opinion, the political construction for which we can prepare now, twelve years after the Treaty of Rome, cannot be confined to the present members of the Community. We believe that the re-examination of Europe's situation made possible by the forthcoming summit should facilitate this development."[44]

6 November

The German Foreign Affairs Minister W. Scheel declares that the government in Bonn will endeavour to ensure that the summit in The Hague takes decisive steps towards *economic and monetary union.* However, he does not believe that it is possible to set a date for achieving that at this stage.

14 November

In the French newspaper *L'Aurore* the Dutch Foreign Affairs Minister Luns states that European *political union* is now desirable. He would not object to the establishment of the political secretariat in Paris.

1-2 December

Conference of heads of state and government in The

[44] Communications, *Bulletin of the European Communities*, 1969, no. 12, p. 137.

Hague. In the *communiqué* they express their willingness to proceed towards the final phase of the European Community and to finalise the financial arrangements for the CAP towards the end of 1969. It is agreed that, on the basis of the memorandum submitted by the Commission in February, the EC Council of Ministers will devise a plan for achieving *Economic and Monetary Union (EMU)* by stages. The development of monetary co-operation must be based on the harmonisation of economic policy. In that connection it is decided to examine the possibility of setting up a European Reserve Fund as the culmination of a common economic and monetary policy. The President of the Commission J. Rey[45] regrets that there has been hardly any mention of political union and no discussion of strengthening the Community institutions, which he considers crucial to the progress of the Communities.

22 December  Basic agreement between the EC Member States on the future financing of the *CAP*.

1970

18 January  At a meeting in the French town of Nice, Hallstein – then chairman of the International Bureau for the European Movement – discusses the question of *sovereignty*. He says that the classic problem for a federation is the installation of a central authority taking account of the national units. The French are afraid that the nations will cease to exist. That is not so; according to the chairman, centralisation is necessary but the identity of the state must also be preserved. As regards economic and social policy he mentions the merging of sovereignty already achieved. Political integration is yet to be created, but it is there in spirit. The rest will just be a question of waiting for the right moment, he says.

[45] President of the Commission between 1967 and 1970.

9 February

Agreement between the central banks of the six EC Member States on providing *short-term monetary assistance*. The support for funds made available short-term will total 2 billion dollars. The quotas fixed at 1 billion dollars represent the amount of support which each central bank can expect (debtor quota) and the amount that it is prepared to provide by way of support for other central banks (creditor quota).

5 March

The Commission publishes a *plan in stages* for EMU. It refers to four main areas which are of particular strategic importance: a) short- and medium-term economic policy and monetary and budgetary policy; b) Community capital markets; c) taxation; and d) strengthening monetary solidarity to establish the Community as a separate monetary entity in the international monetary system. On the basis of these principles it defines three stages: an introductory stage (1970-1971), a preparatory stage (1972-1975) and the final stage for the creation of EMU (1976-1978).

6 March

The EC Council of Ministers sets up a working group headed by the Prime Minister of Luxembourg, P. Werner, to work out this plan in detail. In addition, senior officials are instructed to compile a report on European *political co-operation*, led by E. Davignon of France.

16 March

In a memorandum to the four major European powers (the Federal Republic of Germany, France, Italy and the United Kingdom), Count Coudenhove-Kalergi states that in his opinion Europe can no longer wait for the enlargement of the Common Market but should make an immediate start on a common foreign policy. The founder and chairman of the Pan European Movement believes that this *quadripartite alliance* should enable Western Europe to present a united front against Eastern Europe at the Helsinki conference.

19 March

As part of the *policy of détente*, a meeting is held in Erfurt, East Germany, between the heads of government of the two German states. This is the first official meeting since the creation of the FRG and the GDR.

22 April

Signing of the agreement on reinforcement of the powers of the *European Parliament* and the endowment of the EC with its own resources.

29 April

In an interview with an American journalist the Chairman of the Action Committee for the United States of Europe, Monnet, explains his view of the British candidacy: "In 1950 the British were not convinced by our ideas; they wanted to wait and see whether they would become reality. We had nothing to show them. Now they want to join the Common Market, not just for economic reasons but also because, via Europe, they can exert a real influence in the world which they can no longer do on their own. I do not doubt that they want to put a British stamp on the Community. But that is true of the French and Germans as well. This rivalry will have its benefits."[46] As regards the *United States of Europe*, Monnet says that this is partly a dream, but one which is becoming reality simply because it is necessary.

4 May

Following an official visit to London the Dutch State Secretary of Foreign Affairs H. de Koster announces that it is difficult if not impossible to achieve real progress in *political integration* unless the United Kingdom joins in. His Luxembourg counterpart, G. Thorn, wholeheartedly agrees.

9 May

Celebration of the 20<sup>th</sup> anniversary of the *Schuman Declaration* (the date on which the new-style Europe was born). Taped extracts are played from a speech made by Schuman on 10 December 1951 at the

---

[46] Sources, References and Communications, 1. "From day to day", *Bulletin of the European Communities*, 1970, no. 6, p. 123.

Consultative Assembly of the Council of Europe. They include the following passage: "We have never doubted the need for political integration. Our declaration of 9 May 1950 in which we proposed establishing a European coal and steel community already stated that the ultimate objective was to create a European federation, though the word 'federation' need not be taken in the strict legal sense."[47]

11 May

Proposal by the Commission to the EC Council of Ministers for introduction of a *mechanism for medium-term financial assistance*. This proposal was based on the memorandum dated 12 February 1969 concerning the co-ordination of economic policy and monetary co-operation in the Community. The maximum amount of aid is to be 2 billion units of account,[48] with individual commitments assigned as follows (amounts in millions of European Units of Account[49]): Germany: 600, Belgium/Luxembourg: 200, France: 600, Italy: 400, the Netherlands: 200.

29 June

A preferential *trade agreement* is signed in Luxembourg between the EC and Spain and Israel.

30 June

Negotiations begin in Luxembourg with Denmark, Ireland, Norway and the United Kingdom on *accession to the EC*.

2 July

At a press conference the French President G. Pompidou[50] talks of *political union* in Europe. He considers that there will be a European policy as soon as a European confederation, at least, has been

---

[47] Documents, Facts and Studies, 1. "Twenty years after the declaration by Robert Schuman on 9 May 1950", *Bulletin of the European Communities*, 1970, no. 6, p. 16. Schuman died in 1963 at Scy-Chazelles (Lorraine).

[48] It is proposed that the value of a unit of account be set at 0.88671 grammes of fine gold.

[49] The value of the European Unit of Account was 0.88867088 grammes of fine gold (Article 5 of the Statute of the European Monetary Co-operation Fund).

[50] G. Pompidou (1911-1974) was Prime Minister for France from 1962 to 1968, in which capacity he proved to be a skilful politician in the field of domestic policy. As France's President (1969-1974) he broadly continued De Gaulle's policy though he proved to be less uncompromising on Gaullist principles, especially in European affairs.

established. He discusses the varying approaches adopted by the different countries. The Federal Republic is mainly concerned about its relations with the eastern bloc and the problems caused by the division of Germany. The United Kingdom is constantly referring to its world-wide interests, especially those relating to the Commonwealth. French customs are not necessarily the same as those of its European partners. There is therefore no sense at all in saying that political union will be achieved today or tomorrow, according to Mr. Pompidou.

20 July

The Foreign Affairs Ministers accept the *Davignon Report* on the progress which can be made on political unification and consultation on external policy.

7 October

The group headed by the Luxembourg Prime Minister Werner presents a report *(Werner Report)* which proposes creating EMU in three stages, with the first one lasting until the end of 1973. The process is expected to be completed in 1980. The report refers to a "Community system of central banks" and a "centre for economic policy decision-making". The report has the following to say about the latter: "This centre must be independent, directed by the interests of the Community, and must exercise a decisive influence on the general economic policy of the Community. Since the Community budget will carry too little weight as an instrument of economic policy, the centre must be able to exert influence over national budgets, particularly on whether they should be in surplus or in deficit and by how much, and on how surpluses are spent or deficits funded."[51]

---

[51] Report to the Council and the Commission on the creation of economic and monetary union by stages in the Community, 8 October 1970, 16.956/II/70-N, p. 10. In fact the Werner Report was a compromise between the Schiller Plan presented by the German government and endorsed by Italy and the Netherlands and the (second) Barre Plan presented by the Commission and supported by France, Belgium and Luxembourg. The Schiller Plan described the route to be followed to the achievement of the ultimate goal: a common currency and complete control exercised by Community institutions, reporting to the European Parliament. The Barre Plan was vague on the precise attributes of the final stage and specified only the measures to be taken in the first stage.

EMU is seen as an intermediate phase on the road to Europe's political union. In an interview Werner acknowledges in so many words that "in the last analysis, the development which has started aims at political unification of Europe. It is true that we need not achieve a European confederation or federation tomorrow. But to arrive at this ultimate goal we must first take the step of creating an economic and currency union".[52] Reactions to the report vary. Unlike France and Belgium, Germany and the Netherlands object to a premature narrowing of the fluctuation margin for the exchange rates and to the creation of a reserve fund, proposed in the report, which is to develop into a kind of common central bank.

20 October

The Werner Plan is welcomed by the West German Minister for Economic Affairs K. Schiller. In his view the *transfer of national powers* to central institutions of the monetary union will constitute partial political union. It demonstrates that the political unification of Europe is no longer being based on theoretical considerations but on economic and political reality, the only way of achieving a viable union, according to the Minister. His Dutch counterpart H.J. Witteveen refers to the need to co-ordinate the Member States' budgetary policy. He considers a common economic policy to be essential. This means that the associated national powers must be transferred to a central Community authority.

27 October

In Luxembourg the heads of state and government approve the *Davignon Report* on political co-operation in the Community. This report expresses the belief that progress in the mutual co-ordination of foreign policy will help to promote the development of the Community and make Europeans more aware of their common responsibility.

---

[52] P. Werner, 1971, "Floating and Monetary Union – Without Monetary Union there is no Political Integration", *Intereconomics*, 6 (8), Hamburg, p. 15.

30 October

Following the Werner Report the Commission submits proposals to the EC Council of Ministers concerning the *creation of EMU by stages*. In essence, these proposals mean that the content of the intended union cannot yet be defined in detail. Although it is acknowledged that the important decisions on the budgetary policy of the Member States will have to be taken at Community level, the essential question of how and by whom it will be done is left unanswered. Instead of accepting a plan to be carried out in stages, the Commission restricts itself to Stage One which will last for three years and may be extended to five years. Failing agreement on moving on to Stage Two, which depends partly on agreeing amendments to the Treaty of Rome in order to permit the creation of the union, the monetary provisions laid down for the first stage will cease to be valid.

1970

19 November

The first meeting of EC Ministers for Foreign Affairs is held in the German town Munich in the context of political co-operation. These meetings are to take place twice a year as proposed in the *Davignon Report*.

23 November

The *Werner Report* proposals modified by the Commission come in for serious criticism in the EEC Council of Ministers, particularly from the Germans. The criticism focuses on the fact that the concept of political union has been pushed totally into the background and there is no guarantee that economic and monetary integration will take place in parallel. The proposal whereby the Council of Ministers should issue directives on monetary policy is vigorously rejected with a view to the *Bundesbank*'s independence. In the German government's opinion, this should be preserved in its entirety until the end of Stage Three.

1971

4 January

In an interview with a Paris weekly the French Minister for Defence M. Debré declares that there is no such thing as a *monetary Europe*. The Minister says that either you have a political Europe which then has a currency, or you have no Europe and no currency.

21 January

At a press conference the French President Pompidou discusses the question of Europe: "Because I believe that it is possible and necessary to construct Europe, I instigated the conference in The Hague. But what sort of Europe? ... What has been created so far can only be used as a starting point for constructing a *confederation of states* wishing to harmonise their policy and achieve economic integration. If we look at it this way, we find that the wrangling over supranationality is really senseless. If a European confederation is ever created, then it will naturally need a government whose decisions apply to all member states. The only question concerns the method of setting up such a government and what form it could take. To think that this can be achieved with technical bodies, committees, is an illusion which has already been refuted by the facts." The next important point is argued by the French President on voting procedures in the EC Council of Ministers: "How can the Council of Ministers take decisions? I would like to ask everyone, and especially our partners, to investigate how a coalition government works. If a difficulty arises and everyone is agreed on the solution, then there is no problem; otherwise you have a majority and a minority. In that case the minority may consider that it is not a matter of life and death and acquiesces to the majority decision; if that is not the case, then it breaks up the coalition. However, in our European arrangement there is clearly no possibility of a break-up, because everything would collapse. From that I infer that the important decisions have to be passed unanimously; that is an obvious political fact rather than a legal rule, and if people fail to see that, then everything is lost."[53] Following this speech, the Dutch State Secretary of Foreign Affairs De Koster declares that his government will continue to strive for a genuine European federation with supranational bodies. In this regard, Pompidou's confederation can only be regarded as an intermediate stage.

1971

24 January

Two-day consultations between the Federal Republic of Germany and France. Both countries express their willingness to create *EMU* with the four other EC partners, but no date is fixed.

8-9 February

The EC Council of Ministers approves the *plan in stages* for EMU. The Resolution which takes the Werner Report as the starting point essentially means that the content of the future EMU cannot yet be defined in detail. Although it is acknowledged that the main decisions on the budgetary policy of the Member States will have to be taken at Community level, the essential question of how and by whom this will be done is left unanswered. Instead of a plan to be carried out in stages, only Stage One is considered; this will last for three years and may be extended to five years. Failing agreement on moving on to Stage Two, which depends partly on agreeing amendments to the Treaty of Rome, the monetary provisions laid down for Stage One will cease to be valid.

14 February

In Teheran an agreement is concluded between the oil-producing countries of the Persian Gulf and the cartel comprising 23 companies, mainly American, which was set up on 16 January to conduct the negotiations. The agreement contains an increase in *oil prices*. According to the London *Times*, this agreement is a turning point in the history of the oil industry.

[53] Communications, Sources and References, 1. "From day to day", *Bulletin of the European Communities*, 1971, no. 3, pp. 105-106.

15 March            In Kiel the West German Minister for Foreign Affairs
                    Scheel tells journalists that Europe can never be
                    unified without Britain. He adds that the *accession* of
                    the United Kingdom will be possible on 1 January
                    1973 provided that the formal negotiations can be
                    concluded by the end of this year and the transitional
                    provisions can take effect in 1972.

22 March            EC Council of Ministers adopts the Werner Report in
                    its *Resolution on the creation of Economic and
                    Monetary Union* by stages. There is "political
                    willingness to realise economic and monetary union
                    within the next decade in accordance with the plan
                    which takes effect on 1 January 1971". Under
                    pressure from France, the final date is left open. The
                    Council also adopts three decisions concerning
                    greater co-ordination of short-term economic policy,
                    closer co-operation between the central banks an the
                    establishment of the mechanism for medium-term
                    financial assistance for a four-year period, starting on
                    1 January 1972 (to be automatically renewed, in
                    principle, for five years at a time thereafter). The
                    decision about the financial mechanism stipulates that
                    if a Member State faces problems or the serious
                    threat of problems concerning its balance of
                    payments, it can invoke the Community system for
                    granting mutual assistance. The Council of Ministers
                    will decide by a qualified majority on the granting of
                    such credit. The decision also sets out the
                    commitments which the beneficiary Member State
                    must enter into as regards economic policy.

29 April            In an address at the European Day in Hanover the
                    Luxembourg Prime Minister Werner suggests the
                    possibility of introducing the *future European
                    currency* as an additional reserve currency in the
                    international monetary system.[54]

5 May               *Currency crisis*: in Austria, Belgium, the Federal

[54] Communications, Sources and References, 1. "From day to day", *Bulletin of the European Communities*, 1971, no. 6, p. 143.

Republic of Germany, the Netherlands and
Switzerland the central banks abandon intervention,
causing the currency markets to close.

9 May

The Federal Republic of Germany and the
Netherlands decide to let the *German mark and the
guilder* float against the dollar. Two days later
Schiller, the West German Minister for Economic
Affairs, states that these decisions will not cause the
failure of EMU.

12 May

Since several Member States have adopted floating
exchange rates, the EC Council of Ministers proposes
a system of *Monetary Compensatory Amounts*
(MCAs) for intra-Community trade in agricultural
products, in order to preserve a common agricultural
market.

17 May

In a speech at the Paris business school the French
politician P. Mendès France and the Vice President
of the Commission R. Barre examine the problems of
Europe. Both are concerned about the lack of
*political will* in the construction of Europe. In their
opinion, the governments of the Six have not
achieved their objectives because they have not made
any effort to encourage a European political will in
their people. They also criticise the Americans' lack
of concern about the dollar.

19 May

In an interview with the Belgian newspaper *Le Soir*
the French President Pompidou makes the following
remarkable statement: "I do not pretend that Europe
should be French, nor that it should speak French.
What I do say is that, if Britain joins the common
market in the near future (which I consider likely)
and French ceases to be what it is at present,
Europe's first *working language*, then Europe will
never be really European. Because English is no
longer just the language of Britain, for the whole
world it is primarily the language of America. So

Europe will not be Europe if it is indistinguishable from America."[55]

15 August          US President R. Nixon suspends *dollar convertibility*. Europe's leading foreign exchange markets are closed from 17 to 23 August.

23 August          In the *Benelux arrangement* the Benelux countries agree to support each other's currencies to prevent the exchange rate from deviating by more than 1.5% against each other.

                   Owing to destabilising *capital movements*, France introduces a dual exchange market.

3 September        The ambassadors of France, the United Kingdom and the United States, resident in Bonn, sign the *Berlin Agreement* with the Soviet ambassador; this stipulates that transit traffic of civilians and goods between the Berlin sectors and the Federal Republic via the territory of the GDR will not be impeded.

8 September        In an interview with the French weekly *L'Expresse* the West German Minister for Economic Affairs Schiller[56] comments on German *monetary policy* and states: "Freedom means that everyone does as they like, deciding what is best in their own interests." The Minister says that, like Chancellor Brandt,[57] he has always believed that "General De Gaulle was quite right to invite Europeans to protect their

---

[55] Communications, Sources and References, 1. "From day to day", *Bulletin of the European Communities*, 1971, no. 7, p. 134.

[56] K. Schiller (1911-1994): Minister for Economic Affairs from December 1966; also Finance Minister from May 1971. When the cabinet disagreed on the introduction of foreign exchange restrictions – advocated by the Bundesbank and rejected by Schiller – on account of the dollar crisis, the Federal Government supported the Bundesbank, causing Schiller to resign in July 1972. He was in favour of letting the DM float freely.

[57] W. Brandt (1905-1993) was the Federal German Chancellor from 1969 to 1974. Under his leadership the German policy of *détente* became reality with the signing of the 1970 agreements with the Soviet Union and Poland, the *Vier-Mächte-Abkommen* [Four Power Agreement] on Berlin in 1971 and the *Grundvertrag* [Basic Treaty] between the Federal Republic and the GDR in 1972. He was awarded the Nobel Peace Prize in 1972. Brandt resigned on 7 May 1974 when his adviser, G. Guillaume, was exposed as an East German spy.

national assets".[58] Monnet, Chairman of the Action Committee for the United States of Europe, rejects this statement and says that if we go down that road it will be the end of Europe and before long the end of freedom.

17 September

25th Anniversary of *Churchill's speech* of September 1946. This is the occasion for the British Prime Minister Heath, speaking in Zurich, to draw attention to Britain's support for the creation of EMU to enable Europe to play an essential role in the new international monetary system.

1 November

In Hamburg K. Klasen, the Governor of the *Bundesbank*, advocates a small devaluation of the dollar and a modest revaluation of the other currencies. He considers that this move should be accompanied by an increase in the *fluctuation margin* to a maximum of 3%.

3 December

Summit meeting between the Federal Republic of Germany and France (this is in addition to the *regular Franco-German consultations*). Both countries urge Europe to return to realistic exchange rates with fixed parities. Franco-German co-operation will be assigned the highest priority.

18 December

*Washington Agreement (Smithsonian Agreement)* on the restructuring of exchange rates. The Japanese yen is revalued by 7.66%, the German mark by 4.61% and the guilder and the Belgian franc by 2.76%. The gold parities of the French franc and sterling remain unchanged, while the Italian lira and the Swedish crown are devalued by 1% and the US dollar by 7.89%. On the basis of the new central rates the revaluation against the dollar is 13.57% for the DM, 11.57% for the Benelux currencies, 8.57% for the French franc and 7.84% for the lira. It is also agreed to widen the margin to 2.25% on either side of the

---

[58] Communications, Sources and References, 1. "From day to day", *Bulletin of the European Communities*, 1971, no. 11, p. 131.

central dollar rate, instead of the ±1% stipulated by the IMF rules.[59] This means that at any time the margins between the EC currencies can fluctuate by a maximum of 4.5% (i.e. 9% over time).

1972

22 January

Signing of the *Treaties of Accession to the EC* by Denmark, Ireland, Norway and the United Kingdom at the Egmont Palace in Brussels. The treaties are signed by the parliaments of the Member States, except in Norway where a referendum rejects the accession.

25 January

In the French daily *Le Monde* the American professor R. Triffin expounds the view that widening the fluctuation margins as decided in Washington is liable to endanger economic union. The first step should be to define maximum fluctuation margins between the Community currencies. According to Triffin, the second step should be to reduce these margins gradually, but as quickly as possible, until they are totally abolished, as the precondition for creating the monetary union proclaimed as the ultimate objective by the Summit Conference in The Hague.

11 February

Two-day consultations between the Federal Republic of Germany and France. The French President Pompidou urges for a *European Europe* which must prove its independence of the United States. Both statesmen declare that EMU must be given a new impetus and on that account they agree on the following principles: narrowing of the fluctuation margins between the European currencies, intervention by the central banks of the EC Member States in Community currencies in the case of excessive fluctuations by one currency against another, and co-ordinated action by the central banks

---

[59] In practice a fluctuation margin of ± ¾% was maintained.

in the case of destabilising short-term capital movements. It is also decided to hold a summit in Paris shortly after the referendums in Norway and Denmark. Finally, following a plan launched by Bonn, Paris agrees to the establishment of a permanent secretariat to strengthen political co-ordination in Europe.

3 March

The Norwegian government decides that the *referendum* on joining the EC will be held on 24 and 25 September. The referendum will be consultative and parliament will take the final decision soon afterwards. The Danish referendum will be held on 2 October.

16 March

At a press conference the French President Pompidou announces that the French ought to express their views on European policy, and particularly on the enlargement of the Community, in a *referendum*. A Commission spokesman states that this is an internal matter for France, in accordance with its constitution. On 5 April the French cabinet approves the wording of the question. The referendum will be held on 23 April.

21 March

Resolution by the EC Council of Ministers on the application of the Resolution dated 22 March 1971. One of the points agreed there is that the *fluctuation margin between the currencies* of two Member States must be limited to a maximum of 2.25% by no later than 1 July 1972.

10 April

In the Basle Agreement the central banks of the six EC Member States decide to limit the fluctuation margin between the EC currencies to 2.25%. This means that the maximum fluctuation over time is 4.5% instead of the previous 9%. The agreement is known as the *European snake arrangement*. They also conclude an agreement for the very short-term financing of intervention in Community currencies.

12 April

In the British House of Commons the Labour Party

approves a motion in favour of Britain holding a *referendum* on joining the EC by 129 votes to 96.

17 April

The Chairman of the Pan European Movement Count Coudenhove-Kalergi states in an interview that a start will be made on the *political union* of Europe in 1972, though he warns against a political union extending from Lisbon to Moscow.

23 April

In the *French referendum* on the enlargement of the EC, almost 68% of the electorate are in favour of enlargement.

24 April

The European *snake arrangement* takes effect. Since the EC currencies still have margins of fluctuation against the dollar, it is called the *snake in the tunnel*.

27 April

In a speech before the French Senate, the Vice President of the Commission Barre proposes establishing a *European Fund for monetary co-operation*. The technical significance of Economic and Monetary Union is that the exchange rates between the currencies of the countries taking part are fixed and cannot be changed. This fundamental reality may automatically lead to the introduction of a single currency. The main problems which need resolving, according to the speaker, therefore do not concern the superstructure (establishment of a single central bank or a decision-making centre for economic and financial policy) but the infrastructure. The question is which structural and economic policy conditions should be met if the Union is to work without intolerable tension and not run the risk of collapsing at the first crisis, says Barre.[60]

1 May

Denmark, Ireland and the United Kingdom join the *snake arrangement*.

3 May

The Dutch Foreign Affairs Minister N. Schmelzer

[60] Communications, Sources and References, 1. 'From day to day', *Bulletin of the European Communities*, 1971, no. 6, p. 137.

announces in Paris that the Dutch government will shortly submit a working paper to the EC Council of Ministers on strengthening the Community institutions and *political co-operation*. He advocates general direct elections to the European Parliament but acknowledges that this is still a remote objective.

4 May

The 50th anniversary of the *Pan European Movement* is celebrated in Vienna. On this occasion Count Coudenhove-Kalergi calls for the creation of one great European nation.

10 May

By a majority vote of 83%, in a *referendum* the Irish opt for the accession of the Irish Republic to the EC.

18 May

In a statement before the Council of Europe, the Luxembourg Prime Minister Werner says that the decisions of 21 March 1972 mean the entry into effect of *Stage One* of EMU which will end on 31 December 1973.

22 May

Norway joins the *snake arrangement*.

18 June

In response to a question about the *United States of Europe* in a Dutch television interview, the French President Pompidou makes the following comments: "I do not believe that we shall see the end of the national states in the near future. Even if we get a United States of Europe with a single president, there will always be responsible governments. Further-more, a European Parliament chosen by general elections is certainly not in the interests of the thinly populated countries of Europe, because they would be completely trampled underfoot."[61]

22 June

Denmark, Ireland and the United Kingdom leave the *snake arrangement*. However, Ireland maintains its fixed parity with sterling.

---

[61] Communications, Sources and References, 1. "From day to day", *Bulletin of the European Communities*, 1971, no. 8, p. 156.

13 July

The British House of Commons passes the bill on *accession to the EC* at the third reading by 301 votes to 284. On 20 September the House of Lords passes the bill by 161 votes to 121.

10 August

Celebration of the 20th anniversary of the establishment of the *High Authority of the ECSC*. The Luxembourg Prime Minister Werner pays tribute to the political courage of twenty years ago and hopes that the same degree of courage will be maintained on the new road towards EMU.

21 August

The Benelux countries maintain the 1.5% fluctuation margin between their currencies *(worm within the snake)*.

8 September

The Danish parliament passes the bill on *accession to the EC* at the third reading by 141 votes to 34. This decision will be subject to the 2 October referendum.

12 September

In Rome, the EC Council of Ministers decides to establish the *European Monetary Fund (EMF)* before the end of Stage One.

26 September

In Norway almost 54% of the population votes against *accession to the EC* in a referendum.

2 October

In the Danish referendum, 63.5% of the electorate votes in favour of *accession to the EC*.

10 October

Denmark rejoins the *snake* after a positive outcome to the referendum on accession to the EC.

19-20 October

The first Summit of the enlarged Community is held in Paris. The heads of state and government confirm that during 1973 the necessary decisions are to be taken to allow transition to Stage Two of the unification process on 1 January 1974, in accordance with the aim of creating EMU by 1980. It is again confirmed that economic and monetary integration will proceed in parallel. They decide to set up a *European Monetary Co-operation Fund (EMCF)* before 1 April 1975, as the forerunner of a federal system of central banks to be established in the final stage. They also agree that political consultation must be intensified and that the Foreign Affairs Ministers should meet four times a year from now on instead of twice. Since the delegates have stated that their primary objective is to convert all relations between the Member States into a European Union (EU) by the end of the decade, in full observance of the existing agreements, they request the Community institutions to draw up a report on this subject by the end of 1975 for submission to a subsequent summit.

24 October  The OECD Council decides to end the *EMA* as from 31 December 1972.

30-31 October  Resolution by the EC Council of Ministers in which the Member States declare their aim of limiting the increase in *consumer prices* to 4% in 1973 (excluding the effect of changes in indirect taxation).

4 November  In a letter to the Dutch parliament, the Dutch Foreign Affairs Minister Schmelzer states that the Netherlands will only co-operate on the transition to *Stage Two* of EMU if it can be sure that the Community will have substantially wider decision-making powers and the European Parliament can exert a decisive influence on policy.

22 November  In a lecture held in Rome, Fouchet, a former French Minister, talks about the *political unification* of Europe. He believes that the supranational Europe is inevitably doomed to failure. Fouchet regrets that the recent Summit Conference did not yield any political conception. Achieving that would have been the first step towards a united Europe. Without a united Europe, Fouchet foresees a less than glorious future for all European countries.

5 December  In the *Revue de Défense Nationale* the French Defence Minister M. Debré writes that there can be no clearly defined European policy because there is

not and cannot be a European defence system. He attributes the controversy over the Community institutions primarily to the absence of solidarity. If there were a constant threat, then people would feel the need for a common defence system and hence their connection with their European homeland, but that situation does not apply, according to Debré.

18 December

The Committee of Central Bank Governors takes measures to increase the elasticity of the *EC intervention system*. Intra-marginal intervention is allowed, i.e. intervention before the currencies reach their bottom rate. The Committee also agrees to the more flexible application of the settlement rules.

1973

1 January

Denmark, Ireland and the United Kingdom join the *European Communities*. The EC's free trade agreement with Austria, Portugal, Sweden and Switzerland takes effect.

8 January

The central banks of Denmark, Ireland and the United Kingdom accede to the *agreement of the central banks* of the EC dated 9 February 1970.

18 January

In a commentary on his government policy statement the West German Chancellor Brandt confirms that the creation of European unity as defined by the latest Summit in Paris is the primary objective of his foreign policy. In that connection he mentions the 10th anniversary of the *Franco-German Treaty* which, in his opinion, has led to a fundamental understanding between the two countries.

22 January

Italy introduces a *dual exchange market* as a result of destabilising capital movements.

27 January

The French Finance Minister V. Giscard d'Estaing says that the American plan for automatic exchange rate regulation is impracticable. According to the Minister, the *international monetary system* is sick because gold has been banned; gold should therefore be reintroduced. In principle, gold is the natural foundation of the system and France will endeavour to create a single gold market as soon as possible. If the gold price is increased and dollar convertibility is restored, France will abolish the dual exchange market, the Minister says.

7 February

In view of the currency crisis, the West German Chancellor Brandt stresses in Brussels that it is high time to look for a European solution and that *European monetary union* is more than just words.

12 February

*Devaluation* of the dollar by 10% (new official gold price: 42.2 dollars per fine ounce). The crisis on the international currency markets forces the German government to impose capital restrictions at the beginning of February. Nevertheless, the *Bundesbank* is obliged to intervene on a massive scale, buying the equivalent of almost 6 billion dollars in the first nine days of February.

13 February

Italy leaves the *snake arrangement.*

26 February

According to the Belgian Deputy Prime Minister W. de Clercq the Community Member States should negotiate as a bloc with the United States on reform of the *currency system*. The essential aim should be to end the role of the dollar as a reserve currency, which enables America to cover its deficit by issuing its own currency.

1 March

The *currency crisis* comes to a head. The US dollar reaches its lower limit on the European currency markets. The German *Bundesbank* intervenes to the tune of 2.8 billion dollars. The next day the currency markets are closed, and remain so until 19 March. The EC Council of Ministers meets on 4 March and 8 March to discuss the situation.

6 March

In the House of Commons the British Chancellor of the Exchequer A. Barber sets out the conditions on

1972/73

which the British government will accept *a fixed parity* for sterling: unlimited and unconditional support by the Community Member States and their acceptance that the United Kingdom may reserve the right to adjust the parity subsequently after consulting the EC Council of Ministers.

11-12 March    The EC Council of Ministers publishes a *communiqué* announcing the *decisions* to take effect on 19 March:
− the maximum fluctuation margin between the German mark, the Danish crown, the Dutch guilder, the Belgian franc, the Luxembourg franc and the French franc is kept at 2.25%. For Member States operating a dual exchange market, this obligation applies only to the regulated market;
− the central banks are no longer required to intervene if the fluctuation margins against the dollar are reached;
− to protect the system against destabilising capital movements, the directive of 21 March 1972 will be more rigorously applied and new control instruments will be introduced if necessary.

The British, Irish and Italian members state that their governments will conform as soon as possible to the decision to maintain the Community fluctuation margins. To that end the Commission will submit the proposals which it deems necessary by 30 June 1973. Prior to that date it will present its report on the modifications to short-term monetary assistance and the conditions for the gradual pooling of national reserves.

The German government's representative announces that a limited adjustment to the central rate of the DM will be made before the currency markets open.

15 March    In the local press, Luxembourg's Prime Minister Werner comments on the *currency crisis*: "At first sight, the worst was avoided, namely Community currencies floating individually against one another

and against the dollar. A very solid and significant core of European currencies has been formed and we are continuing with the essential work for the first step along the road to monetary union, namely reducing the fluctuations between the European currencies."[62]

19 March

The currency markets re-open and the measures adopted on 11 and 12 March take effect. The central rate of the DM is revalued by 3% against the other five snake currencies and the currencies of Denmark and Norway. The Benelux countries maintain their mutual fluctuation margin of 1.5%. The United Kingdom, Ireland and Italy allow their currencies to float. Sweden links its currency to the snake. Introduction of this system marks the end of the *Bretton Woods System*, the "snake in the tunnel" becoming a "snake in space".

30 April

The Commission presents the EC Council of Ministers with the action programme for *Stage Two* of EMU which will last from 1 January 1974 to 31 December 1976. The programme includes the preparation of flexible, quantitative five-year estimates of the main economic variables. For the purpose of implementing some of the recommended measures, a directive will be drawn up to promote stability, growth and full employment in the Community. The co-ordination of budgetary policy will be reinforced, particularly by a regular examination of the execution of government budgets. In the monetary sphere, the co-ordination of monetary policy is to be reinforced and the exchange rate system extended to all Community currencies. The EMCF will be in charge of own resources. The introduction of a monetary unit of account is also envisaged, which is gradually to be assigned more extensive functions than just those of a unit of account.

[62] Communications, Sources and References, 1. "From day to day", *Bulletin of the European Communities*, 1973, no. 3, p. 134.

11-14 May          At the European Congress in London, Monnet is awarded the European Movement Prize for his contribution to European unification. In his speech of thanks he says that the crucial question is whether Western Europe can bring itself to agree to the *transfer of decision-making power* from the national states to the Community institutions.

22 May             In the British *Financial Times* Commissioner A. Spinelli[63] talks about co-operation between Europe and America. He warns that *European Union* is still in its infancy. This means that Europeans will have to make an extra effort to prevent the European body of thought from degenerating into a rag-bag of divergent and often conflicting points of view.

1 June             The *EMCF* takes effect. In its first phase of operation the Fund is to ensure a) the mutual consultation necessary for the Community's exchange rate system to function properly; b) pooling of the balances resulting from central bank intervention in Community currencies; and c) management of very short-term financing as regulated by the agreement of 10 April 1972 and short-term monetary assistance under the agreement of 9 February 1970 (to which the central banks of Denmark, Ireland and the United Kingdom acceded on 8 January 1973).

22 June            Italy has recourse to *short-term monetary assistance* totalling 1.8 billion dollars.

28 June            In accordance with the conclusions of the European Council on 19-20 October 1972 and the decision by the EC Council of Ministers on 14 February 1973, the Commission has drafted a report on the

---

[63] A. Spinelli (1907-1986) was a lifelong supporter of federalism. In June 1941, with a small group of Italian Resistance fighters, he wrote a *Manifesto* on cigarette papers, giving rise to the *Movimento Federalista Europeo* which was established in August 1943. His contribution to the *Draft Treaty establishing the European Union* (drawn up in the early 1980s and adopted in February 1984) was his last positive action without which, according to J. Delors, the *Single European Act* adopted in the 1990s could never have come about. See: T. Bainbridge with A. Teasdale, 1995, *The Penguin Companion to European Union*, Harmondsworth, p. 422.

*adjustment of short-term monetary assistance and the gradual pooling of reserves.* As regards short-term monetary assistance, it proposes raising the maximum debtor positions to six times the current quotas.[64] The official reserves are to be pooled by 20% stages, starting on 1 January 1974, so that total pooling will be achieved in 1980.

1973

29 June

*Snake realignment*: the central rate of the DM is revalued by 5.5% against the other snake currencies.

3 July

Opening in Helsinki of the *Conference on Security and Co-operation in Europe (CSCE)*. Thirty five countries take part.

10 July

In an article published in the French journal *Preuves* the West German Minister for Economic Affairs Scheel wonders whether a genuine Economic and Monetary Union can work without transferring any significant powers to the Community: "Our hopes are founded on a European government which, whenever the interests of the Community so require, can take action and make prompt, effective decisions involving everyone. But to have a European government we must have real control by a democratic parliament. It is time to rectify the *parliamentary deficit* in Europe, i.e. to extend the powers of the European Parliament.[65]

26 July

In the French journal *Le Monde* Commissioner Spinelli discusses the content of *European Union* in detail: "Of course, if we want a European Union, we cannot demand that the details of its external policy, social policy, etc. be specified in advance. Where the governments need to reach mutual agreement is on the need to entrust the definition and execution of all

---

[64] These quotas are as follows (in million European Units of Account): 300 each for Germany, France and the United Kingdom, 200 for Italy, 100 each for the Benelux countries, 45 for Denmark and 17.5 for Ireland.
[65] Communications, Sources and References, 1. "From day to day", *Bulletin of the European Communities*, 1973, no. 7/8, p. 120.

these policy functions to European governmental, parliamentary and judicial institutions in which all our peoples feel represented and associated. The Summit Conference has committed itself to discussing this Union in 1975 and creating it by 1980. However, we cannot wait that long. There is only one European institution which, by its nature and the traditions of our democracies which it represents, can draw up and approve the design of a constitution for the Union and thereby ensure that all public authorities of our countries will have taken part. That is the European Parliament. If people argue that its members were not sent to Strasbourg with that mandate, then we only need to invite all national parliaments to confirm or renew their delegations and give them the mandate. This need only take two weeks. No other Community institution would have the necessary qualities to be the constitutive legislative body for the Union. The Commission is supranational but does not have adequate political roots. The Council does have this quality, but because it is not at all supranational in character it is unsuited to this task. If it were to take this on, it would very soon hand over the job to diplomats who would ruin everything. The European Parliament is therefore the institution which the nine Community governments should invite to draw up the draft for a European Union that would then be ratified by the national parliaments. It would undoubtedly take one or two years to bring this work to a successful conclusion."[66]

10-11 September

At their meeting in Copenhagen the EC Ministers for Foreign Affairs present a second report[67] on political co-operation (*Copenhagen Report*). It centres on the European identity and the dialogue between Europe and the United States. One of the points made is that

[66] Communications, Sources and References, 1. "From day to day", *Bulletin of the European Communities*, 1973, no. 7/8, p. 124-5.
[67] The first report was published on 27 October 1970 and is known as the "Luxembourg Report".

the co-operation between the Nine in the foreign policy sphere must be such as to enable Europe to make its own contribution to international equilibrium. Openness, progress, peace and co-operation are part of Europe's mission. According to NATO-Secretary General Luns the progressive unification of Western Europe and the confirmation of its own identity are especially evident in the economic sphere, while the same cannot yet be said of political unity. He says that this lack of political unity threatens to be a serious obstacle in the search for a solution to the issues arising in relations between Western Europe and the United States. He proposes that the Foreign Affairs Ministers should meet four times a year. Also, a group will be set up comprising European correspondents working in the national ministries of foreign affairs; it will be called the "Group of Correspondents" and its task will be to monitor the implementation of political co-operation. According to the wording of the Luxembourg Report, it was envisaged that, in cases where the Ministers' work had implications for the activities of the European Community, the Commission would be asked to give its opinion. The Ministers welcome the fact that these contacts have now become reality and have led to a constructive, on-going dialogue.

17 September

*Snake realignment*: the central rate of the guilder is revalued by 5% against the other snake currencies (the new central rate of the guilder is SDR 0.298056, corresponding to 0.264874 grammes of fine gold). In a *communiqué* the Commission regrets that the Dutch government did not first consult with the authorities of the other Member States and the Commission in the spirit of the arrangements for creating economic and monetary union.

27 September

At a press conference the French President Pompidou puts forward the proposal that the heads of state and government of the Member States should henceforth meet at set times to discuss *political co-operation*. The British Prime Minister, Heath, takes up the idea, proposing that the heads of state and government should meet twice a year to determine the broad outline of European policy. Bonn announces that the German government is prepared to hold regular summit meetings. The Dutch government is afraid that such meetings will create a "board of directors" of the great powers in the Community.

**6 October**

The attack by Egypt and Syria on Israel (Yom Kippur War) heralds the first global *oil crisis* in which OPEC (Organisation of Petroleum Exporting Countries) decides on massive price increases. The price per barrel soars rapidly from $1.80 to $5.12 and in December it is raised to $11.65 by the Gulf States belonging to the OPEC cartel.

**26 October**

The former President of the Commission J. Rey urges France to review its negative attitude towards *European integration* and to resume the leading position in Europe which it had held twenty years before. In his opinion, the process of European integration falls down on two points: the stagnation in the decision-making process (he asserts that nothing has changed since 1952) and the absence of political will, so that the visionary spirit of the 1950s is lacking.

**9 November**

The Commission puts forward new proposals to speed up the *process of integration*. France and the Netherlands are against proceeding to the Stage Two: France because three Member States have floating exchange rates, and the Netherlands because of the inadequate democratic structures.

**13 November**

In the European Parliament the German Chancellor Brandt presents an impassioned plea for *European Union*. In his speech the German Chancellor makes the following statement: "We must bring forward the deadlines which we have set ourselves, both for EMU and for what I have called social union as well as political union. According to the resolution by the Paris Summit[68], European Union is to become reality by the end of this decade. The classical model of the nation state is a form of life which belongs to yesterday. Our future no longer lies in the nation state as a separate entity. My government wants to see a new, clear step on the road to a European government by the end of this year."[69]

15 November

*Snake realignment*: the central rate of the Norwegian crown is revalued by 5%. The Commission submits detailed *proposals* for realising "a" second stage in EMU to the EC Council of Ministers. In that connection it presents a directive on stability, growth and full employment in the Community. The earlier proposal for pooling national reserves is watered down: the initial payment will total only 10% of the gross foreign exchange reserves as at 31 December 1973. There is no further mention of subsequent stages.

16 November

Report by a study group of economists and experts[70] set up by the Commission at the end of 1972 on the development of Economic and Monetary Union. It emphasises the fact that the creation of EMU requires simultaneous progress in a number of areas: internal and external monetary policy, economic policy, budgetary policy, social policy and industrial policy. As regards monetary policy, it is proposed that *a* new *European currency unit* be created in the near future, defined as a basket of currencies. This new currency would have to be more than just an instrument for official settlements. Its introduction would therefore require an issuing institution empowered to pursue a policy in support of that currency. This can only be done by applying instruments at European level. In contrast, budgetary policy could continue at Member

[68] This is a reference to the summit conference in Paris in October 1972.
[69] "Mr. Willy Brandt at the European Parliament", *Bulletin of the European Communities*, 1973, no. 11, pp. 7-9.
[70] The economists of this group are H. Giersch, J. Meade, R. Mundell, Th. Peeters and R. Triffin.

State level, though care would be needed to ensure adequate flexibility in the fiscal sphere.

23 November

At a symposium on "Programme for Europe" Commissioner Spinelli asks the heads of state and government to initiate a procedure for designing a *European identity*. This should be done by giving the European Parliament a mandate for drawing up a draft treaty establishing the political union which would embrace the existing Communities.

14-15 December

The heads of state and government meet in Copenhagen. In the official statement the nine countries confirm their common will to let Europe speak with a single voice on important world affairs. They accept the statement regarding the European identity and decide to accelerate the work necessary to define the European Union. In that connection they agree to ask the Community institutions to take the necessary measures whereby, on the basis of the existing decisions, they will speed up progress towards completion of Economic and Monetary Union, increase the resources of the EMCF and co-ordinate action against destabilising capital movements in order to create *a zone of monetary stability* in Europe. The participants will meet more often, whenever the situation makes that desirable, or if it proves necessary to establish new lines of policy for the construction of Europe. The country holding the presidency will convene the meeting and make proposals regarding its preparation and organisation.

17 December

Decision by the EC Council of Ministers to start *"a" Stage Two* which will end on 31 December 1976. The objective of this stage is to achieve essential progress in establishing EMU to permit its completion on the agreed date of 1 January 1980. Short-term monetary assistance is also to be increased. The proposed initial deposit — now 10% of the gross foreign exchange reserves as at the end of December 1973 — will be examined.

The EC Council of Ministers passes the *resolution* concerning the prevention of price increases and maintenance of a high level of employment. The wording chosen is such that the recommendations and provisions leave national governments a great degree of freedom. For instance, in the case of monetary policy Member States may choose from quantitative control over the money supply, a more selective approach to bank lending, non-compensation for an outflow of liquidity or promoting saving by adjusting the interest rate structure.

1973/74

## 1974

21 January

France leaves the *snake arrangement* for a period of six months. The five remaining Member States (Benelux countries, Denmark and the Federal Republic of Germany) decide jointly with the associated countries, Norway and Sweden, to maintain the mutual fluctuation margin of 2.25%.

13 February

In the European parliament, Commissioner R. Dahrendorf gives a warning on the *economic problems* in the Community: while the real rate of growth is 2 to 3%, inflation is predicted to be close to 10%. Dahrendorf deeply regrets the fact that the Member States have still not reached agreement on progressing to Stage Two of EMU.

18 February

Resolution by the EC Council of Ministers on the realisation of a high degree of convergence in the economic policy of the Member States (*convergence decision*). The Council cannot decide on proceeding to Stage Two of EMU.

18 March

Italy uses the *short-term monetary assistance* agreed in July 1973.

*History of the European Union*

21 March

France abolishes the dual *currency market*. The next day Italy also abolishes its dual currency market.[71]

2 April

A joint statement by the Presidents of the EC Council of Ministers and the Commission says that the outline decision on proceeding to an *EMU consolidation phase* should be prepared without delay. To speed up the decision-making process, the statement says that members of the Council of Ministers should endeavour to facilitate the decision, e.g. by abstentions, especially where a clear majority emerges.

18 April

The Commission requests a group of fifteen economists and experts to examine the problems which will arise when EMU is created. The group is headed by the Frenchman Marjolin and is called the *Study Group on Economic and Monetary Union, 1980*. The group plans to study the institutional and structural disparities between the Member States which are hampering creation of the union. The group will also discuss the national and Community instruments of economic policy which are necessary to satisfy the EMU criteria.

25 April

In Portugal, the *dictatorship* which has existed since 1928 is overthrown.

29 April

The Italian government informs the Commission of the *safeguard measures* which it has taken on the basis of Article 109 of the EEC Treaty. The measures consist of the introduction of a compulsory, non-interest-bearing deposit with the *Banca d'Italia* equivalent to 50% of the value of imports for a six month period. On 6 May the Commission recommends the Council of Ministers to grant mutual assistance (in accordance with Article 108 (2) of the EEC Treaty).

---

[71] France introduced the dual market on 21 August 1971; Italy did so on 22 January 1973.

7 June

The first meeting of the *Economic Policy Committee* is held in Brussels, amalgamating the EEC Committees on economic policy, budgetary policy and medium-term economic policy.

8-9 July

Two-day *consultation* between the Federal Republic of Germany and France. The two countries agree that the fight against inflation is a vital prerequisite for economic and political integration in Europe.

24 July

In Greece the *military junta* collapses, whereupon the EC ministers for Foreign Affairs issue the following statement: "The Nine are glad that individual and political freedom has been restored in Greece and wholeheartedly applaud the efforts to achieve that by the Karamanlis administration."[72]

16 September

At the EC Council of Ministers meeting in Brussels the French Minister for Economic and Financial Affairs J.P. Fourcade submits a number of proposals for a *rélance monétaire européenne*. One of his proposals favours revision of the exchange rate mechanism whereby Member States not taking part in the snake should be offered a *structure d'accueil*. This would enable those countries to adapt gradually to the European model. However, the promotion of economic convergence which this requires is hardly considered. The proposals find little support among the other Member States.

21 October

Resolution by the EC Council of Ministers on the creation of *Community loans* of up to a maximum of 3 billion dollars (principal plus interest) to finance balance of payments deficits caused by oil price rises.

18 November

After the short-term monetary assistance has twice been extended for three months, the EC Council of Ministers decides to grant Italy a loan within the

[72] Community activities in September 1974, 5. "Institutional questions – European policy", *Bulletin of the European Communities*, 1974, no. 9, p. 95.

framework of the *mechanism for medium-term financial assistance* totalling 1.2 billion European Units of Account (EUAs) with an average maturity of 3½ years. The United Kingdom does not participate but states that it is willing to grant extension loans equal to the amount of the British participation in short-term monetary assistance (EUA 0.4 billion). The loan is effected on 18 December.

9-10 December

In Paris, the European Council decides that the heads of state and government will meet three times a year with the EC Ministers for Foreign Affairs, or more often as necessary to discuss *political co-operation.* The Council of Ministers considers that, in order to operate more effectively, it should abandon the practice of requiring the Member States to be unanimous on decisions on any question whatsoever, regardless of their individual positions on the conclusions set out in Luxembourg on 28 January 1966. The European Parliament's powers will be strengthened in particular by the assignment of certain powers in the Community's legislative process. Agreement is reached on the establishment of a regional development fund with effect from 1 January 1975, which is allocated 1.3 billion EUAs for the first three years. L. Tindemans, head of the Belgian government, is also requested to produce a report by the end of 1975 on the prospects for EMU.

## 1975

4 March

Signing of a joint declaration by the European Parliament, the EC Council of Ministers and the Commission on the introduction of a *consultation procedure* for decisions of general purport which have substantial financial implications.

8 March

The "Study Group on Economic and Monetary Union, 1980" set up by the Commission in April 1974 publishes the *Marjolin Report* which says that "Europe is no nearer to EMU than in 1969", adding that "national economic and monetary policies have never in 25 years been more discordant, more divergent than they are today". Marjolin says the fact that in all those years no significant progress has been achieved means that "the authority of the European institutions has been weakened and that they are no longer regarded as the prefiguration of the institutions which would watch over the destiny of a united Europe."[73] The report attributes the failure to three causes: a) setbacks such as the international monetary crises since the end of the 1960s and the abrupt increase in oil prices in 1973; b) the absence of political will on the part of governments, which means that, instead of prompting a leap forward, these crises caused a general relapse into an individualistic policy, with each country trying to secure its own salvation as far as possible; c) intellectual myopia causing people to enter on the road to EMU without any clear idea of what they were undertaking.

10-11 March

The Community heads of state and government together with their Ministers for Foreign Affairs meet in Dublin for the first time as the *European Council* in accordance with the decision taken at their meeting on 9 and 10 December 1974. The President of the Commission F.X. Ortoli[74] talks about the role of the European Council. It should hold top level discussions on matters of importance to the Community. The Council must not become an appeal body or an arbitration board. A declaration is adopted relating to the Conference on Security and Co-operation in Europe.

18 March

Establishment of the *European Regional Development Fund (ERDF)* which takes effect on 16 October 1975.

---

[73] R. Marjolin, 1989, *Architect of European Unity. Memoirs 1911-1986*, London, p. 362.
[74] F.X. Ortoli (1925- ), French politician who championed the European cause in France from the end of the 1950s. From 1973 to 1976 he was the President of the European Commission. In France he was awarded the honour of commander of the *Ordre national du mérite* and received the *Croix de Guerre* 1939-1945.

19 March          The Lomé Convention leads to formal definition of
                  the *EUA*. It consists of a basket of nine EC currencies
                  (Netherlands share 9%, Germany 27.3%). The EUA
                  is used as the accounting unit by a number of
                  European institutions from 21 April.

24 March          The Italian government terminates the *safeguard
                  measures* adopted in May 1974 requiring a
                  compulsory deposit for imports of certain goods.

3 April           In Vienna, the Commission President Ortoli gives a
                  speech on European Union in 1980. He advocates the
                  *principle of subsidiarity* as follows: "I certainly do
                  not mean … That I want to bring about unification at
                  any price. If people want to establish a European
                  Union, then the economic harmonisation which that
                  requires and the desired social unity must not impair
                  the identity and individual character which are
                  Europe's heritage. By that I mean that artificial and
                  unjustified barriers should be avoided and that we
                  should aim at a uniform concept while preserving the
                  diversity of situations. This means greater flexibility
                  in the realisation of European integration and
                  participation on totally equal terms at various other
                  levels, such as institutions of a future European
                  Union, countries, regions, local authorities and
                  citizens, so that their respective initiatives do not
                  conflict with one another but instead are mutually
                  supportive."[75]

9 May             25th Anniversary of the *Schuman Declaration* of 9
                  May 1950, celebrated in the *Salon de l'Horloge* at
                  the Quai d'Orsay in Paris, attended by 150 public
                  figures including seven heads of state or government.
                  The French President Giscard d'Estaing says that the
                  work of bringing about a genuine union is still a long
                  way from completion. According to the Federal
                  German President Scheel the idea that political unity
                  will   necessarily   result   from   progress   towards

---

[75] "The European Union in 1980: the opinion of citizens, local authorities and regions on the
proposal by the governments", *Bulletin of the European Communities*, 1975, no. 4, p. 9.

economic integration has too often been used as an excuse for postponing political decisions.

| | |
|---|---|
| 5 June | Referendum in the United Kingdom in which over 67% of the electorate favour staying in the *EC*. |
| 12 June | Greece submits a formal application for *accession to the EC*. |
| 25 June | The Commission publishes the *report on European Union* produced on behalf of the heads of state and government. In the monetary sphere, creating monetary union on time is still a condition for achieving internal economic integration and ensuring that the Member States present a united front to the outside world. The ultimate aim should be for the Union to hold monetary powers. To improve the political cohesion of the Union, the report proposes assigning wider powers to the Union than it currently holds at European level, though it is only to be given those functions which the Member States can no longer perform effectively themselves. |
| 8 July | The central banks of the EC Member States agree to extend the financing period under the *very short-term credit mechanism* excluding the use of gold for settling debts. |
| 10 July | France returns to the *snake arrangement* at the old parity of the franc. The EC Council of Ministers and the central bank Governors invite Switzerland to a discussion on possible association with the "snake" countries. |
| 16-17 July | In Brussels the European Council discusses the *economic outlook* and urges the EC Council of Ministers to strengthen the co-ordination of the economic and financial policy of the Member States. The Council of Ministers for Foreign Affairs is asked for a report by the end of the year on the election of the European Parliament by direct universal suffrage. |

22 July

A Treaty giving the European Parliament *wider budgetary powers* is signed. It enters into force in June 1977.

23 July

The Commission passes a decision authorising the United Kingdom to maintain the existing *safeguard measures* temporarily in the form of restrictions on direct investment by residents of that country in other Member States and certain capital movements (pursuant to Article 108 (3) of the EEC Treaty).

1 August

In Helsinki the *Final Act of the CSCE* is signed by the thirty five countries taking part.

24 August

In Venice the EC Council of Ministers decides on *co-ordinated action* in support of business activity, to combat inflation and to improve growth opportunities in the long term. Thus, measures to stimulate the economy are taken or announced in various Community countries (Denmark, the Federal Republic of Germany, France, Italy and the Netherlands).

22 September

Report by the Belgian Finance Minister De Clercq on Switzerland's participation in the Community's exchange rate system. Switzerland and the Community agree on participation by the Swiss franc in the *snake arrangement* because this extends the European zone of monetary stability.

14 October

Commission Vice President W. Haferkamp presents the European Parliament with a statement on the economic situation in the Community. He focuses particularly on the divergent rates of *inflation* that is running at 6 to 7% in some Member States but sometimes over 20% in others.

20 October

Meeting of the *Benelux Economic Union*.

1 November

*The Economist* publishes the *All Saints' Day Manifesto* in which nine prominent European economists recommend the EC central banks to issue a "Europa" which should be a European money of constant purchasing power. In the article the experts put forward ten proposals for reforming the European monetary system: "Whatever the details of the arrangement, it would be wise to keep in mind one guiding principle: we must give the monetary authorities the same independence from political control and the same responsibility to the rule of law we have accorded the judicial system. It follows that the new institution or institutions should be removed from the jurisdiction of treasuries, and monetary authorities should be appointed or elected for long periods of time, if not for life."[76]

15-17 November     Summit of the Big Five (Federal Republic of Germany, France, Japan, the United Kingdom and the United States) in *Rambouillet* where the Franco-American compromise on the international exchange rate system is accepted. This compromise means accepting that it is legitimate for currencies to float but distinguishing between random and fundamental exchange rate fluctuations in the market: intervention may be used to tackle the former but not the latter.

20 November     The Swiss parliament decides to postpone Switzerland's possible *association* with the snake. Objections to such association are expressed by France.

28 November     For the time being, Italy does not return to the *snake arrangement*, partly because of the large inflation rate differential vis-à-vis Germany.

---

[76] "All Saints' Day Manifesto for European monetary union", *The Economist*, 1 November 1975, pp. 33-38. The nine economists are: G. Basevi (*Università di Bologna*), M. Frattianni (Indiana University, USA), H. Giersch (*Institut für Weltwirtschaft an der Universität Kiel*), P. Korteweg (*Erasmus Universiteit Rotterdam*), D. O'Mahoney (University College Cork), M. Parkin (University of Manchester), Th. Peeters (*Katholieke Universiteit Leuven*), P. Salin (*Université Paris-IX.Dauphine*), N. Thygesen (*Københavens Universitat*).

1-2 December

The European Council meets for the third time since the consultations in December 1974.[77] The meeting is held in Rome where the economic situation in the Community is discussed. The Council confirms the policies laid down in Rambouillet regarding closer *international co-operation*. Apart from that, direct elections for the European Parliament will be held in May-June 1978.

8-9 December

Following the *Rambouillet conference*, the governors of the central banks of the snake countries and the US Federal Reserve Bank decide to consult each other on a daily basis on the foreign exchange market situation, the objective being to prevent large fluctuations in the exchange rate of the dollar.

22 December

Extension of *the mechanism for medium-term financial assistance* by four years, on account of Italy's recourse to this mechanism.

29 December

The Belgian Premier Tindemans sends his *report on European Union* to the other EC heads of state and government and to the President of the Commission.

1976

7 January

Publication of the *Tindemans Report*. The report finds that little progress has been made in recent years in the efforts to consolidate the Community by creating Economic and Monetary Union without which the European Union is pointless. Since 1969 the heads of state and government have repeatedly expressed their desire to create EMU, and in 1971 this was specified as a currency union. However, the

---

[77] Unlike the summit conferences of December 1969 (The Hague), October 1972 (Paris) and December 1973 (Copenhagen), since the summit meeting of December 1974 (Paris) people speak of the "new-style" summit which has clearly defined characteristics. These are summarised as follows in a *communiqué* published on 10 December 1974: "the heads of government recognise the need for a general approach to the internal issues associated with the construction of Europe and the problems between Europe and the outside world, and consider that an effort should be made to develop cohesion between the activities of the Communities and work on political cooperation".

Member States have never agreed on what that single currency means for the autonomy of the individual Member States as regards budgetary and economic policy. In this connection Tindemans refers to the need to pursue a common economic and monetary policy. However, the report finds that there is no real political consensus on bringing this about because there is insufficient mutual trust to hand over to Community controlling authorities the powers which they must necessarily be granted. In his foreword Tindemans says that he has deliberately refrained from issuing a blueprint for the ideal Europe because that would be liable to become utopian. He merely proposes measures and objectives which can restore the momentum of European union. Tindemans says that he is keeping to what is realistic and feasible. In line with that standpoint the report formulates proposals whereby the "Community snake, the core of monetary stability" should form the basis for a new approach.

| | |
|---|---|
| 16 February | During the meeting of the EC Council of Ministers, the Belgian Minister for Finance De Clercq calls the existing *exchange rates* realistic and correct. According to his French colleague Fourcade "Rambouillet" has functioned perfectly. |

The CMEA proposes an agreement with the EC.

| | |
|---|---|
| 15 March | France leaves the *snake arrangement* again. |

The *Benelux arrangement* (the worm) is cancelled.

The EC Council of Ministers grants *Community loans* to Ireland (300 million dollars) and Italy (1 billion dollars). The grant of these loans is associated with economic policy conditions to be respected by both countries.

| | |
|---|---|
| 18 March | The Italian government takes a number of *safeguard measures* aimed at halting the decline in the value of |

the lira and restoring sound public finances. Since 20 January the lira has fallen by 22% against the dollar.

1-2 April

In Luxembourg the European Council fails to reach agreement on directives to counter *economic and monetary problems*. However, there is unanimous confirmation of the resolve to create EMU despite the very difficult circumstances. The heads of state and government stress that the exchange rate relationship between their currencies is due merely to the unfavourable economic situation and that this evil must therefore be rooted out.

12-13 July

The European Council affirms in Brussels its approval of the allocation of seats in the *European Parliament* to be formed in 1978 via direct general elections. There are 410 seats altogether which are allocated as follows: Belgium 24, Denmark 16, Ireland 15, Luxembourg 6, the Netherlands 25 and the four large countries, France, Germany, Italy and the United Kingdom, 81 seats each.

21 July

Commission decision authorising Italy to maintain the *compulsory import deposit* introduced on 5 May 1976 until 5 November 1976.

The negotiations for Greece's *accession to the EC* are opened formally.

26 July

At the EC Council of Ministers meeting the Dutch Finance Minister W. Duisenberg proposes reducing the exchange rate differentials between snake currencies and other currencies by introducing *target zones (Duisenberg Plan)*.

27 July

Commission decision whereby the *safeguard measures* introduced by the United Kingdom in July 1975 are extended until 30 June 1977.

20 September

Signing by the EC Ministers for Foreign Affairs of the texts on *direct general elections* to the European Parliament.

29 September

Commission decision extending the period of validity of the Italian *import deposit* to 15 April 1977, with the compulsory deposit being reduced gradually from mid October 1976.

18 October

*Snake realignment*: The official central rate of the German mark is raised by 2% against the guilder and the Belgian franc, the central rate of the Norwegian and Swedish crowns is raised by 1% and that of the Danish crown is reduced by 4%. The Commission points out that the consultation procedure in respect of exchange rate realignments, agreed in the resolution of 18 February 1974, has not been complied with. As a result of the currency turbulence, the German *Bundesbank*, in particular, has intervened in the period from the end of July to mid October, with purchases totalling around DM 8 billion.

9 November

The EC Council of Ministers discusses the *Duisenberg Plan* on exchange rate target zones. The proposal is considered to be a good idea but one which is not feasible for the time being. The German proposal to publish reference data on the expansion of the money supply is applauded by the majority of the Council. It is decided that the Monetary Committee will examine at set times the monetary objectives laid down by the Member States.

22 November

Within the framework of the *Community loans*, the EC Council of Ministers decides to place a loan for the benefit of Italy because the United Kingdom terminates its credit granted to Italy by way of short-term monetary assistance. According to the Council the policy conditions agreed with Italy for 1976, like those of a year earlier, have been substantially infringed, particularly in the monetary sphere. For that reason the Italian authorities feel obliged to resort to measures at the border, including reintroduction of the import deposit, later followed by announcement of a temporary levy on foreign exchange purchases by residents.

29-30 November

In The Hague, the European Council passes a resolution on the *Tindemans Report*. The ministers for foreign affairs will produce an annual report on the results achieved and possible progress towards European Union in the immediate future. This will be realised gradually by consolidation of the Community's achievements, with the existing treaties forming the basis for new kinds of policy. The creation of EMU is vital to consolidating Community solidarity and realising European Union. High priority should be accorded to the policy to combat inflation and unemployment. Furthermore, the Council requests the Monetary Committee and the Committee of Central Bank Governors to elaborate on the Dutch proposal on exchange rate target zones and to examine how and under what conditions it can be put into practice.

1977

21 January

The French President Giscard d'Estaing sends a letter to the heads of state and government of the Member States and to the President of the Commission in which he sets out his ideas on the operation of the *European Council* and makes suggestions on possible improvements.

25 March

20th Anniversary of the signing of the *Treaties of Rome*. On this occasion President G. Leone of Italy talks about the political significance of the Treaties and the European identity: "The Treaties of Rome have given us economic progress and peace in Europe for twenty years. We must now prepare to take a new step which, once internal solidarity becomes reality, means that we really concentrate on creating conditions for the advent of the "European", a person who will find his spiritual, cultural and social equilibrium in a new society. We hope that if that can be achieved, then just as people once proudly said *"Civis romanus sum"*, so they will be able to say "I am a European". That is the desire expressed by Winston Churchill ten years before the Treaties of Rome were signed.[78]

28 March            Portugal formally applies for *accession to the EC*.

4 April            *Snake realignment*: the official central rate of the Swedish crown is reduced by 6% and that of the Norwegian and Danish crowns by 3% against the other snake currencies.

18 April            The EC Council of Ministers approves a *Community loan* of 500 million dollars to Italy, bringing this loan to its maximum level.

Decision by the EC Council of Ministers to instruct the competent bodies to examine at regular intervals whether the proposed *budgetary and monetary policy* can be considered in keeping with the requirements for external and internal monetary stability.

7-8 May            At the third economic summit conference of the Western industrial countries (*"Downing Street Summit"*) the Community takes part as such for the first time in some of the talks.

15 June            The Commission proposes the creation of a *new Community borrowing instrument* to finance structural investment

1 July            End of the transitional period leading to full abolition of intra-Community *customs tariffs* for the three new Member States (Denmark, Ireland and the United Kingdom) which joined in 1973.

28 July            Spain submits a formal application for *accession to the EC*.

28 August            Sweden suspends its association with the *snake*. The

---

[78] Main events 2. "Twenty years ago: Signing of the Treaties of Rome", *Bulletin of the European Communities*, 1977, no. 3, p. 13.

central rate of the Norwegian and Danish crowns is reduced by 5% against the other snake currencies.

17-18 September

Informal Commission meeting discussing matters which include the failure to create EMU and the loss of credibility, though this must not lead to the conclusion that its objectives have become pointless and utopian. In a *communiqué* the Commission says that there will be no *European Political Union* unless substantial progress is achieved on the road to EMU. It is therefore necessary to confirm the ultimate objective once again, to explain it better and adapt it to the changed circumstances resulting from the enlargement of the Community.

25 October

In Luxembourg the inaugural meeting takes place of the *Court of Auditors* of the European Communities, replacing the Board of Auditors of the EEC and Euratom and the financial commissioner of the ECSC.

27 October

To mark the 20th anniversary of the Community, Commission President R. Jenkins[79] gives the first *Jean Monnet Lecture* in Florence on the prospects for monetary union. Among other things, he talks about monetary union and political integration: "It is a purely political argument that Monetary Union can be used as an instrument for European political integration. In 1949 J. Rueff said '*L'Europe se fera par la monnaie ou ne se fera pas*' [Europe will be created via its currency, otherwise it will not happen]. Even though I do not want to be as categorical as that, it is still clear that successful creation of European Monetary Union would help Europe to cross the political threshold ... We must not only do what is best under the present circumstances. We must give our peoples a goal which goes beyond what is immediately possible. Politics is not just the art of the possible, but as Jean

---

[79] R. Jenkins was appointed President of the European Commission in 1976 as the successor to Ortoli; he held that post from 1977 to 1981.

Monnet said, it is also the art of making possible tomorrow what cannot yet be done today."[80]

31 October

The British authorities decide to cease opposing a further appreciation of *sterling*.

16 November

Commission communication to the European Council on the "Necessity and current relevance of Economic and Monetary Union". In its *Thoughts on method* the Commission considers that the crisis is an insufficient explanation for the failure of attempts to construct EMU. The problem lies more in the two types of approach adopted in the past. The first is known as persisting in and intensifying the progressive method, which means improving the co-ordination of economic policy, continuing the integration of the market and applying common policy measures and instruments. The second approach consists in speeding up the decision on integration and considering the conditions whereby significant economic and monetary powers can be transferred to the Community. The Commission now wants to combine the two methods and presents the European Council with a five-year action programme which is to be set out in detail each year. At the end of each year, after evaluating the results achieved, the Council proceeds to the next year's action plan. This method would not only be more flexible but would also have the advantage of seeking at the highest level the control and permanent political momentum without which no programme has any chance of being fully implemented.

5-6 December

The European Council urges in Brussels for closer *co-ordination* of the economic policy of the Member States and stronger financial solidarity by adjustment of the Community's short and medium-term credit mechanisms. The Council says that, in view of the

[80] Main events, 1. "A challenge and a prospect for Europe, speeches on Monetary Union given in Florence on 27 October by Mr. Roy Jenkins, President of the Commission", *Bulletin of the European Communities*, 1977, no. 10, p. 16.

worrying level of unemployment, everything possible must be done to implement the economic growth strategy approved by the EC Council of Ministers on 17 October.

19 December

Decision by the EC Council of Ministers regarding the adjustment of the *mechanism for medium-term financial assistance* (the maximum commitments of the Member States are doubled and expressed in EUA). The stipulations regarding the conditions for assistance and supervision of compliance with those conditions are adjusted. As regards short-term monetary assistance, the central banks agree to consider by March 1979 whether the quotas should be revised in accordance with the February 1970 agreement which provides for revision of the quotas every five years.

21 December

The Commission authorises Denmark, Ireland and the United Kingdom pursuant to Article 108 of the EEC Treaty, to apply *safeguard measures* relating to investment in securities, and in the case of the United Kingdom also relating to direct investment and certain capital transfers.

1978

13 February

*Snake realignment*: the Norwegian crown is devalued by 8% against the other snake currencies.

14 February

In a speech before the European Parliament, Commission President Jenkins gives a new impetus to the aim of monetary union. He refers to the arguments developed over the past few months in support of a renewed effort to achieve this goal: "What we need is a new economic impetus on a historic scale, and we believe that this can be achieved in the Community by a renewed and accelerated effort to attain *Economic and Monetary Union.*"[81]

20 March

On the basis of a Commission communication the EEC Council of Ministers reports on the policy pursued by the Member States in 1977 and has examined the adjustment of the *guidelines for policy* in 1978 in accordance with the convergence decision of February 1974. The Commission finds that the economic growth target of 4-4.5% is not attainable for the Community as a whole.

28 March

The Portuguese government submits an official application for *accession to the EC.*

7-8 April

The meeting of the European Council in Copenhagen focuses on boosting *economic growth* and combating unemployment. The Council considers it essential for the Community to achieve an annual growth rate of 4.5% by mid 1979 and urges for additional specific measures to boost employment particularly for young people. The Council agrees for the first direct elections to the European Parliament (7 and 10 June 1979).

5 June

The Monetary Committee starts discussions on alternative forms of *monetary co-operation.* It talks about pooling part of the national foreign exchange reserves, determining monetary growth objectives in the individual Member States and expanding the role of the EUA. According to the Belgian Chairman J. van Ypersele the EMCF should be revived and the EUA should be converted into a European currency unit.

19 June

The EC Council of Ministers puts forward proposals for an *alternative monetary system*: (1) maintenance of the snake with the possibility of accession for non-snake countries; (2) a new monetary arrangement

[81] Italics as in the text. "Commission Programme of Work for 1978", *Bulletin of the European Communities*, 1978, no. 2, p. 9.

with a currency basket, the exchange rate being allowed to fluctuate within a certain margin against the basket; and (3) creation of a Fund modelled on the IMF.

6-7 July

In Bremen the European Council discusses proposals prepared earlier by the French President Giscard d'Estaing and the German Chancellor H. Schmidt.[82] These concern a new monetary system which is to lead to a *zone of monetary stability in Europe*. The finance ministers are instructed to draw up the necessary guidelines for the competent Community authorities so that they can devise the necessary measures around the end of October. The heads of government of Belgium, the Federal Republic of Germany, Denmark, Luxembourg and the Netherlands confirm that the snake was not and is not under discussion.

24 July

The EC Council of Ministers elaborates on the decision in principle regarding the new European monetary system but does not go into technical details. It is referred to as a *European Monetary System (EMS)*.

18 September

The EC Council of Ministers agrees that the *European Currency Unit* (ECU) will be the keystone of the European monetary system by use of the ECU in both the European Monetary Fund and the exchange rate system, where the central rates of currencies in the system will be expressed in ECUs.

The Italian government repays the third tranche within the framework of the *mechanism for medium-term financial assistance*. At the end of September the fourth tranche is repaid (due on 19 December 1978 according to the directive) so that Italy has paid back all the loans taken out under the EC facility.

---

[82] H. Schmidt (1918- ) succeeded Schiller as Minister for Economic and Financial Affairs from July to December 1972. After that he became the Minister for Finance. From 1974 to 1982 he was the Chancellor of the Federal Republic of Germany.

15 October

*Snake realignment:* the central rate of the German mark is revalued by 4% against the Danish and Norwegian crowns and by 2% against the Belgian franc and the guilder. This is the seventh revaluation of the German currency since its creation in 1948.

16 October

Decision in principle by the EC Council of Ministers whereby, under the *New Community Instrument (NCI)*, the Commission is empowered to raise loans in order to promote investment in the Community up to a maximum of EUA 1 billion (Ortoli facility).

27 October

The Commission presents two proposals forming the legal basis permitting introduction of the *EMS* with effect from 1 January 1979. The first concerns the value of the new accounting unit, set at 0.8867088 grammes of fine gold. The Commission considers that any reference to gold for fixing the value of the currency is out of step with the current rules in the international monetary system. The new European accounting unit is the ECU defined as a basket of currencies of the Member States.[83] The second proposal deals with the implications of accepting the ECU as the accounting unit in the European Monetary Co-operation Fund.

10 November

The European Parliament discusses the political unrest in Iran heralding the *second oil crisis*. The official price per barrel of "Arabian light" increases from an average of $12.70 in 1978 to $22 in 1979 and $34 in 1982, partly because of the war which breaks out between Iran and Iraq in September 1980.

20 Novemberer

As a result of the studies and discussions on the introduction of the *EMS,* the EC Council of Ministers has now reached agreement on most aspects and there are only a few issues which still need to be

---

[83] The ECU is made up as follows: 0.828 German marks + 0.0885 pounds sterling + 1.15 French francs + 109 Italian lire + 0.286 Dutch guilders + 3.66 Belgian francs + 0.14 Luxembourg francs + 0.217 Danish crowns + 0.00759 Irish pounds.

discussed at the forthcoming European Council meeting.

15 November

In a speech before the European Parliament the German Foreign Minister H.D. Genscher[84] (acting President of the EC Council of Ministers) expatiates on *political co-operation* in the Community. He points out that political co-operation between the Nine has become increasingly important and that this tendency is bound to persist in the years ahead. The accession of the candidate countries should not be considered primarily from an economic angle but should be seen as a genuine political decision in the light of the strengthening of democracy in Europe.

4-5 December

In Brussels the European Council adopts a resolution whereby the EMS will be introduced as from 1 January 1979. All Member States will participate (Ireland, Italy and the United Kingdom decide to join at a later date) including Denmark as an associate member. The core of the EMS is the *Exchange Rate Mechanism (ERM)* providing for stable but adjustable exchange rates. In this arrangement joined by all Member States except the United Kingdom, every participating currency has a central rate against the ECU. In principle the fluctuation margin is set at 2.25% either side of the central rate. Countries with previously floating exchange rates may opt for a wider margin of up to ±6%. The ECU is used as an indicator to monitor divergences between the participating currencies. Initially the composition of the ECU is identical with that of the EUA. Later, the Council instructs a "Committee of Three Wise Men" to formulate proposals permitting progress towards the European Union. This committee consists of B.

---

[84] H.D. Genscher (1927- ) was the Federal German Minister for Foreign Affairs from 1974 to 1992. Born in the former GDR, he worked particularly hard to bring about German reunification and improve relations between Eastern and Western Europe after the collapse of communism in 1989.

Biesheuvel of the Netherlands, R. Marjolin of France and E. Dell of the United Kingdom.[85]

12 December

Norway leaves the *snake arrangement* so that only the Benelux countries, Denmark and the Federal Republic of Germany remain in this arrangement.

29 December

Problems with France regarding the *CAP* lead to failure of the attempt to set the new central rates on 29 December, so that the EMS cannot take effect on 1 January.

30 December

Decision by the EC Council of Ministers regarding extension of the *mechanism for medium-term financial assistance* until the end of December 1980.

1979

1 January

France takes on the *Presidency* of the EC for the next six months.

5 January

The negotiations on Spanish *accession to the EC* formally open in Brussels.

15 January

The EC Council of Ministers (for foreign affairs) discusses the *agro-monetary problems* which must be solved before the EMS is introduced. The 12 February session is devoted entirely to this without achieving any results.

6 February

The EC Council of Ministers adopts guidelines for Community regional policy and amendments to the 1975 Regulation establishing ERDF.

5-6 March

The EC Council of Ministers (for foreign affairs) reaches consensus on the measures to be taken in the

---

[85] B. Biesheuvel (1920-   ) was Prime Minister (1971-1973), Vice-Premier and Minister for Agriculture (1963-1967) of the Netherlands. R. Marjolin's main posts in France were as *Commissaire général adjoint au Plan* (1946-1948) alongside J. Monnet, Deputy Secretary General of the OECD (1948-1955) and Vice President of the EEC Commission (1958-1961). E. Dell was formerly the Secretary of State for Trade, and from 1966 held various government posts in Britain.

agro-monetary field. This consensus concerns in particular the abolition of the existing *MCAs* and rules regarding the new MCAs. This clears the way for effective entry into operation of the EMS.

13 March          The EMS takes effect. The *ECU central rate* of the guilder is set at 2.72077, for the DM it is 2.51064.[86] The United Kingdom does not participate for the moment. Italy opts for a wider margin of ±6%. At that time the 20% of their national gold and currency reserves which participants in the EMS have to deposit in the form of a three-month revolving swap with the EMCF represents around ECU 24 billion. The British journalist, D. Marsh, makes the following comments on the role of Germany, and especially Chancellor Schmidt, in the establishment of the EMS: "The EMS was part of what Schmidt liked to call, in later years, his 'grand strategy for integrating Europe'. In 1987, Schmidt revealed that a vital, though unspoken, reason behind the creation of the EMS was his wish to provide an additional 'anchor' for West Germany's ties to Western Europe. Since the time of Konrad Adenauer, the desire to bind the country into an irreversible commitment towards the west has been one of the more permanent features of post-war European foreign policy." With regard to the then *Bundesbank* Governor K.O. Pöhl, Marsh says that, looking back in 1991, he commented that, "The *Bundesbank* turned the original concept (for the EMS) on its head by making the strongest currency the yardstick for the system."[87]

---

[86] The ECU acted as the accounting unit in the EMS. With the exception of Belgium, where gold and silver ECU coins were minted in denominations of 5 and 50 ECUs to commemorate the 30th anniversary of the EEC Treaty in 1987, the ECU was legal tender nowhere. In the following text the new ECU exchange rate of the Dutch guilder and the German mark due to a realigment is published. These currencies are chosen because of the anchor role of the mark in the European exchange rate mechanism and the close relationship of the guilder to the mark which was the aim of Dutch monetary policy since the establishment of the EMS.

[87] David Marsh, 1992, *The Bundesbank. The Bank that Rules Europe*, London, p. 233.

16 March

On the death of Monnet [88] the Commission President Jenkins makes the following statement. "Europe without Jean Monnet is almost unthinkable. His death is sad news for the European Community and for everyone who has tried for more than a generation to realise the *European idea*. No-one has done more than Jean Monnet to help establish and develop the Community. No-one has done more than him to combine original ideas with practical achievements. He knew moments of disappointment and disillusionment, but he never lost his faith and hope in Europe and he always managed to find new ways forward."[89]

12-13 May

In Paris the European Council confirms that while the *economic and social situation* in the Community does have its positive side, it is still not very satisfactory in certain respects. Since there are again signs of tension on the prices front in the first few months of 1979, the Council feels that controlling inflation must remain the primary goal of the Member States' economic policy. Bringing inflation successfully under control is said to be crucial to achieving stable, sustainable growth. The implementation of the EMS should be based on greater convergence in economic policy. To that end, the Council requests the EC Council of Ministers, on the proposal of the Commission, to reinforce the means of co-ordinating the economic policy of the Member States.

14 May

Within the framework of the *Ortoli facility* the Commission is authorised to place a first tranche of EUA 500 million on the capital market.

28 May

The Greek act of *accession to the EC* is signed in

[88] J. Monnet (1888-1979). His *Mémoires* published in 1976 reveal that he was guided by two principles in his tireless efforts to achieve European unification: (1) Europe must not be built on visions or generalities but on *réalisations concrètes* [real achievements]; (2) Community institutions – and not intergovernmental co-operation – are the key to a lasting Europe.
[89] "Jean Monnet", *Bulletin of the European Communities*, 1979, no. 2, p. 5.

Athens. Greek duties on manufactured goods will be reduced in six stages, beginning on 1 January 1981, leading to the customs union on 1 January 1986. The drachma will be included in the ECU basket within this five-year transitional period.

| | |
|---|---|
| 7-10 June | First *election to the European Parliament* by direct suffrage. |
| 21-22 June | In Strasbourg, now that the EMS has been in effect for three months, the European Council concludes that the initial results are favourable and stresses the political significance of the system. The Council also develops policy guidelines for the harmonisation of *economic policy* between Member States, the co-ordination of their budgetary policies and the fight against inflation and unemployment. |
| 28 June | The Greek parliament ratifies the *Treaty of Accession to the EC.* |
| 1 July | Ireland takes over the *Presidency* of the EC. |
| | The United Kingdom takes part in the *revolving swaps* in the EMCF. As a result, the value of the initial transfer of gold and dollars increases to the equivalent of over ECU 29 billion, of which ECU 18 billion is in the form of gold. |
| 17-20 July | First meeting of the European Parliament appointed by the first *direct elections.*[90] |
| 9 August | The EC Council of Ministers decides to use the *ECU as the accounting unit* for the CAP. |
| 24 September | First *realignment in the EMS:*[91] the German mark revalues by 2% and the Danish crown devalues by |

[90] Although the Treaties of Rome provided for direct elections, the formal agreement on the matter was not concluded until 12 July 1976.
[91] The realignment decision is taken pursuant to a resolution by the ministers of economic and financial affairs and the governors of the central banks of the Community countries taking part in the EMS.

3% against the other EMS currencies (ECU central rate of the guilder: 2.74748, DM: 2.48557).

1979

Publication of the *Spierenburg Report*. This report considers that integration must proceed simultaneously in the monetary and general economic spheres in order to create the currency union − the *conditio sine qua non* for the success of the European Union. This implies the rejection of the monetarist approach while specifically dismissing the idea of introducing a parallel currency as an intermediate link. According to the report, creating economic and monetary union entails transferring essential monetary and budgetary powers; if the national governments lack the political will for that, then they should cease paying lip service to the objective of monetary union. Following this report the Commission decides to set up two working parties (headed by Ortoli and Jenkins respectively) to submit proposals on the Commission's administrative policy and institutional questions.

23 October

The United Kingdom announces the total abolition of *foreign exchange controls*. According to Article 108 of the EEC Treaty. This means that the authorisation to take safeguard measures, granted by the Commission on 21 December 1977, has lapsed and the United Kingdom is fully complying with its obligations with regard to capital movements.

29-30 November

In the Irish capital Dublin the European Council stresses the convergence of Member States' economic performances and budgetary questions. The Council acknowledges that insufficient progress has been made in co-ordinating *economic policy* as agreed at the European Council in Bremen of July 1978. The objectives pursued, notably sustained growth and the fight against unemployment, have not been fully attained. A common approach is essential, and priority should be assigned to controlling inflation. The current difficulties necessitate better co-ordination of the Member States' economic and monetary policy. With that in mind, the European Council confirms its intention to create the European Monetary Fund in accordance with the planned timetable.

The Committee of Three Wise Men set up by the European Council in December 1978 presents its *"Report on the European Institutions"* to the Council. This report severely criticises the way in which the Community has operated so far. It has moved steadily in the direction of an intergovernmental system and hence further and further away from the original intention of the Common Market. The Committee offers suggestions for maintaining the role of the Council of Ministers, increasing the co-operation between the Commission and the heads of state and government and establishing direct relations between the European Council and the European Parliament in order to integrate the European Council as far as possible into the normal framework of inter-institutional relations. But the Committee says that the Council must do more: "The European Council must keep a close watch on all joint action by the Member States, regardless of whether it is Community action in the strict sense. This applies particularly to political co-operation. The Article 235 procedure must be given priority. However, should this procedure prove unworkable, then other forms of joint action enabling the Community to make progress should not be ruled out in principle."[92]

30 November

*EMS realignment:* the central rate of the Danish crown is reduced by 5% against the other EMS currencies (ECU central rate of the guilder: 2.74362, DM: 2.48208).

13 December

Commission proposals for replacing the EUA by the *ECU* in a number of areas, including the general

---

[92] "Working of the European Institutions, Conclusions of the 'Committee of Three Wise Men' ", *Bulletin of the European Communities*, 1979, no. 11, pp. 27-28.

budget, all Community actions and arrangements which come under the ECSC Treaty.

1980

1 January

Italy takes over the *Presidency* of the EC.

29 January

The Commission proposes a second tranche of loans totalling EUA 500 million via the *Ortoli facility*.

27-28 April

In Luxembourg the European Council under its Italian President meets without resolving the main question on the agenda: Britain's contribution to the *Community budget*. The meeting which should have been held four weeks earlier was postponed because at that time, too, the political climate in Europe offered little prospect of agreement being reached. As regards the EMS, the Council welcomes the fact that the system has managed to withstand the movements on the foreign exchange market. The Council notes serious economic and monetary disturbances leading to a general rise in interest rates, higher inflation, larger inflation rate differentials and increasing balance of payments disequilibrium in the Member States. One of the Council's conclusions is that, against that background, the currencies of the Member States participating in the EMS have shown a degree of mutual cohesion not seen since 1972.

9 May

On the initiative of the European Movement, the "Congress of Europe" is organised in Paris in commemoration of the *Schuman Declaration* of 9 May 1950. The following passage in the conclusions of the statement approved by the Congress is relevant: "... In view of the clear risks of collapse and decline facing the European Community as a result of the global economic crisis and the new nationalistic tendencies, it is urgently necessary for the Community institutions once again to be guided by the spirit of the great political vision which, by creating the Community, revived the hopes of the peoples, and which, by founding the United States of

Europe tomorrow, will confirm their will from now on to share their destiny in inextricable solidarity. The Congress of Europe which records the marked failure of the intergovernmental approach to the political unification of Europe ends with an urgent plea to the institutions of the European Communities and the governments of the Member States to take the necessary measures to enable the Community to develop into a federal structure."[93]

30 May

The EC Council of Ministers reaches a compromise agreement for the *United Kingdom's contribution to the Community budget.*

12-13 June

In Venice the European Council discusses the international situation which is dominated by repeated *oil price* rises. The Council considers that controlling inflation must be the primary short-term objective of economic policy, and must be achieved by an appropriate monetary and fiscal policy.

1 July

Luxembourg takes over the *Presidency* of the EC.

15 July

The EC Council of Ministers decides to authorise the Commission to issue a new tranche of EUA 400 million via the *Ortoli facility.* By way of exception, the remaining EUA 100 million of this second tranche will be used for purposes other than infrastructure and energy (EC Council of Ministers decision dated 20 October 1980).

11 November

The CSCE opens in Madrid; this is the second meeting of the thirty five countries which signed the Helsinki Final Act in 1975.

17 November

The EC Council of Ministers decides that the transition to a *consolidated EMS,* which was to take place after two years, will be postponed indefinitely. The agreement on the pooling of reserves, applicable

[93] "Thirty years after the Schuman declaration", *Bulletin of the European Communities*, 1980, no. 5, p. 19.

for the transitional period, will remain in force for a further two years after 13 March 1981.

28 November

Commission proposal on extending the *mechanism for medium-term financial assistance* by two years, i.e. until the end of December 1982 or until the final phase of the EMS takes effect.

1-2 December

In Luxembourg the European Council decides to extend the *transitional stage* of the EMS for a period of time yet to be determined. The Council notes the intention of the EC Council of Ministers and the Committee of Central Bank Governors to extend the mechanism for medium-term financial assistance and the swap agreements which are an integral part of the EMS.

15 December

The EC Council of Ministers decides to extend the *mechanism for medium-term financial assistance* to 31 December 1982 unless the final stage of the EMS starts before that date.

16 December

EC Council of Ministers regulation whereby the EUA will be replaced by the *ECU* in Community decisions with effect from 1 January 1981. However, any rights and obligations still denominated in EUA on that date will be preserved.

## 1981

1 January

Greece joins the *European Communities* which now comprise ten countries. Greece takes part in the EMS but not in the ERM.

6 January

The German Foreign Affairs Minister Genscher proposes reinforcing political co-operation and security in the European Union. Part of this plan is adopted by the German government and by his Italian colleague, E. Colombo, so historians refer to it as the *Genscher-Colombo Plan*. The plan is intended as a European Act supplementing the EEC Treaty, and provides for a common foreign policy and co-ordination of the policy on security, with the EC Council of Ministers only accepting a Member State's right of veto in exceptional cases.

23 March
*EMS realignment*: the lira devalues by 6% against the central rates of the other EMS currencies (new ECU central rate of the guilder: 2.81318, DM: 2.54502).

23-24 March
In Maastricht the European Council considers it desirable to strengthen the dialogue with the United States with the aim of mutual consultation on *monetary policy* and interest rates.

29-30 June
In Luxembourg the European Council stresses that the EC should accord top priority to co-ordinated measures against *unemployment and inflation*.

5 October
*EMS realignment*: the Belgian franc, the Danish crown and the Irish pound are devalued by approx. 5.5% against the central rates of the German mark and the guilder. The French franc and the Italian lira are devalued by approx. 8.5% (new ECU central rate of the guilder: 2.66382, DM: 2.40989).

19 October
In Luxembourg the French Finance Minister Delors[94] says that transition to *Stage Two* of EMU is unrealistic.

6, 12 November
The German and Italian governments present the Genscher-Colombo Plan to the other Member States. In an explanatory statement to the European Parliament, Genscher argues for a *European Act* which should form the general framework for revising decision-making. The aim is that it should again become the norm for the Council of Ministers to decide by a majority vote as prescribed by the

---

[94] J. Delors (1925- ) was the French Minister for Economic and Financial Affairs from 1981 to 1984. In 1985 he was appointed President of the European Commission, a post which he held until the beginning of 1995. Delors is regarded as one of the most influential Commission Presidents since Hallstein.

EEC Treaty, and that "compelling interests" should only be invoked in exceptional cases. His colleague Colombo emphasises the need for an indissoluble link between politics and economics, which together should culminate in a specifically European strategy. The proposal for a European Act represents neither a new treaty nor a legally binding document, although it is a solemn declaration. Denmark, France and the United Kingdom do not wish to give up the right of veto.

26-27 November
In London the European Council urges for better co-ordination of economic and monetary policy and the promotion of the use of the ECU for EC loans. Delors is emphatically in favour of strengthening the ECU and monetary co-operation. The Council of Ministers (for foreign affairs) also requests dis-cussions with the Commission on the proposals formulated in the *Genscher-Colombo Plan* for a European Act converting relations between the ten Member States into a *European Union* in which economic integration should be paralleled by political development. Commission Vice President Ortoli states that it is not currently possible to start the institutional phase of the EMS.

14 December
Proposal by the Commission for granting it the authority to raise *loans* of ECU 1 billion to stimulate investment in the Community.

19 December
The Governor of the Belgian central bank Baron C. de Strycker presses for the termination of the *transitional phase* of the EMS. In the past thirteen months the dollar has risen by 45% against the ECU.

### 1982

15 February
The EC Council of Ministers debates the Commission's proposals for deepening the *EMS*. This includes the settlement of intervention debts in ECUs and expansion of intra-marginal intervention.

Deepening should simultaneously reinforce the internal discipline of the system.

22 February

*EMS realignment*: devaluation of the Danish crown by 3% and the Belgian franc by 8.5% against the central rates of the other EMS currencies (new ECU central rate of the guilder: 2.67296, DM: 2.41815). Luxembourg was only informed of the Belgian intention at the last minute. This leads Prime Minister Werner to conclude that the Belgian-Luxembourg monetary agreement, known as the BLEU Convention of May 1935, needs amending.

15 March

The EC Council of Ministers considers it possible and desirable to deepen the *EMS* by activating the co-ordination of the economic and monetary policy of the Member States, strengthening the technical mechanisms for mutual assistance in a pragmatic manner, encouraging and extending the use of the ECU and improving monetary co-operation between the Community and third countries. The proposals to that effect made earlier by the Commission are supported by France and Italy but encounter serious resistance from the Federal Republic of Germany in particular.

29-30 March

25th Anniversary of the signing of the EEC Treaty. In Brussels the European Council commemorates the signing of the Treaties establishing the EEC and Euratom on 25 March 1957. During the discussion of the economic situation the Council talks of a serious *structural crisis* in global economic development and in that connection it highlights the need for a co-ordinated policy to promote investment and combat unemployment.

26 April

The EC Council of Ministers approves the Commission's proposal for granting the Commission the authority to raise a *single loan tranche* of ECU 1 billion.

14 June

*EMS realignment*: the French franc is devalued by

10%, the Italian lira by 7% and the other EMS currencies by 4.5% against the central rates of the German mark and the guilder (new ECU central rate of the guilder: 2.57971, DM: 2.3379).

1982/83

28-29 June

In Brussels the European Council discusses the *accession negotiations* with Portugal and Spain.

5 July

The meeting between Belgium and Luxembourg results in the agreement on closer *consultation* in the case of potential realignments and establishing a link with the strongest currency, if possible.

9 July

The Commission submits a number of proposals aimed at strengthening the *internal market*. This concerns simplifying the formalities for freight transport and relaxing border controls for people travelling between Member States.

8 October

*Devaluation* of the Swedish crown by 16%.

19 October

Commission proposal to authorise a new *loan* of ECU 3 billion.

10 November

The Benelux Summit (the first since 20 October 1975) advocates closer *co-operation* which will help to bring about European integration.

3-4 December

In Copenhagen the European Council instructs the EC Council of Ministers to reach a decision by the end of March 1983 on the measures proposed by the Commission to strengthen the *internal market*.

17 December

Decision by the EC Council of Ministers to extend the *mechanism for medium-term financial assistance* by two years unless the final stage of the EMS enters into effect during this period.

1983

1 January

Germany takes over the *Presidency* of the EC.

| | |
|---|---|
| 10 January | *Devaluation* of the Greek drachma by 15.5% against the other currencies. |
| 7 February | The EC Council of Ministers agrees to the Commission's proposal that it be authorised to raise loans of up to a maximum of ECU 3 billion via the *NCI* to promote investment in the Community. |
| 21 March | *EMS realignment:* the Irish pound is devalued by 7%, the French franc and the Italian lira by 6%, the Belgian franc by 2% and the Danish crown by 1% against the central rate of the guilder. The central rate of the German mark is increased by 2% against the guilder (new ECU central rate of the guilder: 2.49587, DM: 2.21515). |
| 16 May | The EC Council of Ministers decides to grant France a Community loan of ECU 4 billion. This puts into effect the *mechanism of Community loans to provide balance of payments support*, laid down by a Regulation on 16 March 1981. |
| 17 May | The EC Council of Ministers and the Committee of Central Bank Governors decide to assign a fictitious ECU exchange rate to *sterling* based on the market rate of 17 May (new ECU central rate of the guilder: 2.52595, DM: 2.24184). |
| 20 May | The revision of the 1935 BLEU Convention culminates in the establishment of the *Luxembourg Monetary Institute (LMI)* as the central bank of Luxembourg. The LMI has no powers over credit policy, which is still controlled by the National Bank of Belgium. However, the LMI will manage Luxembourg's foreign exchange reserves, be the central monetary authority and represent Luxembourg in international monetary discussions (Luxembourg remains a member of the BLEU). |
| 17-19 June | At the European Council meeting in Stuttgart the ten heads of state and government sign the *Solemn Declaration on European Union* in which the |

Member States confine themselves to promising to give a general political impetus to European integration, in other words the Genscher-Colombo Plan has been watered down. According to the President of the Commission G. Thorn no-one expected any miracles from the European Council of Stuttgart. Personally, he would have liked something more than a programme of work. The German Chancellor H. Kohl[95] talks of "a first step which will certainly not satisfy everyone but which is a step in the right direction and at the right time".[96]

1 July

Greece takes over the *Presidency* of the EC.

4-5 December

At the European Council in Athens, differences of opinion on the reform of the agricultural policy and financing of the Community are not resolved, thus blocking any chance of reaching a decision on re-launching the *Community* and enlarging it to include Portugal and Spain. In the final sentence of the *communiqué* the Council notes that the Community of Europe should have gained speed but has been held back in an extremely dangerous way.

## 1984

1 January

France takes over the *Presidency* of the EC.

Abolition of the last *tariff barriers* and quantitative restrictions on trade in manufactured goods between the EC and EFTA. This creates the world's largest free trade area with a market numbering some 312 million consumers.

---

[95] H. Kohl (1930- ), Chancellor of the Federal Republic of Germany for the period 1979-1998, is known as a convinced pro-European in the tradition of Adenauer. His friendship with the French President Mitterand was important for Franco-German co-operation. In 1987 in Karlsruhe they announced the establishment of a Franco-German Security Council which was formalised the following year. Kohl will go down in history as the Chancellor who brought about German reunification and who was the driving force behind the success of the Treaty of Maastricht.
[96] Main events, 5, "The European Council of Stuttgart", *Bulletin of the European Communities*, 1983, no. 6, p. 25.

*History of the European Union*

12 March

The EC Council of Ministers evaluates the experience of *five years EMS*. It confirms that the main objective of "Bremen", namely to create "a zone of monetary stability in Europe", has been achieved. This is the Council's response to a Commission communication drawing attention to some significant weaknesses which still remains. For instance, little use is made of the official ECU which is not seen as a component of the reserves, and intervention on the currency markets is still effected mainly in dollars. Technical defects and particularly the importance that Member States attach to certain bilateral parities hamper the effectiveness of the convergence indicator.

19-20 March

In Brussels the European Council focuses on the *financing of the Community*. The United Kingdom and the other nine Member States disagree on the extent to which the United Kingdom should be compensated for its contribution to the Community budget, which London considers to be excessive.

9 April

For the first time since the free trade agreement was signed between the EC and EFTA, the ministers of the seventeen member countries meet. In a joint statement they emphasise the importance of further measures to consolidate and strengthen co-operation with the aim of creating a dynamic *European Economic Area (EEA)* for their countries.

25-26 June

In Fontainebleau the European Council decides to set up an ad hoc Committee for Institutional Questions (*Dooge Committee*) comprising representatives of the heads of state and government, modelled on the Spaak Committee. It's job is to suggest ways of improving European co-operation both on Community matters and in the sphere of political co-operation.[97]

---

[97] The Fontainebleau Agreement provides a solution to the problem of the British contribution to the EC budget, during the negotiations on which the British Prime Minister M. Thatcher spoke the legendary words: "I want my money back." Apart from that, the Fontainebleau meeting also decided on the establishment of a committee to prepare and co-ordinate the measures to be taken by the Community with a view to a "Citizens' Europe" (Adonnino Committee).

Agreement is reached on the reduction of the British contribution to the Community budget.

1984

1 July

Ireland takes over the *Presidency* of the EC.

16 July

The Commission presents a report on the allocation of the loan tranches already drawn via the *NCI*. The document reveals that the loan requests allowed by the Commission already exceed ECU 1 billion and are being used to help to effect investments totalling ECU 2.5 billion.

15 September

The EC Council of Ministers decides to revise the *composition of the ECU* in accordance with the European Council Resolution of 5 December 1978 providing for the establishment of the EMS. This revision does not alter the ECU central rates. The Council accedes to the Greek government's request to include the drachma in the ECU. The drachma is still not participating in the ERM.[98]

29 November

The Commission presents a draft resolution to the EC Council of Ministers containing measures to strengthen the *EMS*. The resolution has three aims: a) economic convergence in the EMS, particularly by adjusting the mechanism for medium-term financial assistance; b) the revival of the financial integration process; and c) strengthening of the EC mechanisms, particularly by expanding the use of the ECU.

3-4 December

In Dublin the European Council expresses its concern about the delay in the integration process. It urges the strengthening of the *EMS*. The Commission's draft resolution to that effect is favourably received and the Monetary Committee and the Committee of Central Bank Governors are asked to examine this draft.

10 December

The EC Council of Ministers decides to extend the

---

[98] The ECU central rate of the drachma was set at 84.4813 per ECU while the fictitious ECU central rate for sterling was slightly modified and fixed at £0.585992 per ECU.

mechanism for medium-term financial assistance until 31 December 1986 unless the final stage of the EMS starts before that date.

19 December        The Commission passes three decisions authorising France, Ireland and Italy to continue to apply certain *safeguard measures* to capital movements.

1985

1 January          Italy takes over the *Presidency* of the EC.

7 January          *New Commission* takes office, with J. Delors as President.

14 January         Commission President Delors states that he refuses to join in the *euro pessimism*. Speaking about the institutional operation of the Community he refers to differences of dogma that everyone can use as an excuse for doing nothing. Delors argues that those differences must be eliminated, and the Commission should offer a helping hand by giving inspiration and encouragement.

9 March            The Dooge Committee recommends convening an intergovernmental conference to negotiate a draft treaty on *European Union*.

13 March           Signing of the agreement by the ten Member States whereby *Greenland* is no longer part of the European Community but remains associated as an overseas territory.[99]

29-30 March        European Council in Brussels. In order to improve the decision-making process, the majority of the Dooge Committee favours acceptance of a new general principle whereby decisions are to be passed

[99] When Denmark joined the EC, Greenland also became a member. On 1 May 1979 the system of autonomy for Greenland took effect, providing for the gradual transfer of certain powers from Denmark to Greenland. In a referendum on 23 February 1982 the majority (52%) of the population of that territory voted in favour of Greenland's withdrawal from the Community.

by a qualified or ordinary majority. Unanimity is still required in certain exceptional cases, far fewer in number than under the Treaties. The committee also favours strengthening the Commission's powers and the role of the European Parliament. A report to the European Council contains the following comments: "A qualitative leap forward should now be made and the various proposals should be presented as a whole, to express the common political will of the Member States. That will should ultimately find expression in the establishment of a genuine *political entity* between European countries, i.e. a European Union ...".[100] The European Council decides to continue developing these proposals in bilateral contacts so that final conclusions may be reached at the meeting in Milan. Political agreement is also reached on the accession of Portugal and Spain to the EC.

14-15 April

In an informal meeting at Palermo, the EC Council of Ministers approves the agreement by the Committee of Central Bank Governors on strengthening the *EMS*. The rate of interest paid on the ECU, which has hitherto been linked to the official discount rates, is raised to the market level. The agreement also makes it possible for central banks outside the EC and international monetary institutions to hold official ECUs in their reserves. In addition, the obligation to accept ECUs in settlement of mutual intervention debts is widened.

8 May

Recommendation by the European Parliament on enlargement of the EC to include Portugal and Spain. As prescribed in the *Solemn Declaration* of Stuttgart, the Parliament was consulted by the EC Council of Ministers for the first time before the signing of the treaties of accession.

10 May

Commemoration of the 25th anniversary of *EFTA* in Vienna. Commission President Delors talks about the

1984/85

---

[100] Documentation, 5: "Report of the ad hoc Committee for Institutional Questions", *Bulletin of the European Communities*, 1985, no. 3, p. 111.

common market and co-operation in the field of technology, aspects which in his view already mean the institutional strengthening of Europe.

21 May

Italy presents a draft mandate whereby the *Intergovernmental Conference* will negotiate a treaty on the gradual establishment of the EU. The Netherlands proposes that the conference objective should be to revise the EEC Treaty in accordance with Article 236 and to draw up a protocol for the consolidation and institutionalisation of political co-operation.

8-9 June

Informal meeting of the EC Council of Ministers (for foreign affairs) during which the United Kingdom submits a document on the decision-making process (adjustments not requiring amendment of the EEC Treaty) and a draft agreement on *political co-operation*.

12 June

The *Treaties of accession* of Portugal and Spain are signed in Lisbon and Madrid. In his speech the Italian Foreign Affairs Minister G. Andreotti states that as a result of this accession, the geographical Europe will increasingly coincide with the political and institutional Europe.

14 June

The Commission publishes a *White Paper on the completion of the internal market*. It develops measures to be taken up to 1992 to eliminate all physical, technical and fiscal barriers within the EC. One of the report's conclusions reads as follows: "Just as the customs union had to precede economic integration, so economic integration must precede European Union. This White Paper therefore proposes that the Community should now take a new step in the direction so clearly defined by the Treaties." In this connection it refers to the preamble to the EEC Treaty which speaks of the determination "to lay the foundations of an ever closer union among the peoples of Europe".[101]

The Schengen Agreement on elimination of border controls is signed by Belgium, the Federal Republic of Germany, France, Luxembourg and the Netherlands in Schengen (Luxembourg).

28-29 June

In Milan the European Council holds detailed discussions on convening an *Intergovernmental Conference* in order to work out the following: a) a Treaty on a common policy on foreign affairs and security based on the Franco-German and British draft; b) the amendments to the EEC Treaty (in accordance with Article 236) which are necessary for implementing the institutional changes as regards the decision-making process of the EC Council of Ministers, the executive powers of the Commission and the powers of the European Parliament. The Council welcomes the White Paper and instructs the Council of Ministers to draw up an action programme so that a genuine single market can be completed in the Community no later than 1992 by set stages which conform to predetermined priorities and a binding timetable.

1 July

Luxembourg takes over the *Presidency* of the EC.

Greece joins the *EMS* but does not take part in the ERM for the time being.

22 July

*EMS realignment*: the Italian lira is devalued by 8% against the other EMS currencies (new ECU central rate of the guilder: 2.52208; DM: 2.23840). The Greek drachma is also devalued by 15%. Greece is granted a Community loan of ECU 1.75 billion.

---

[101] Commission of the European Communities, 1985, *The completion of the internal market*, Commission White Paper for the European Council, CCOM (85)310 final, p. 55. This report is known as the *Cockfield White Paper*, named after Lord Cockfield, Commissioner for Trade. The report contains a list of 300 statutory measures necessary to create an internal market.

The EC Council of Ministers approves convening a Conference of Representatives of the Member States to *make amendments to the EEC Treaty* and to draft a common foreign and security policy.

9 September    First meeting of the Intergovernmental Conference in Luxembourg, attended by the Foreign Affairs Ministers of the Ten plus Spain and Portugal. The conference has the task of revising the *EEC Treaty* and drawing up a Treaty on foreign policy and common security. Commission President Delors proposes that the Community's powers be extended in four areas: the large European market, technical know-how, economic and social cohesion and "certain monetary powers".

22 September    *Plaza Agreement*: the five major industrial countries (the Federal Republic of Germany, France, Japan, the United Kingdom and the United States) issue a joint statement in which they acknowledge that "considerable progress" has been made in promoting the convergence of economic development between the member countries, but that serious external imbalances could potentially cause problems. These countries state their policy intentions to obtain greater balanced growth. Exchange rates are needed which more accurately reflect the underlying economic factors. Further orderly appreciation of the other currencies against the dollar is considered desirable.

21 October    At the second meeting of the Intergovernmental Conference the draft treaty on *political co-operation* is not yet discussed. Commission President Delors says that all members regard the internal market as the decisive factor for *relaunching* the construction of Europe.

28 October    The EC Council of Ministers approves a regulation amending the EMS as regards the use of the ECU by third parties. The aim of this regulation is to enable the central banks of the Community to transfer ECUs

bilaterally and temporarily from the EMCF to the central banks of third countries and international monetary institutions. On that occasion Commission President Delors attempts to get the EMS incorporated in the *EEC Treaty*. This would confirm the powers of the EC institutions in Community monetary matters and give the Commission the right of initiative with regard to the future development of monetary co-operation in the Community.

2-3 December

In Luxembourg the European Council reaches agreement in principle on the reform of the *Community institutions*. The agreement provides in particular for increasing the number of decisions taken by a majority vote so that a single, internal market can be created in the Community by the end of 1992. It is decided to undertake a limited revision of the EEC Treaty and to prepare a draft treaty on European co-operation in the field of foreign policy. The European Parliament has more say, but the EC Council of Ministers will still have the last word. The ministers may present the outcome of the conference on the amendments to the EEC Treaty and the text on political co-operation in the form of a single act.

16-17 December

The seventh Intergovernmental Conference in Brussels puts the finishing touches to all the texts of the European Council of Luxembourg which are combined in a *Single European Act (SEA)* which will be presented to the Member States for signature at the end of January 1986. This is the first time that both the development of the Community by a revision of the EEC Treaty (most importantly by extending  the scope of qualified majority voring) and the development of political co-operation are regulated in a single act. However, it proves impossible to incorporate the objective of EMU as a new Treaty obligation. The text finally agreed stresses the need for co-operation in the economic and monetary spheres. A new amendment to the Treaty will be necessary for institutional changes relating to economic and monetary policy. The

1985

Common Provisions (Title 1 of the European Act) accord the European Council institutional status. Denmark and Italy uphold their general reservation while the United Kingdom maintains a reservation regarding the social chapter.

31 December

The *oil price* is $27 per barrel. A fall sets in, and the price reaches a low of $9 per barrel in July 1986.

1986

1 January

The Netherlands takes over the *Presidency* of the EC.

Portugal and Spain join the *EC.*

21 January

The Danish parliament passes a resolution stating that the *SEA* is unacceptable in its current form.

7 February

The ministers for foreign affairs of nine Member States ratify the *SEA.* Denmark, Greece and Italy have not yet decided their position. According to the Dutch minister H. van den Broek the Act is "primarily an instrument in the service of a political will …".[102]

17, 28 February

The *SEA* is signed in Luxembourg and The Hague

22 February

*Louvre Accord*: the seven industrial countries (Canada, the Federal Republic of Germany, France, Italy, Japan, the United Kingdom and the United States) issue a joint declaration announcing that their currencies are now at a level consistent with their economic situation in relation to one another, given the agreed policy objectives. Further substantial exchange rate fluctuations could damage the prospects for growth and adjustment. Agreement is reached on closer co-operation to secure stable exchange rates at around the current level.

---

[102] Main events, 1. "Signing of the European Act", *Bulletin of the European Communities*, 1986, no. 2, p. 8.

28 February

Denmark, Greece and Italy ratify the *SEA* following a referendum in Denmark on 27 February in which 56% of the electorate agreed to the proposal.

5 March

In accordance with the convergence decision of 18 February 1974, the Commission issues a communication on the economic situation in the Community. Despite the economic recovery, *unemployment* is described as a very serious problem. The Commission therefore considers it urgently necessary to apply without delay the co-operative strategy for growth and employment which it proposed previously.

7 April

*EMS realignment*: all other EMS currencies are devalued against the German mark and the guilder: the French franc by around 6%, the Belgian franc and the Danish crown by around 2%, the Italian lira and the Irish pound by around 3% (new ECU central rate of the guilder: 2.40935, DM: 2.13834). Belgium seeks to link its economic policy with that of Germany and the Netherlands.

21 May

The Commission adopts a communication addressed to the EC Council of Ministers setting a programme for the *liberalisation* of capital movements in the Community. The creation of a homogeneous financial area is one aspect of the large internal market to be created by 1992 according to the objective stated in the SEA.

26-27 June

European Council meeting in The Hague which is also attended by Portugal and Spain. The Council welcomes the *proposals for* the *liberalisation* of capital movements and encourages the Council of Ministers to place these proposals high on the agenda.

1 July

The United Kingdom takes over the *Presidency* of the EC.

4 August

*EMS realignment* as a result of the continuing

weakness of the Irish pound, which is devalued by 8% against the other EMS currencies (new ECU central rate of the guilder: 2.37833; DM: 2.11083).

17 November         The EC Council of Ministers approves the directive providing for the amendment of the First Directive of 11 May 1960 and the extension of the Community obligations to *liberalise* capital movements.

5-6 December        In London the European Council confirms the commitment entered into in The Hague to pursue a *joint growth strategy*. The EC Council of Ministers is invited to continue the talks on the EMS in order to reinforce the convergence of the economic policy of the Member States and monetary stability in Europe.

15-16 December      The EC Council of Ministers agrees to amend its rules of procedure to facilitate *majority decisions*. In 1986 the Council decided on around one hundred issues in this way, representing major progress in comparison with the past.

1987

1 January           Belgium takes over the *Presidency* of the EC.

12 January          *EMS realignment*: the Belgian franc is devalued by 1% against the German mark and the guilder while the French franc, the Italian lira, the Danish crown and the Irish pound are devalued by 3% (new ECU central rate of the guilder: 2.31943, DM: 2.05853).

18 February         Commission President Delors presents the Commission's programme for 1987 to the European Parliament, accompanied by the "Single Act: A new frontier for Europe" setting out the conditions for achieving the aims of the SEA and proposals for completing the reform of the CAP, the structural investments and the Community's financial arrangements.

25 February         The Commission decides to extend the scope of the

*safeguard measures* for Greece, Ireland and Italy to include transactions covered by the Council Directive of 17 November 1986 on the liberalisation of capital movements.

25 March

30th Anniversary of the signing of the *EEC Treaty*. Acting Chairman of the EC Council of Ministers L. Tindemans notes that "what the pioneers wanted to achieve is still our objective. Europe remains a concept consisting of many different elements which can be combined into a specific identity. It is therefore obvious that this set of cultural, political, economic and social values must be given a structure which unites Europeans ... If an oath should be sworn here in Rome invoking the ideals which were already partly embodied in a treaty in 1957, then it is that we shall not rest until European Union is achieved. Let our commemoration form an oath of allegiance – the Capitol oath of allegiance to such a Union".[103]

14 April

The Turkish government submits an official application for *accession to the EC.*

23 April

Publication of a report on the strategy for developing the economic system of the EC by a group of independent experts chaired by the Italian T. Padoa-Schioppa. Recommendations in the report include the *co-ordination of monetary policy* and a considerable reinforcement of the EMS mechanisms in order to maintain freedom of capital movements and discipline on the exchange markets.

11 May

In its second report on the implementation of the *White Paper on the completion of the internal market* the Commission considers the results disappointing but not discouraging.

---

[103] "Commemoration. Passages from the speeches on 25 March 1987 at the Capitol in Rome during the official celebration of the thirtieth anniversary of the signing of the Treaties of Rome", *Bulletin of the European Communities*, 1987, no. 2, supplement 2/87, pp. 9-10.

13 May    The *Banco de España* signs an official act whereby Spain becomes a party to the *EMS agreement*. After depositing 20% of its gold and foreign exchange reserves with the EMCF, Spain will hold a position similar to that of the United Kingdom and Greece, with the exception of the peseta which is not yet included in the ECU basket of currencies.

16 June   The German *Bundesbank* decides to allow the *ECU* to be used by individuals to the same extent as foreign exchange. Since Portugal has accepted the ECU for stock market listing with effect from 15 September 1985, the ECU is now recognised *de facto* or *de jure* in all Member States.

19-20 June   In Brussels the European Council asserts that one of the Community's primary tasks is to create a *common economic area* which includes realising the internal market and economic and social cohesion. Reference is made to the importance of the White Paper on the completion of the internal market. In order to keep to the 1992 deadline, the Council requests the competent bodies to take the necessary decisions, including the complete liberalisation of capital movements.

1 July    Denmark takes over the *Presidency* of the EC.

          The *Single European Act* enters into force.

31 July   The Commission withdraws the authorisation granted to Italy in December 1984 to continue applying certain *safeguard measures*. This withdrawal follows the relaxation of foreign exchange controls by the Italian authorities on 15 May, when they abolished the non-interest-bearing deposit that residents had to make when purchasing securities and property abroad.

12 September   Informal meeting of the EC Council of Ministers in Nyborg (Denmark). The Ministers approve the agreement by the Committee of Central Bank

Governors to improve the functioning of the EMS without any institutional changes. Pursuant to this *Basle-Nyborg Agreement*, adequate interest rate differentials will be implemented promptly while the full permitted band width will be used to discourage speculative capital flows. There will also be closer mutual surveillance of developments in the EMS.

28 October

The Commission approves proposals for the full *liberalisation* of capital movements in the Community. In that connection it has abolished the safeguard clause which some countries were permitted to apply. From now on only Greece, Ireland, Portugal and Spain may maintain their restrictions on capital transactions, the first two countries pursuant to the EEC Treaty (Article 108) and the last two pursuant to the Act of Accession.

10 November

The *Banco de Portugal* signs an official act whereby Portugal becomes party to the *EMS* agreement. After depositing 20% of its gold and foreign exchange reserves with the EMCF, Portugal will hold a position comparable to that of Greece, Spain and the United Kingdom with the proviso that the escudo, like the peseta, is not yet part of the ECU basket.

4-5 December

In Copenhagen the European Council decides to hold an additional meeting in February 1988 as there is evidently no political will to resolve the difficulties over the Commission's proposals for *reforms* in the Community. The acting President P. Schlüter puts the problem as follows: "… It is the art of persuading a number of independent nations to co-operate. We can very meaningfully call this the art of co-operation."[104]

17 December

Publication of a progress report on the EMS and the liberalisation of capital movements drawn up by the

---

[104] Main Events, 1. "Implementation of the Single European Act, Passages from the addresses by Mr. Schlüter and Mr. Delors before the European Parliament", *Bulletin of the European Communities*, 1987, no. 12, p. 8.

Commission on the request made by the European Council at the end of 1985. According to this report, the completion of the internal market, the strengthening of the EMS in 1987 and the achievement of free movement of capital are closely interdependent. It refers to the two-fold need to extend the EMS to the whole Community and create a genuine European financial area, including freedom to provide financial services. Finally, the Commission advocates the creation of an *Economic and Monetary Union*, the only way of increasing the Community's prosperity in the long term and enhancing its contribution to international economic and monetary equilibrium.

22 December     *Telephone agreement* by the seven industrial countries (Canada, the Federal Republic of Germany, France, Italy, Japan, the United Kingdom and the United States) in which they reconfirm the fundamental economic policy objectives as agreed in the Louvre Accord. They also declare that the recent monetary policy decisions and the reduction in interest rates are regarded as desirable and that large exchange rate fluctuations or further changes in the dollar exchange rate, producing a destabilising effect, may be counter-productive for world economic growth prospects.

1988

1 January       The Federal Republic of Germany takes over the *Presidency* of the EC.

11-13 February  In Brussels the European Council reaches agreement on all the conclusions realing to "The Single Act: A new frontier for Europe".[105] The conclusions smooth

---

[105] In the same month the *Cecchini Report* was published as the outcome of the "Programme of research on the costs of a non-united Europe" undertaken by the Commission in 1986. This report demonstrated not only the extent of the costs of having twelve separate markets (around ECU 200 billion per annum) but also showed what tremendous potential prospects were offered by completing the internal market.

the way for the completion of the *internal market* because compromises have been reached on the following subjects: level of Community resources, budgetary discipline and budget control, system of own resources, complementary policies (including reform of the structural funds) and the reform of the agricultural policy. According to the Commission President Delors, this confirms the success of the approach adopted by Jean Monnet: "This approach means that the greater the number of decision parameters ... The greater the effort that everyone must make to achieve a higher goal that creates momentum according to a precise timetable accepted by everyone."[106]

29 March

The Commission publishes results of "Europe 1992 – The overall Challenge", a study carried out by a group of independent experts to assess the advantages of the SEA. So far the Commission has submitted 208 of the 300 proposals mentioned in the White Paper to the EC Council of Ministers.

20 May

Commission proposal for an *integrated mechanism for financial support for the balances of payments of the Member States*. This proposal combines the medium-term credit facility with the Community loan instrument. The total contribution by Member States in the medium-term mechanism (ECU 13.9 billion) remains unchanged. The proposal sets a maximum of ECU 16 billion for granting loans, regardless of the source of finance, and a sub-maximum of ECU 14 billion as the limit on loans financed by the Community via the capital market.

24 June

To promote the *European financial area*, the EC Council of Ministers approves a directive and a regulation which respectively concern the full liberalisation of capital movements with effect from 1 July 1990 and the establishment of an integrated

[106] Main Events, 1. "Implementation of the Single European Act", *Bulletin of the European Communities*, 1988, no. 3, p. 9.

mechanism for medium-term financial support for the balances of payments of the Member States. As regards the liberalisation of capital movements, a transitional period will apply until the end of December 1992 to Member States with a less developed money and capital market (Greece, Ireland, Portugal and Spain). Belgium and Luxembourg abolish their dual exchange market on the same date.

25 June

A joint declaration is signed establishing *official relations* between the Community and the CMEA.

27-28 June

In Hanover the European Council decides to set up a committee (*Delors Committee*) whose task will be to examine concrete steps that may lead to EMU. The United Kingdom declares that neither a European Central Bank (ECB) nor a European currency are required for the establishment of EMU. The Federal Republic of Germany sees the ECB as the culmination of progressively closer monetary co-operation. The Council agrees to reappoint Delors President of the Commission.

1 July

Greece takes over the *Presidency* of the EC.

The *Interinstitutional Agreement* (between Council of Ministers, Commission and European Parliament) on budgetary discipline and improvement of the budgetary procedure approved in June, enters into force.

8 July

In a regulation the EC Council of Ministers agrees to the establishment of an *integrated mechanism for financial support for the balances of payments of the Member States*.

16 September

The Commission adopts a proposal for a regulation on the application of the decision of 24 June with regard to the Community's *own resources*. The aim of this proposal is to replace the system of Member

States' own contributions with effect from 1 January 1989.

15 November         Portugal and Spain join the *WEU*.

22 November         The Commission decides that the authorisation granted to Greece in November 1985 to apply certain *safeguard measures* in capital transactions should continue to the end of 1989.

2-3 December        In Rhodes the European Council reports on progress in implementing the SEA, placing the emphasis on the *social dimension* and the associated policy measures. The single market cannot be regarded as an end in itself, but is aimed at a broader objective of ensuring that the social progress which is part of Europe's historical tradition ensures optimum prosperity for everyone. The Council confirms that the process of completing the internal market has given a new impetus to the European economy by stimulating economic reforms and reviving growth.

### 1989

1 January           Spain takes over the *Presidency* of the EC.

13 March            The EC Council of Ministers commemorates the 10th anniversary of the *EMS*. It is unanimous in stating that the EMS has led to lower inflation and more stable exchange rates, and thus contributed to sound economic growth. A Commission communication to the Council of Ministers calls the EMS the focal point of the Community's efforts to bring about greater convergence. The greatest divergences between EMS countries concern budgetary policy. According to the Commission, the monetary financing of budget deficits has decreased greatly in recent years, "a development in which the EMS has undoubtedly played a central role".[107]

---

[107] Main Events, 1, "The Tenth Anniversary of the European Monetary System", *Bulletin of the European Communities*, 1989, no. 3, p. 8.

12 April                    Presentation of the *Delors Report* describing the most
                            important elements of EMU and how it can be
                            achieved in the EC. It proposes achieving EMU in
                            three stages. Stage One centres on economic
                            convergence and equally on closer co-ordination of
                            policy. Stage Two is the transitional stage which can
                            begin once the necessary amendments have been
                            made to the EC Treaty. In Stage Three, exchange
                            rates must be irrevocably fixed. After a time, the
                            national currencies can be replaced by the ECU and
                            the single currency. The report concludes that only
                            one monetary policy can be pursued in the union, and
                            that will require the establishment of the European
                            System of Central Banks (ESCB). In contrast, no new
                            institution is considered necessary for non-monetary
                            policy "because the required institutional framework
                            has already been provided by the Treaty of Rome.
                            However, some expansion and adjustments to the
                            functions of the existing institutions will be
                            necessary".[108]

19 June                     Spain joins the *ERM* with a fluctuation margin of
                            ±6% (ECU central rate of the peseta: 133.504).
                            Sterling, the Greek drachma and the Portuguese
                            escudo do not yet take part in the mechanism.

26-27 June                  In Madrid the European Council adopts conclusions
                            on EMU. The Council decides to start Stage One on
                            1 July 1990. At the same time, preparations for the
                            later stages, including the Intergovernmental
                            Conference, will begin. The Council stresses the need
                            to eliminate material and fiscal barriers with a view to
                            creating an *area without internal borders.*

1 July                      France takes over the *Presidency of the EC.*

17 July                     The Austrian government submits an official
                            application for *accession to the EC.*

---

[108] Main Events, 1. "Report by the Committee for Studying Economic and Monetary Union",
*Bulletin of the European Communities*, 1989, no. 4, p. 8.

9-10 September

In Antibes, France, the EC Council of Ministers agrees on the need to review the *Decision of 8 May 1964* on co-operation between the central banks of the Member States and the Decision of 18 February 1974 on the convergence of economic policy.

21 September

The Spanish peseta and the Portuguese escudo are included in the *ECU basket*. As from that date the weightings in the ECU are as follows: Belgian franc 3.301, Danish crown 0.1976, German mark 0.6242, Greek drachma 1.440, Portuguese escudo 1.393, French franc 1.332, Dutch guilder 1.2918, Irish pound 0.008552, Luxembourg franc 1.130, Italian lira 151.8, Spanish peseta 6.885 and pound sterling 0.08784.

9 November

The fall of the *Berlin Wall* marks the collapse of communism in Europe. A publication issued in 1992 discusses the possible implications for the countries of Western Europe:

" ... since the autumn of 1989 the Twelve's declared commitment to proceed to political union did not find clear expression in the pronouncements of West European leaders like Mrs. Thatcher, President Mitterand or Chancellor Kohl on their political pilgrimages to East European capitals. Quite often their statements and policy objectives did not give the impression that they formed part of a coherent whole. Arguably, therefore, the revolutions in Eastern Europe and the retreat of the Soviet Union present the danger of reopening Europe's Pandora Box which, if unchecked, might spill over to Western Europe ... In other words the revolutions of Eastern Europe and the likely disintegration of the Soviet Union and Yugoslavia have raised the pertinent question whether ... instead of moving towards 1992 we are not heading towards 1914. Whether a Balkanization or Libanization etc. could be averted or contained. Whether the EC, and other West European institutions, have grown strongly enough to stand together and help the Eastern European

1989

countries to gradually close the gap and join with the prosperous half of Western Europe. Or, whether the gap has indeed become unbridgeable in which case one should not rule out an alternative nightmarish scenario whereby Western Europe becomes 'East Europeanized', 'Third Worldized' or simply thrown back to its heroic or barbaric past, complete with new religions and new wars, new prophets and new Caesars."[109]

| | |
|---|---|
| 14-15 November | The EC Council of Ministers takes note of the report by a *High Level Working Party*. This report defines the main technical, institutional and political issues to which a solution must be found in order to draw up a treaty on EMU, and as such is a suitable instrument for convening an intergovernmental conference. |
| 8 December | In Strasbourg the EC Council decides that an *Intergovernmental Conference* will be held before the end of 1990 to draft amendments to the EEC Treaty for the final stage of EMU. It also decides to set up the European Bank for Reconstruction and Development (EBRD). The EC and its Member States own 51% of its capital. |
| 19 December | In a joint statement the EC Council of Ministers and the Ministers of the EFTA countries decide to open *formal negotiations* as early as possible in the first half of 1990 on the subject of an agreement concerning better structured co-operation between the Community and all EFTA countries. |

1990

| | |
|---|---|
| 1 January | Ireland takes over the *Presidency* of the EC. |
| 5 January | *EMS realignment.* Italy reverts to the narrow fluctuation margin of ±2.25% following a 3.68% devaluation of the central rate of the lira. This is the |

---

[109] P. Tsakaloyannis, 1992, "Risks and opportunities in the East and South" in A. Pijpers, ed., *The European Community at the Crossroads*, Dordrecht, p. 186.

twelfth realignment since the EMS started in March 1979 (new ECU central rate of the guilder: 2.30358, DM: 2.04446).

28 March

The (fifth) annual Commission report on the implementation of the *White Paper on the completion of the internal market* confirms the irreversibility of the establishment of the internal market by about 1992. There are still some problems, e.g. as regards taxation and the abolition of border controls for persons.

19 April

President F. Mitterand[110] and Chancellor H. Kohl propose that *political unity* in the EC should start around 1 January 1993. The proposals comprise: increasing democratic control to provide a legitimate basis for political unity, improving the efficiency of the EC institutions, ensuring economic, monetary and political cohesion in the EC and establishing a common foreign and security policy. Shortly afterwards, the two men call on the European Council to convene an Intergovernmental Conference by December 1990 on the subject of political unity, to coincide with the planned summit on EMU.

28 April

In Dublin an extraordinary meeting of the European Council results in unanimous agreement on a common approach to *German unification* and relations with the countries of Central and Eastern Europe. In response to the proposals presented by Mitterand and Kohl on political union, the Council decides on the following measures: a) a detailed examination of whether amendments could perhaps be made to the Treaties to strengthen the democratic legitimacy of the Union; b) proposals by the foreign

---

[110] F. Mitterand (1916-1996) was France's President from 1981 to 1995. Thanks to his efforts, a solution was found at Fontainebleau in June 1984 to the problem of the British contribution to the EC budget (see footnote 97). On European affairs, Mitterand responded to the challenge of German unification by strongly advocating European integration, with Germany and France bound closely to one another as the main pillars for the development of the European Union under the Maastricht Treaty.

affairs ministers for examining whether a second intergovernmental conference might be held at the same time as the conference on EMU.

8 May

The Commission reports to the Council of Ministers on the preparations which have begun with the EFTA countries. It requests permission to open negotiations with these countries (including Liechtenstein) to conclude an agreement on the creation of a *European Economic Area (EEA)*.

9 May

40th Anniversary of the *Schuman Declaration*. The chairman of the European Parliament E. Baron Crespi refers to EMU and EPU discussed at the European Council meeting in Dublin as the final aims which Schuman had in mind in 1950. The Political Union which has been permanently claimed by the European Parliament since 1984 creates a new dimension for Europe. Crespi firmly believes that Schuman would have said now: "let it be realised as soon as possible."[111]

21-23 May

The *Treaty on economic and monetary union between East and West Germany*, signed on 18 May, is approved by the West German parliament. Following ratification by the two German parliaments, the German mark is introduced into the unified currency area as the single currency from 1 July.

29 May

Signing of the constituent agreement of the *EBRD* whose objective is to finance industrial and economic development in the East European countries by funding loans, guarantees and investments and to promote the transition by these countries to the free market economy.

---

[111] "Commemoration of the Schuman Declaration", *Bulletin of the European Communities*, 1990, no. 5, p. 135.

| | |
|---|---|
| 11 June | The *Bundesbank* Governor K.O. Pöhl[112] submits a proposal to the EC Council of Ministers for achieving EMU by a *"two-speed process"*. His plan envisages that a small number of low-inflation countries (Benelux, the Federal Republic of Germany and France) will join the ECB. The other countries which have not achieved the same degree of economic convergence or are not prepared to surrender sufficient autonomy will be invited to join later. |
| 18 June | The EC Council of Ministers (for general affairs) approves the guidelines for negotiations between the EC and EFTA on the creation of the *EEA*. |
| 19 June | The Benelux countries, the Federal Republic of Germany and France sign the *Schengen Application Convention*[113] whereby these countries agree to eliminate all border checks for people. |
| 20 June | The United Kingdom submits proposals for a gradual transition to EMU by introduction of a *parallel currency*, the "hard" ECU. |
| | The EC and EFTA start *formal negotiations* for the creation of the EEA. |
| 25-26 June | In Dublin the European Council lays down the guidelines for full implementation of the *SEA*. The Council also agrees to convene an intergovernmental conference on EPU. It also discusses the preparations for the intergovernmental conference on EMU which |

1990

---

[112] K.O. Pöhl (1929- ) succeeded O. Emminger in 1980 as President of the German Bundesbank. His reticence on monetary union between the two German states was at odds with Chancellor Kohl's determination to effect the rapid introduction of the D-Mark in East Germany. The growing tension between the two prompted Pöhl's resignation in 1991, though in his official statement he did not mention any direct connection between that decision and the (accelerated) introduction of monetary union in the GDR.

[113] The official name is "Convention applying the Schengen Agreement of 14 June 1985 [...] on the gradual abolition of checks at their common borders". The most striking feature of this Convention is its failure (despite some visa harmonization) to harmonize national legislation on criminal and security policies (see J. Th. Leerssen and M. van Montfrans, 1993, p. 61).

has already been agreed. The opening dates for the two conferences are fixed for 13 and 14 December.

1 July

Italy takes over the *Presidency* of the EC.

Start of *Stage One* of EMU. Most Member States abolish all restrictions on capital movements. For Greece, Ireland, Portugal and Spain there is a derogation giving them time to comply with the directive until the end of 1992.

*Monetary Union* between East and West Germany becomes reality.

4 July

Cyprus submits an official application for *accession to the EC*

12 July

The Greek government announces its intention that *Greece* shall join the *EMS* in 1993 if the government's tax measures are successfully implemented.

16 July

Malta submits an official application for *accession to the EC*.

21 August

The Commission proposes that *Stage Two* of EMU should start on 1 January 1993. This stage is to be one of intensive preparation in which the ESCB will be set up. The start of Stage Three will have to form the subject of a political agreement by the European Council: "If Economic and Monetary Union is to be totally efficient, then there must be institutional progress which will bring the Community much closer to political union. The intergovernmental conference on EMU should therefore be viewed in conjunction with the intergovernmental conference on political union. Economic union should be based on the completion of the internal market, closer co-ordination of economic policy measures and the development of common policies. In addition, the Treaty should prohibit the monetary financing of government budget deficits as well as the provision of surety for a Member State. The principle of running an excessive budget deficit is not acceptable."[114]

8 September

The EC Council of Ministers fails to reach agreement on the *speed of integration*. Spain proposes starting Stage Two on 1 January 1994 and completing the transition to Stage Three within a maximum of five to six years.

12 September

Signing in Moscow of the *"Treaty on the Final Arrangements with regard to the Federal Republic of Germany"* by the two German states, France, the Soviet Union, the United Kingdom and the United States.

19 September

Governor Pöhl of the *Bundesbank* sets absolute requirements for EMU: it must be based on economic and financial co-ordination between Member States, especially as regards anti-inflation policy and contractually enforced *budgetary discipline*. In the final stage of EMU to be achieved via a "long-term transition process" he envisages that the ESCB's independence will be guaranteed and that it will be able to impose sanctions on governments which fail to comply with the budgetary discipline.

3 October

The Treaty on *German Unification* takes effect. As a result, five East German Länder (Brandenburg, Mecklenburg/West Pomerania, Saxony, Saxony-Anhalt and Thüringia) and East Berlin join the Federal Republic of Germany and therefore become members of the Community family.

8 October

Sterling joins the *ERM*. The value of the pound can fluctuate ±6% against the central rate (new ECU central rate of the guilder: 2.31643, DM: 2.05586).

---

[114] Activities in July-August 1990, 2. "The unified market and the economic and social area in the Community", *Bulletin of the European Communities*, 1990, no. 7/8, p. 15.

19 October                  Norway links the crown to the *ECU* (fluctuation margin ±2.25%) as a step towards closer co-operation with the EC.

27-28 October               Extraordinary meeting of the European Council in Rome (Rome I). All Member States except the United Kingdom agree to the start of *Stage Two* on 1 January 1994. As regards EPU, the Council confirms its aim of gradually transforming the European Community by developing its political dimension. This transformation should be accompanied by expansion of the legislative role of the European Parliament and the strengthening of the other institutions. The Council notes that there is a consensus on the objective of a common foreign and security policy.

19-21 November              In Paris the 34 heads of state or government of the CSCE sign a charter for a *new Europe*.

21 November                 The Commission issues a progress report on the programme for completion of the internal market set out in the 1985 *White Paper*.[115] It asserts that the attainment of the 1992 objective increasingly depends on the elimination of fiscal borders.

27 November                 Italy signs the *Schengen Agreement*.

6 December                  The Federal Republic of Germany and France submit proposals for *political union*, particularly for the development of a common foreign policy and a common security policy. A clear organisational link should be established between the WEU and the new political union, which the WEU should eventually join. The proposal is criticised by the Dutch Prime Minister R. Lubbers who considers that it will disturb the existing balance between the EC institutions.

---

[115] The Single European Act has made it possible to initiate legislation in areas not formally covered by the White Paper. This concerns in particular the implementation of the structural funds and the action programme on the social charter.

| | |
|---|---|
| 14-15 December | In Rome the European Council (Rome II) agrees to continue playing an essential role in setting the political pace in important issues. It stresses that the extension of the *Union's powers* must be accompanied by a stronger role for the Commission. The possibility of majority voting becoming the general rule for decisions by the EC Council of Ministers will also be examined. |
| 15 December | First session of the *Intergovernmental Conference* in Rome. The European Council confirms that the two conferences will continue to work side by side and can be concluded by the end of 1992. |
| 19 December | The EEC/EFTA meeting of ministers achieves a breakthrough in the negotiations on the establishment of the *EEA* by the summer of 1991. |

1990/91

1991

| | |
|---|---|
| 1 January | Luxembourg takes over the *Presidency* of the EC. |
| 8 January | The British Chancellor of the Exchequer N. Lamont presents detailed proposals for creating a new currency, the hard ECU, as a *parallel currency*, and regulating it by a European Monetary Fund. |
| 28 January | At the second session of the Intergovernmental Conference on EMU, France and Spain submit proposals for "hardening" the existing ECU, as the precursor to the eventual *single currency*, rather than creating a thirteenth currency. France stresses the need for "fully democratic management", which will be concentrated in the EC Council of Ministers, to control a future ECB. Spain assumes that the monetary institution to be set up during Stage Two will be a clear precursor to a fully-fledged ECB. |
| 4 February | The second session of the Intergovernmental Conference on EPU discusses a plan by the German and French Ministers for foreign affairs. According to this plan (*Genscher-Dumas Plan*) EMU should – if |

unanimous agreement can be reached – determine which aspects of foreign policy are to be included in the common policy. The EC Council of Ministers will then decide on these issues by majority vote. Initially, the WEU (comprising all Member States except Denmark, Greece and Ireland) can act as a link between the EC and NATO. The proposals are rejected by the non-WEU countries and by the United Kingdom and the Netherlands, which are both concerned about their relationship with the United States.

22 February

The EC Council of Ministers (for foreign affairs and defence) approves a provisional report in which the *WEU* is regarded as a bridge between the European integration process and NATO.

25 February

At the third meeting of the Intergovernmental Conference on EMU, all except the British Minister agree on rules concerning the *budgetary policy* of the Member States. The delegates are aware of the need to stipulate sanctions for cases where a Member State runs an excessive budget deficit.

4 March

The third Intergovernmental Conference on EPU discusses involving the European Parliament in the appointment of Commission members and the establishment of a *joint decision-making procedure* for the Parliament and the Council of Ministers. The Dutch State Secretary of Foreign Affairs P. Dankert makes the following comments on the differences of opinion which emerge at both Intergovernmental Conferences: "The differences of approach among the member states go to the very heart of the Community: should it develop in a more federal direction, or should the emphasis be more on intergovernmental operation." In response to the French demands for maintaining co-operation on an intergovernmental basis, Dankert puts the Dutch position as follows: "Obviously, such a development would conflict with the Netherlands' desire to pursue the ultimate objective of creating a federal and democratic Europe based on a Community legal order ... More generally speaking, I believe that a Community legal order provides better guarantees that the interests of all member states will be taken into account in a balanced manner. This internal balance could ensure that the member states are more willing to transfer powers or sovereignty to Community institutions and procedures. This is the essence of European integration and it is a necessary precondition for the gradual and evolutionary process which is ultimately intended to lead to the *finalité politique* [political objective] of European Union. The Netherlands' concern at this stage is that this evolutionary process towards a federal Community should not be interrupted or blocked by introducing forms of inter-governmental co-operation which do not lend themselves to subsequent incorporation in a Community legal order. In the view of the Netherlands, an essential element in such a legal order – indeed a precondition for it – is that the role of the European Parliament be strengthened as the powers of the Community – that is sovereignty – must be accompanied by a corresponding strengthening and expansion of the powers of the Parliament."[116]

13 March | The Commission favours letting the *ECSC* end on schedule, i.e. in 2002. It considers that this option offers a long enough transitional period to prepare for the integration of the coal and steel sector into the EEC Treaty after 2002. Furthermore, during this transitional period the Commission can adapt some of the provisions of the ECSC Treaty on which work has already begun.

18 March | The fourth meeting of the Intergovernmental Conference on EMU discusses the Luxembourg proposal to let the EC governments draw up general *guidelines* for exchange rate policy. However, the

[116] P. Dankert, 1992, "Challenges and Priorities" in A. Pijpers, ed., *The European Community at the Crossroads*, Dordrecht, p. 9.

ECB will have to be consulted beforehand to reach a consensus in accordance with the objective of price stability. The proposal attempts to strike a balance between the German preference for a politically independent ECB with a statutory obligation to pursue an anti-inflationary policy, and the greater government control preferred by France and other countries.

19 March        In the European Parliament *Bundesbank* Governor Pöhl warns against the introduction of a European currency without greater *economic convergence*.

22 March        The German Foreign Minister Genscher and his French counterpart R. Dumas discuss the timetable for the *various stages* of EMU. In a joint statement they propose that the ECB should be established at the start of Stage Two. The bank can then begin to operate in January 1994. In Stage Three the new independent central bank will carry sole responsibility for implementing monetary policy and protecting the stability of the currency.

26 March        The EC Council of Ministers (for foreign affairs) discusses a Dutch proposal regarding Europe's role in *security and defence* with the maintenance of "a continued North American political and military commitment to the security of Europe".

8 April         At the fifth meeting of the Intergovernmental Conference on EMU the Federal Republic of Germany, supported by the Netherlands, advocates allowing S*tage Two* of EMU to start on 1 January 1994 only if, as agreed by the European Council of Rome II, the national economies have converged to a sufficient degree, particularly as regards controlling inflation and balance of payments deficits.

9 April         The Committee of Central Bank Governors approves the *draft Statute of the ECB*.

14 April        Inauguration of *EBRD*.

15 April

At the fourth meeting of the Intergovernmental Conference on EPU the Luxembourg government presents two documents in the form of draft articles on joint *decision-making* by the Commission and the common foreign and security policy. Joint decision-making would have to apply to subjects on which the Council of Ministers can decide by a qualified majority.

10-11 May

At an informal meeting of the EC Council of Ministers the discussion focuses on three aspects of the *transitional period*, namely the programmes encouraging greater convergence, the institutional content of Stage Two and the transition to Stage Three. Commission President Delors draws attention to the fact that the Commission would prefer a brief Stage Two. The ministers reach a broad consensus on two basic principles: no right of veto for any Member State and no possibility of imposing the single currency on any Member State. In the presence of the Committee of Central Bank Governors Delors proposes including an *opting-out clause* in the text of the EMU Treaty allowing the United Kingdom to leave a future parliament to decide on the ultimate goal of Stage Three.

13-14 May

The fifth meeting of the Intergovernmental Conference on EPU focuses on *social policy*.

17 May

Sweden links the crown to the *ECU*.

4 June

Finland links the mark to the *ECU*. The proposed fluctuation margin corresponds to the actual range of fluctuation between the Finnish mark and the basket of currencies.

10 June

At the sixth meeting of the Intergovernmental Conference on EMU the ministers lay the foundations for an agreement on the role of the *European Council*. This is not only to initiate the transition from Stage Two to Stage Three but must also promote the definition of the broad lines of economic policy.

| | |
|---|---|
| 17 June | Sixth meeting of the Intergovernmental Conference on EPU. It discusses a document from the Luxembourg government proposing a new text for the common and final provisions of the *Union Treaty*. The proposal seems to represent real progress, though some ministers consider that the three-part structure (Community, Union and intergovernmental co-operation) still allows some ambiguity. |
| 20 June | Proposal by the Luxembourg government for a *draft treaty on European Political Union*. This contains references to a "federal objective", a possible joint defence policy, a slimmed down Commission and a European Parliament which would "have a say" in the EC Council of Ministers. |
| 24-25 June | Ministerial meeting in Salzburg on the *EEA*. The delegates note that the majority of the legal and institutional issues relating to the EEA have been resolved and promise to conclude the negotiations on outstanding questions in the near future so that the signing of the Treaty on European Union can take effect on 1 January 1993. The toughest problems concern fisheries, the cohesion fund and trans-Alpine transit traffic. |
| 24 June | The EC Council of Ministers approves the mutual alignment of rates of VAT and excise duty. This opens the way to an *area without borders* with effect from 1 January 1993. |
| 25 June | Spain and Portugal sign the *Schengen Agreement*. |
| 28-29 June | The European Council meets in Luxembourg to discuss the results of the intergovernmental conferences. The final decision on the text of the *Treaty on European Union* will be taken at the European Council of Maastricht so that the results of the two conferences can be confirmed simultaneously in 1992 and the new Treaty can take effect on 1 January 1993. |

1 July

The Netherlands takes over the *Presidency* of the EC.

Sweden officially applies for *EC membership*.

8 July

The EC Council of Ministers concludes that, clearly, over the past two years, no progress has been made towards the necessary *convergence* and that the current degree of convergence in many Member States is totally inadequate. The Council acknowledges that convergence is harder to achieve under relatively unfavourable economic conditions, but the policy measures for stimulating economic growth are the same as the measures for promoting convergence: improving the allocation of the resources to encourage sustainable, non-inflationary growth in the medium term.

9 September

The seventh meeting of the Intergovernmental Conference on EMU is devoted to a draft text presented by the Netherlands in which the Community transition to Stage Three is replaced by an *accession procedure* open to Member States which meet the conditions required for the transition to that stage.

21-22 September

Informal meeting in Apeldoorn where the ministers for foreign affairs and finance reach a consensus on a number of *outstanding issues*. They agree that Stage Two will start on 1 January 1994. The transition to Stage Three takes place as follows: no later than three years after the start of Stage Two the Council of Ministers will determine, on the basis of objective criteria, what progress has been made towards convergence. That examination will form the basis for deciding whether the transition to Stage Three is possible and which countries meet the criteria. The final decision will be taken by the European Council. The ministers then approve the establishment of the European Monetary Institute (EMI) in Stage Two.

24 September

The Netherlands publishes a *draft Treaty on political union*. It advocates greater powers for the

Commission and the European Parliament, which should be entitled to veto EC Council of Ministers decisions by a majority vote. The draft attracts serious criticism from most Member States. Some, including the United Kingdom, consider it too radical; others, such as France, believe it does not go far enough. The Federal Republic of Germany and Spain support the text.

30 September

At the seventh meeting of the Intergovernmental Conference on EPU a majority of the ten Member States rejects the *Dutch proposal*. Most delegations feel that the draft text submitted by Luxembourg should be used as the basis.

7 October

At the eighth meeting of the Intergovernmental Conference on EMU the ministers consider the *objective convergence criteria* for progressing to the final stage of EMU. They pay special attention to the problem of the procedure to be followed in the case of excessive deficits, whether sanctions should be imposed and, if so, what they should be. Agreement is reached on a number of procedural provisions for the future treatment of the institutional aspects of EMU. They also examine the scope for possible reduction of the narrow fluctuation margin in the ERM with effect from 1 January 1995.

21 October

The EC Council of Ministers reaches agreement on the establishment of *EEA*.

28 October

The eighth meeting of the Intergovernmental Conference on EPU concentrates mainly on the *decision-making procedure*.

4 November

The ninth meeting of the Intergovernmental Conference on EPU is dominated by discussion of the *provisions* which should be accepted regarding justice, home affairs and social policy. As regards the first two aspects, most delegations agree with the proposed division between questions subject to intergovernmental co-operation and Community questions. This means that the draft treaty should provide for the possibility of transferring a number of specific questions from intergovernmental co-operation to the Community.

11-12 November

At the ninth meeting of the Intergovernmental Conference on EMU the Commission President Delors presents the *Delors II package*. This takes account of all factors favouring cohesion, including structural policy and the reform of the CAP. The conference also tackles an agreement on the EMI which will have control over its own resources and be able to manage foreign exchange reserves within certain limits to be decided, the reserves being made available voluntarily by the Member States. The ministers agree on the need to adhere to the ECU as determined and composed in Stage Two and reject the idea of an ECU with a stronger basket of currencies ("hard" ECU).

23-27 November

The Commission discusses the *draft treaties on EPU and EMU*. In its view the European Union should safeguard the powers accorded to the Community, the Member States and the regions, taking full account of the principles of subsidiarity and diversity. Using the term "federal" to describe this future vision reflects the interlinking of the attainments of the Community construction and the expected future developments. The Commission stresses its concern about the treaty on political union. In its proposed form the union develops alongside the Community without referring, as does the Single European Act, to the desire to amalgamate into a single entity the powers that the Member States wish to exercise jointly in the political and economic sphere. The union also lacks any legal personality in the context of international law. The Commission believes that it should be possible to overcome these problems by clearly stating that all action covered by the treaties should converge towards the realisation of a political Community.

25 November

At the tenth meeting of the Intergovernmental Conference on EMU agreement is reached on the *excessive deficit procedure*. Effectively, this means that the Council of Ministers will determine the existence of such a deficit on the recommendation of the Commission. The rules, except for the sanctions, should also apply from Stage Two of EMU.

9-10 December

The European Council in Maastricht concludes the Intergovernmental Conferences on EMU and EPU. Agreement is reached on a draft treaty on the European Union, known as the *Treaty on European Union (Maastricht Treaty)*. This takes Economic and Monetary Union into an irreversible and gradual process by the introduction of the single currency no later than 1 January 1999 and by the establishment of a procedure for the transition to Stage Three by no later than 1 July 1999. Before the start of Stage Two, which will commence on 1 January 1994, the Member States are to lay down long-term programmes on convergence while the Council of Ministers is to assess the progress made towards convergence. Member States are also to proceed with total liberalisation of capital movements. During Stage Two, Member States must already endeavour to avoid excessive budget deficits and should start the process leading to central bank independence. This stage will also see the establishment of the EMI which will be responsible for co-ordinating the monetary policy pursued by the Member States and will prepare for Stage Three before the end of 1996. Before the start of the final stage the ESCB is to be set up, comprising the new ECB which will determine monetary policy, with price stability as its primary task, together with the central banks of the Member States taking part. The ESCB will be independent and cannot accept any instructions from national governments or Community institutions. To be eligible for the final stage, Member States must satisfy a number of conditions known as the convergence criteria. As regards national budgetary policy, it is agreed that the total government deficit must not exceed 3% of Gross Domestic Product (GDP) and that the government debt must not exceed 60% of GDP. Furthermore, a Member State must maintain its exchange rate within the narrow band of the ERM for a period of two years without requesting devaluation. Next, the capital market interest rate must not deviate by more than 2 percentage points from the interest rate in the three countries with the lowest inflation. Finally, inflation itself measured in terms of the consumer price index must not be more than 1.5 percentage points above the average for the three lowest inflation countries. The criteria are intended to guarantee that the participating countries are in a position, in economic terms, to link their currencies irrevocably without endangering the proper functioning of EMU.

As regards EPU, little is achieved. The Treaty on European Union contains provisions on the common foreign and security policy. As regards the institutions, the legislative powers of the European Parliament are widened. The Commission's mandate is extended to five years, making it the same as that of the European Parliament, which is to play a part in appointing the Commission. The scope for deciding by a majority vote is widened. Under pressure from the United Kingdom, the chapter on social policy is left out of the Union Treaty altogether. A special protocol allows this country and Denmark not to participate in Stage Three of EMU ("opting-out" clause).

A biography of J. Monnet published in 1994 contains the following comments on the Treaty of Maastricht: "When the EEC came into operation it was widely assumed that it would lead rapidly to economic union and that this in turn would create the conditions for political union. In fact it has taken over thirty years for the EEC to erect most of the pillars of economic union it was supposed to raise in a decade. But political union, in any real sense, has still escaped its would-be authors. The Maastricht Treaty of

European Union solves few of the problems. It raises all the issues – money, defence, foreign policy, law and order – but in practice is overwhelmingly intergovernmental on all of them. The 1990s have fulfilled the European programme of the 1950s, but found that their political vision remains as elusive as ever. The disappointments of Maastricht echo the failures or shortcomings of the EDC/EPC[117] in 1954, the Werner Plan for monetary union in 1970, the European Council of 1974, and several lesser schemes. There remains ... a qualitative gap between the enunciation of the Monnetist "general view" with which the European Commission and its predecessors have been endowed, and the exercise of sovereign power. Monnet spent his last fifteen years trying and failing to bridge this gap. In short, the founding fathers would have liked to work towards a federal union, but were unable to do so. Now, Maastricht has proved again that the states are more open to politically advanced forms of economic integration than to political union as such."[118]

18 December

The Commission reports on the measures approved in accordance with the *White Paper on the completion of the internal market*. Roughly a year before the date fixed for creating the internal market, over 60% of these measures are being applied in the Member States.

1992

1 January

Portugal takes over the *Presidency* of the EC.

16 January

The European Parliament approves the integration of the content of the *ECSC Treaty and the Euratom Treaty* into the EEC Treaty at the earliest possible opportunity. It expresses the desire for the necessary work to commence without delay and expects it to be

---

[117] This refers to the European Defence Community and European Political Community.
[118] F. Duchêne, 1994, Jean Monnet, The First Statesman of Interdependence, New York, London, p. 407.

completed by no later than the Intergovernmental Conference planned for 1996.

7 February    The ministers for foreign affairs and the ministers for finance of the twelve Member States officially sign the *Treaty on European Union*. On this occasion several of those present indicate that the Treaty is not the final stage in the construction of Europe but rather the start of a new cycle. The Treaty stipulates that any European state with a democratic system of government can apply to join the Union.

The *Bundesbank* urges the national governments to work out the details of the structure of the intended *political union* which it considers essential for creating a successful EMU. It also believes that there should not be a set timetable for compliance with the criteria for membership.

18 March    Finland officially applies for *accession to the EC.*

6 April    Portugal joins the *ERM* with a fluctuation margin for the escudo of ±6%.

7 April    The European Parliament approves the resolution on the *EU Treaty* by 226 votes to 62, with 31 abstentions. However, it also draws attention to the weaknesses of this Treaty. The national parliaments are invited to request their respective governments to examine how these weaknesses can be rectified at future Intergovernmental Conferences; this concerns in particular the lack of democracy and the decision-making procedures.

2 May    Signing of the agreement on the EEA in Porto. This agreement enables nineteen European countries to establish the free movement of goods, persons, services and capital on the basis of the existing EC

*History of the European Union*

legislation *(Acquis communautaire)*[119] as developed over the past thirty years.

14 May    The EC Council of Ministers confirms its commitment to take the necessary measures to attain the objective of creating the *internal market* by no later than 31 December 1992.

15 May    The British Prime Minister Thatcher[120] warns that "the problem of German power has reared its head again". She favours a looser, broader *confederation* in Europe rather than a centralised super-state.

20 May    Switzerland presents official application for *accession to the EC.*

2 June    A *referendum* held in Denmark rejects the EU Treaty by 50.7% of the votes.

3 June    The French President Mitterand announces that a referendum will be held to decide on the ratification of the EU Treaty. In the United Kingdom, *ratification* is suspended following the negative outcome of the Danish referendum.

18 June   In Ireland 68.7% of the electorate in a *referendum* are in favour of ratifying the EU Treaty.

23 June   In France the *Assemblée* approves the amendments to

---

[119] See: T. Bainbridge with A. Teasdale, 1995, *The Penguin Companion to European Union*, Harmondsworth, 1995, p. 4: "The phrase *acquis communautaire*, sometimes translated as 'the Community patrimony', denotes the whole range of principles, policies, laws, practices, obligations and objectives that have been agreed or that have developed within the European Union. The *acquis communautaire* includes most notably the Treaties in their entirety, all legislation enacted to date, and the judgments of the Court of Justice."

[120] M. Thatcher (1925- ) was Britain's Prime Minister from 1979 to 1990. Her views on European integration were broadly in line with those of De Gaulle. Both defended the national state and were therefore fiercely opposed to supranationalism. Her agreement to the United Kingdom's participation in stage one of EMU was extracted under pressure from leading politicians such as N. Lawson and Sir G. Howe, who threatened to resign if she continued to block the progress of the European integration process. In December 1989 she refused to sign the Social Charter. Her obstinacy on Europe was one reason for her resignation in 1990.

the constitution necessary for deciding by *referendum* on the ratification of the EU Treaty.

**26-27 June**

In Lisbon the European Council strongly reaffirms that despite the negative outcome of the Danish referendum the Community will continue on the road to the construction of Europe. The Treaty of Maastricht must be ratified within the prescribed period without new negotiations or amendments so that it can enter into force on 1 January 1993, come what may. The Council considers that the EEA agreement has opened the way to enlargement negotiations with the EFTA countries seeking membership of the EU. The Council also notes the substantial progress which has been achieved towards completing the internal market. Over 90% of the measures necessary for implementing the market without internal borders have now been taken.

**1 July**

The United Kingdom takes over the *Presidency* of the EC.

**2 July**

In *Luxembourg* the Chamber of Representatives approves the EU Treaty by 51 votes to 6 with 3 abstentions.

**17 July**

In *Belgium* the lower house approves the EU Treaty by 1463 votes to 33.

**22 July**

In Spain the lower house approves an *amendment to the constitution* permitting ratification of the EU Treaty. Approval by the upper house follows on 30 July.

**31 July**

In *Greece* the parliament which consists of only one chamber approves the EU Treaty by 286 votes to 8.

**8 August**

*Currency crisis.* On the currency markets, the approaching French referendum increases speculation. Rumours abound when Finland decides to end the link between the Finnish mark and the ECU on the same date.

18 August            The Germany newspaper *Frankfurter Allgemeine*
                     publishes an article on the relationship between
                     monetary and political union. Referring to the
                     monetary unions established in the $18^{th}$ and $19^{th}$
                     centuries, the writer remarks that they failed bit by bit
                     because they created arbitrary currencies. In all cases
                     it was not the stability of the value of money that was
                     the decisive problem; their *inter-state character*
                     made the putative single currencies susceptible to any
                     political crisis.[121]

14 September         *EMS realignment*: the Italian lira devalues by 3.5%,
                     the ten other currencies revalue by 3.5% (ECU
                     central rate of the guilder: 2.29789, DM: 2.03942).

16 September         *Black Wednesday*: sterling, the Italian lira and the
                     Spanish peseta are forced through the floor of the
                     EMS. Sterling leaves the ERM (the interest rate in
                     Sweden soars to 500%).

17 September         Italy leaves the *ERM* while the Spanish peseta
                     devalues by 5% (ECU central rate of the guilder:
                     2.29193, DM: 2.03412).

                     The *Italian upper house* approves the EU Treaty by
                     176 votes to 16 with 1 abstention.

20 September         The *referendum* held in France finds that 51% of the
                     electorate are in favour of ratifying the EU Treaty.

8 October            In the Federal Republic of Germany the *Bundestag*
                     approves the ratification of the Treaty at the first
                     reading provided that it has the final say on the
                     introduction of the European currency to complete
                     EMU.

9 October            In Denmark the government publishes a *White Paper*
                     setting out its position following the rejection of the
                     EU Treaty.

---

[121] W. Weimer, "Keine Währung ohne Staat" [No currency without State], *Frankfurter
Allgemeine Zeitung*, 18 August 1992.

1992

| 16 October | At an extraordinary meeting of the European Council in Birmingham, the heads of state and government draw attention to the fact that it is important to complete the ratification process as quickly as possible without interfering with the text of the Treaty. In this connection stress is laid on the importance of greater *economic convergence* between the Member States. By strict adherence to the principles of sound economic policy, the Community can attain its objective. The Council again repeats that it attaches great importance to the EMS as the key to economic stability and prosperity in Europe. |

| 27 October | Commission communication to the Council of Ministers on the *principle of subsidiarity*. The inclusion of this principle in the Treaty imposes an obligation on all Community institutions involved in making decisions. In practice, it implies the application of a simple principle of common sense whereby the Community, in exercising its powers, should do only what can be better achieved at that level. |

In Denmark seven of the eight parliamentary parties reach a "national compromise" on additions to the EU Treaty, on the basis of which they will support a second *referendum* in 1993.

| 29 October | In *Spain* the lower house approves the EU Treaty by 314 votes to 3, with 8 abstentions. |

In *Italy* the lower house approves the EU Treaty by 403 votes to 46, with 18 abstentions.

| 5 November | In *Belgium* the upper house approves the EU Treaty by 115 votes to 26, with 1 abstention. |

| 6 November | Greece signs the *Schengen Agreement*. |

| 9 November | Sweden decides to let the *crown float*. |

| | |
|---|---|
| 12 November | In the *Netherlands* the lower house approves the EU Treaty by 137 votes to 13. Parliament imposes the condition that it must be consulted before the introduction of the single currency. |
| 22 November | *EMS realignment*: the central rates of the Spanish peseta and the Portuguese escudo are reduced by 6% (new ECU central rate of the guilder: 2.21958, DM: 1.96992). Between June and December, the intervention measures of all European central banks (including those of Scandinavia) come to the equivalent of DM 284 billion. |
| 25 November | In *Spain* the upper house approves the EU Treaty by 222 votes with 3 abstentions. |
| | The Norwegian government submits an official application for *accession to the EC.* |
| 2 December | In the *Federal Republic of Germany* the *Bundestag* approves the EU Treaty by 543 votes to 17. |
| 6 December | Switzerland votes against the EEA in a *referendum* so that "technical" adjustments are necessary to facilitate the free trade area of eighteen countries. |
| 10 December | Norway decides to let the crown float. |
| | In *Portugal*, the parliament which consists of only one chamber approves the EU Treaty by 200 votes to 21. |
| 11-12 December | In Edinburgh the European Council approves a resolution which notes that Denmark will not take part in the introduction of a single currency or in arriving at decisions relating to defence. The Council notes three *unilateral declarations by Denmark* which will be attached to the Danish instrument of ratification if the Treaty is ratified. The Council has also approved a global approach to the principle of subsidiarity and the creation of a temporary credit facility of ECU 5 billion. |

| | |
|---|---|
| 15 December | In the *Netherlands* the upper house unanimously approves the EU Treaty. |
| 18 December | In the *Federal Republic of Germany* the *Bundesrat* unanimously approves the EU Treaty. Both approvals are conditional upon the German parliament's approval of the transition to Stage Three of EMU. |

## 1993

| | |
|---|---|
| 1 January | Denmark takes over the *Presidency* of the EC. |
| | The *Single European Market* becomes reality. In all twelve Member States there is virtually total freedom of movement for goods, services, persons and capital. |
| 18 January | The EC Council of Ministers agrees to grant a loan of ECU 8 billion to Italy under the *integrated mechanism for medium-term financial support for the balances of payments* of the Member States. |
| 1 February | *EMS realignment*: the central rate of the Irish pound is reduced by 10% (new ECU central rate of the guilder: 2.20045, DM: 1.95294). |
| | In Brussels the negotiations on *accession to the EC* of Austria, Finland and Sweden are opened. |
| 22 March | In Belgium the government's powers to control the decisions and functions of the *Banque Nationale de Belgique* are amended. The government commissioner appointed at the bank no longer has the right to block monetary policy decisions. Furthermore, monetary financing of budget deficits is prohibited. |
| 30 March | In *Denmark* the parliament approves the EU Treaty by 154 votes to 16. |
| 5 April | Negotiations on *accession to the EC* of Norway open in Luxembourg. |

| | |
|---|---|
| 11 May | The French government submits a bill to parliament on the new statute of the *Banque de France*. |

14 May — *EMS realignment*: the central rate of the Spanish peseta is reduced by 8% and that of the Portuguese escudo by 6.5% (new ECU central rate of the guilder: 2.19672, DM: 1.94964).

18 May — Second *Danish referendum*: 56.7% of the electorate are in favour of the EU Treaty.

21-22 June — The European Council in Copenhagen focuses on the battle against *unemployment*. The Commission is instructed to compile a White Paper on long-term strategy to promote growth, competitiveness and employment. In that connection it is decided that the temporary credit facility adopted in Edinburgh should be increased by ECU 3 billion and extended after 1994. The Council also points out that the accession of Austria, Finland, Norway and Sweden must actually take effect on 1 January 1995 and agrees that the associated countries in Central and Eastern Europe can join the European Union, should they so wish, provided that they satisfy the economic and political requirements.

1 July — Belgium takes over the *Presidency* of the EC.

2 August — Decision by the EC Council of Ministers and central bank governors on a radical *revision* of the ERM. The maximum deviation from the central rate for all currencies is increased from ±2.25% or ±6% to ±15%. The exception is the bilateral agreement between the Federal Republic of Germany and the Netherlands, maintaining the fluctuation margin between the German mark and the guilder unchanged at ±2.25%. In a *communiqué* published on 6 August the Commission draws the following inference: "without close co-ordination of economic policy, no progress can be made towards Economic and

Monetary Union".[122] W. Duisenberg, then Governor of the *Nederlandsche Bank,* makes a similar remark: "Experience in the ERM has clearly shown that fixed and even semi-fixed exchange rates cannot be realised without a considerable degree of convergence, not only of economic fundamentals but also of policy views. In order to restore the credibility of the mechanism, important efforts in both respects have to be made. Further progress in realising central bank autonomy will be helpful in rebuilding credibility. In addition, fiscal consolidation must be given absolute priority."[123]

The *United Kingdom* ratifies the Treaty on European Union after the House of Commons approved a vote of confidence demanded by Prime Minister Major by 339 votes to 299 on 23 July 1993.

1 September

The *Schengen Application Convention* of 19 June 1990 enters into force. As from 1 December 1993 the regulations with regard to the established "Executive Committee" consisting of national ministers of the Schengen countries will be applied.

12 October

The *German Constitutional Court* rules that the EU Treaty is not contrary to the principle of sovereignty enshrined in the German constitution. However, the Court considers that the Treaty can be revoked and reserves the right to decide in any cases where European legislation conflicts with the German constitution.

17 October

The *Schengen Agreement* is postponed. The Treaty was to have taken effect on 1 December 1993.

22 October

In Luxembourg the government passes a law which

---

[122] Activities in July-August 1993, 2. "The single market and the economic and social area of the Community", *Bulletin of the European Communities,* 1993, no. 7/8, p. 22.
[123] W.F. Duisenberg, 1993, "Dinner Speech: To Cut or Not to Cut Interest Rates: Some Remarks on the ERM", in J.O. de Beaufort Wijnholds, S.C.W. Eijffinger and L.H. Hoogduin, 1994, *A Framework for Monetary Stability, Financial and Monetary Policy Studies,* Dordrecht, p. 161.

1993

gives the *LMI* greater independence, as stipulated in the Maastricht Treaty.

29 October

In Brussels the European Council confirms that 1 January 1994 will be the starting date for *Stage Two* of EMU. During this stage, the EMI – the precursor of the ECB – will be launched with its headquarters in Frankfurt, and Baron A. Lamfalussy as President. The EMI ought to step up substantially the co-ordination of the Member States' monetary policy. The Council also stresses that the common foreign and security policy must enable the Union to speak with a single voice and act decisively.

1 November

The *Treaty on the EU* takes effect.

Article 109 G of the EC Treaty irrevocably fixes the proportion of each currency composing the *ECU basket* as at 21 September 1989 (since that date the share of the "hard" currencies has risen from 70.8 to 74.7%).

26 November

The permanent credit facility offered to the Italian treasury by the *Banca d'Italia* is terminated by law.

5 December

The Commission publishes a *White Paper on growth, competitiveness and employment: the challenges and ways forward into the 21st century*. The paper is produced at the request of the European Council in Copenhagen.

10-11 December

In Brussels the European Council decides, in accordance with the Commission White Paper, to implement an action plan to combat *long-term unemployment*. The Council is also pleased to note that all the conditions are fulfilled for actually launching Stage Two of EMU.

13 December

The EC Council of Ministers concludes agreement creating the *EEA*.

## 1994

1 January

Greece takes over the *Presidency* of the EU.

*Stage Two* of EMU takes effect. The EMI is established with its temporary seat in Basle. It will create the necessary conditions for transition to Stage Three by increasing the co-ordination of monetary policy in order to ensure price stability. With the start of Stage Two, the prohibition on monetary financing of the government by the central bank and the prohibition on preferential government access to financial institutions take effect. Also, the EMI controls the loans contracted by the Community under the integrated mechanism for medium-term financial support for the balances of payments. The EMI takes over the functions of the EMCF, whereupon the Committee of Central Bank Governors ceases to exist.

The *EEA* enters into force, without Switzerland.

In France, the new statute of the *Banque de France* takes effect, guaranteeing a degree of independence comparable to that of the *Bundesbank*.

1 March

Enlargement of the *EU.* Agreement is reached with Austria, Finland and Sweden whereby, following ratification by their national parliaments, they will join the EU on 1 January 1995. Norway has not taken a decision.

In Portugal and Spain the *Schengen Agreement* enters into force by signing the Act of Accession to the Schengen Application Convention of 19 June 1990.

31 March

Hungary applies for *membership of the EU.*

5 April

Poland applies for *membership of the EU.*

18 May

The Spanish parliament approves a bill on greater autonomy for the *Banco de España.* The law of 1

June 1994 gives the bank full responsibility for formulating and implementing monetary policy with price stability as the main objective.

| | |
|---|---|
| 1 June | In Italy the *Schengen Agreement* enters into force by signing the Act of Accession. |
| 12 June | *Austrian referendum*: the majority of the electorate vote in favour of joining the EU. |
| 24-25 June | In Corfu the European Council decides to set up a discussion group to prepare for the Intergovernmental Conference of 1996. Also, the *Act of Accession to the EU* is signed by Austria, Finland, Norway and Sweden. |
| 1 July | Germany takes over the *Presidency* of the EU. |
| 15 July | At an extraordinary meeting of the European Council in Brussels the Luxembourg Prime Minister J. Santer is chosen to succeed Delors as President of the Commission. |
| 18 July | *Free-trade agreement* signed with Estonia, Latvia and Lithuania in Brussels. |
| 19 September | Decision by the EU Council of Ministers on excessive budget deficits in Belgium, Denmark, the Federal Republic of Germany, France, Italy, the Netherlands, Portugal, Spain and the United Kingdom. This is the first time that the *excessive budget deficit procedure* has been applied, now that Stage Two of EMU has started. |
| 16 October | *Finnish referendum*: the majority of the electorate vote in favour of joining the EU. |
| 8 November | The EC Council of Ministers adopts the name *Council of the European Union* (EU Council). |
| 13 November | *Swedish referendum*: the majority of the electorate vote in favour of joining the EU. |

| | |
|---|---|
| 15 November | First meeting of the *EMI* in Frankfurt. |
| 28 November | Norwegian *referendum* rejects accession to the EU. |
| 30 November | The EU Council of Ministers adopts the first joint action under Article K.3 of the Treaty on European Union in the area of *co-operation in the fields of Justice and Home affairs.* |
| 9-10 December | In Essen the European Council lays down *lines of action* for strengthening the strategy of the White Paper on growth, competitiveness and employment with special references to measures to combat unemployment. The Council agrees on an overall strategy to bring the associated countries of Central and Eastern Europe closer to the Community. |

1995

| | |
|---|---|
| 1 January | France takes over the *Presidency* of the EU. |
| | Austria, Finland and Sweden join the *EU*. They also join the EMS but not the ERM. Norway remains outside the EU. |
| 9 January | The Austrian schilling joins the *ERM*, but is not yet part of the ECU basket. One fifth of the national reserves (equivalent to around 18 billion schilling) are deposited with the EMI on a swap basis. According to the *Österreichische Nationalbank*, participation will not alter the currency policy pursued hitherto. The bank has maintained a stable rate of exchange between the schilling and the German mark for over fifteen years, and will continue to adhere strictly to this close link. |
| 1 February | The *Association Agreements* establishing an association between the EU and Bulgaria, Romania, the Slovak Republic and the Czech Republic enter into force. |
| 6 March | *Devaluation* of the Spanish peseta and the |

Portuguese escudo by 7% and 3.5% respectively against the ERM currencies (new ECU central rate of the guilder: 2.15214, DM: 1.91007).

7 March

Publication of the first *annual report* of the EMI, criticising the tendency towards increasing budget deficits which has been evident for years. President Lamfalussy stresses that the European countries are a long way from satisfying the criteria laid down in the Maastricht Treaty regarding the size of the budget deficit and the public debt. The annual report mentions the crucial role which budgetary policy will play in the creation of a sustainable, non-inflationary system: "There is a clear need for governments in the EU to take determined structural budget adjustment measures, but there is a risk that consolidation efforts may not materialise in a period in which the cyclical upswing tends to reduce actual deficits. The experience of the late 1980s, when many governments effectively loosened fiscal policy in the face of strong economic growth, must be seen as a lesson in this respect. Progress towards fiscal consolidation is not only needed to bring budgets back onto a sustainable path and help to restore acceptable levels of public debt but also to reduce the interest rates on the capital market. Without continued efforts to bring down the structural part of the fiscal balance, no lasting progress can be made towards a viable fiscal position and a more balance policy mix in the Union as a whole."[124]

20 March

Application of the *excessive deficit procedure*. According to the EU Council of Ministers, ten of the former twelve Member States do not meet the required convergence criteria on public sector finances. Apart from Luxembourg, Ireland is also excepted even though the Irish government debt of almost 90% of GDP is well above the EMU reference value of 60% of GDP.

---

[124] European Monetary Institute, 1995, *Annual Report 1994*, Frankfurt am Main, p. 51 (Dutch version). The foreword by President A. Lamfalussy was signed on 7 March 1995.

26 March

The *Schengen Application Convention* of 19 June 1990 becomes operative. France is granted a transitional period of three months so that 1 July 1995 becomes the effective date.

31 March

The Commission does not want any *big bang scenario* when introducing the third and final stage of EMU, according to the EU Commissioner Y. Thibault de Silguy at a conference of the Federation of European Banks. Rejecting such a scenario means a phased transition to the introduction of the single currency. The Commission wants the EMU scenario to be finalised before considering whether a majority of the Member States can go ahead with EMU next year.

7 April

At a quadri-partite meeting of the European Union and the Council of Europe, the participants decide to give a new impetus to relations between the two bodies. In particular, this means *closer co-ordination* of joint action with the new democracies of the Central and East European countries and the independent states of the former Soviet Union in order to speed up their integration into the Council of Europe.

9 April

In Versailles the EU Council of Ministers drops the idea of 1997 as the starting date for EMU. This informal meeting discusses possible scenarios for the transition to Stage Three. The ministers favour the *delayed big bang* model, which is based on a three year adjustment period in which the ECU will initially be used only in transactions between central banks, and will not come into widespread use for private payments until thorough preparations have been completed. The ministers also agree on the division of the ECU into units. The smallest unit is the ECU 0.01 coin, the largest is the ECU 500 note. The name "ECU" is not yet fixed. *Bundesbank* Governor H. Tietmeyer objects to the name "ECU" because it is identical with the current basket of currencies which has seen its exchange rate plummet in recent years.

Liechtenstein approves the *participation in the EEA* as from 1 May 1995.

15 April

*Bundesbank* Governor Tietmeyer considers 1997 to be unrealistic as the target date for transition to *Stage Three* of EMU. He expressly stresses the political implications of monetary union.

28 April

Austria signs the *Schengen Agreement.*

31 May

European Commission *Green Paper on the creation of EMU.* The Commission favours a phased approach ("mounting wave" model) in which the exchange rates must be irrevocably fixed by no later than 1999. The Commission agrees with the three-year adjustment period proposed in Versailles, starting in 1999, during which the national currencies will remain in circulation alongside the ECU. As regards the use of the ECU, the Commission aims to build up a "critical mass" which includes not only transactions between central banks but also interbank and private transactions.

2-3 June

A Committee of Wise Men *(Groupe de Réflexion)* is set up in Messina, chaired by the Spanish, to prepare for the 1996 Intergovernmental Conference.

12 June

The Baltic states of Estonia, Latvia and Lithuania sign *Association Agreements* with the EU in Brussels. This marks the first formal step towards EU membership. If the agreements are ratified by their national parliaments, the three countries will participate fully in the accession strategy devised by the EU Commissioner Van den Broek. The three Baltic states have gained the same status as Bulgaria, the Czech Republic, Hungary, Poland, Romania and Slovakia with which the EU has already concluded European agreements.

19 June

The EU Council of Ministers expresses its doubts about the *feasibility of EMU* in 1997. The Council does not necessarily regard the Commission Green Paper as the only available scenario. The Dutch Finance Minister G. Zalm considers that the "critical mass" is not necessary for EMU's credibility, stating that for people and businesses the crucial point is that there are no longer any exchange rate risks. The name of the new currency is still undecided.

22 June

The Romanian government submits an official application for *accession to the EU.*

26-27 June

In Cannes the European Council decides to draw up a final scenario for the transition to *Stage Three* of EMU before the meeting to be held in Madrid at the end of 1995. With this decision the European heads of state and government tacitly drop 1997 as the starting date for Stage Three. A group of experts is ordered to study the relationship between EMU members and the EU countries which are unable or unwilling to join. The Council confirms its resolve to keep strictly to the convergence criteria in preparing for the transition to the single currency by no later than 1 January 1999.

27 June

The Slovakian government submits an official application for *accession to the EU.*

France declares that it will abolish border controls as soon as possible, but by no later than 1 December 1995, in accordance with the *Schengen Agreement.*

1 July

Spain takes over the *Presidency* of the EU.

3 July

According to *Bundesbank* director O. Issing monetary union cannot work as a step towards *political union*: "If there is insufficient political will to take the road to political union ..., then there is little reason to trust that the political integration which people in principle desire can be achieved, as it were, via the back door of currency union. A

Europe which ventures into a currency union cannot shirk the decision on the shape of the political union. If concessions are made at random to demands from all sides, then experience teaches us that we can expect a situation in which good money has little prospect and no hope at all of operating as a disciplinary factor in the Community in the long term."[125]

10 August    According to the Italian Prime Minister L. Dini the *"perverse spiral"* of ever-increasing budget deficits has been ended in Italy – partly thanks to reform of the pension system. On those grounds he presses for the lira's speedy return to the ERM.

29 August    The Italian Prime Minister Dini announces that, towards the end of the year, his government will consider whether the lira can return to the *EMS*.

5 September    According to the Spanish Minister for European Affairs C. Westendorp radical plans for rendering the EU more efficient and less bureaucratic will probably not be discussed by the *1996 Intergovernmental Conference*. He bases this conclusion on the resistance among senior officials from the fifteen EU Member States to the proposal that powers should be transferred from the Council of Ministers to the European Commission or the European Parliament.

12 September    According to the Dutch State Secretary of Foreign Affairs M. Patijn the *requirements* for joining EMU should be more flexible, especially the rules on the government debt which he considers impossible for either the Netherlands or Belgium to satisfy.

The Benelux countries want to present a joint memorandum at the *1996 Intergovernmental Conference* which is to decide on the future of Europe. The joint position of the three countries is

---

[125] O. Issing, "Europa: Politische Union durch gemeinsames Geld?". [Europe: Political Union via a single currency?]. Deutsche Bundesbank, 1995, *Auszüge aus Presseartikeln*, no. 50, p. 7.

that further enlargement of the EU, particularly into Central and Eastern Europe, should be preceded by deepening.

14 September

The German Finance Minister Th. Waigel advocates tightening some of the *EMU rules*. When the economy is doing well, the maximum government deficit should not be 3% of GDP but less than that. The same applies to the public debt ratio.

18 September

Sweden states that accession to Stage Three of EMU depends on approval by parliament. This makes Sweden the fourth country (after Denmark, the Federal Republic of Germany and the United Kingdom) with a *formal reservation*.

20 September

According to the German Minister Waigel Italy can forget the idea of joining EMU in 1999. Belgium will also have a hard time in view of its high government debt, and need not expect an easy ride in Brussels. European Commission President J. Santer does not consider that stricter *membership requirements* should be imposed on countries wishing to join EMU.

22-23 September

Informal European Council meeting on Majorca which discusses the preparations for the *Intergovernmental Conference in 1996* which is to revise the Maastricht Treaty. However, the meeting is totally dominated by crisis management following the recent statements by the German Minister Waigel. The Italian Prime Minister Dini considers that the final stage of EMU should be postponed if "not enough" countries are ready to join. Leaving that aside, the British Prime Minister J. Major argues for the earliest possible start to negotiations on enlarging the EU into Eastern Europe. These should start six months after the conclusion of the Intergovernmental Conference scheduled for 1996.

28 September

In the German weekly *Die Zeit*, the former Chancellor Schmidt accuses the *Bundesbank* of *nationalism.* The bank is really against EMU because it does not want to hand over its extensive powers to other bodies. He says that certain gentlemen at the *Bundesbank* are already in the habit of psychologically and politically undermining the monetary union which was agreed in the Maastricht Treaty.[126]

The President of the EMI Lamfalussy advocates *additional agreements* to secure the longer term stability of the European currency.

29-30 September

In Valencia the EU Council of Ministers sweeps away all doubt that EMU will be launched on 1 January 1999. Nor will there be any tampering with the existing strict *membership conditions.* To satisfy the Federal Republic of Germany, it is agreed that EMU members will remain subject to a strict economic and financial policy even after joining. The decision on who will join EMU will be taken at the beginning of 1998 by a European Council conference.

10 October

The Federal German President R. Herzog puts a passionate plea for a *"federal Europe"* before the European Parliament. Monetary union is unthinkable without political union. If Europe rejects EMU, then Herzog fears a return to the 1930s. Then the EU Member States will resort to competitive devaluations, trade wars, protectionism, a return to national economic policies with the threat of deflation if not depression. He implicitly criticises Minister Waigel: "the public bickering over whether EMU can be created on schedule or which countries are ready for it threatens not only Monetary Union but also Political Union".[127]

---

[126] "Schmidt beschuldigt Bundesbank van afkeer tegen EMU" [Schmidt accuses the Bundesbank of aversion to EMU], *De Volkskrant*, 29 September 1995.

[127] P. de Graaf, "Duitse president durft voor federaal Europa te pleiten" [German President dares to advocate a federal Europe], *De Volkskrant*, 11 October 1995.

24 October

In the Federal Republic of Germany, the six leading economic institutes[128] urge the government to adhere less strictly to the *EMU convergence criteria*. They consider that the debt criterion, in particular, merits re-examination. The French President J. Chirac and the German Chancellor Kohl then express their conviction that their countries will constantly satisfy the requirements for joining EMU from the start.

28 October

In September the average rate of *inflation* over the past year in the fifteen EU Member States is 3.1%.

14 November

The Dutch newspaper *Het Financieele Dagblad* describes *monetary union in Benelux* as a happy dream: " ... after all the attempts to co-ordinate policy in the Netherlands and Belgium, all that has been achieved is the Benelux Economic Union and the Language Union. Monetary union has never been achieved, let alone political union".[129]

According to the *Nederlandsche Bank* Governor Duisenberg, the Netherlands will have to cut its *public debt ratio* by 2% per annum to meet the EMU criteria. The reduction by 0.4 percentage points of GDP estimated for 1996 is not enough.

15 November

Commission President Santer supports Waigel's proposal for a *Stability and Growth Pact (stability pact)* to secure budgetary discipline in EMU. The next day when visiting The Hague Waigel gets the backing of the Dutch Minister Zalm, joined a day later by the French Finance Minister J. Arthuis.

27 November

The EU Council of Ministers demonstrates broad support for the German idea of a *stability pact*.

[128] It concerns the following independent research institutions: Deutsches Institut für Wirtschaftsforschung, Berlin, Institut für Weltwirtschaft an der Universität Kiel, Institut für Wirtschaftsforschung, Halle, Institut für Wirtschaftspolitik an der Universität zu Köln, HWWA-Institut für Wirtschaftsforschung-Hamburg, Ifo Institut für Wirtschaftsforschung, München.
[129] F. Gersdorf and S.P. van der Vaart, "Ook in Benelux is monetaire unie een mooie droom" [Even in Benelux, monetary union is a happy dream], *Het Financieele Dagblad*, 14 November 1995.

1995

However, the Council cannot agree on the date for deciding which countries are eligible to join EMU. The French demand for setting a date at the beginning of 1998 is rejected.

28 November              Estonia applies to join the *EU*.

5 December               Publication of the report by the think tank which, headed by the Spanish Minister for European Affairs Westendorp, is to make the preparations for the *Intergovernmental Conference in 1996* to revise the Maastricht Treaty. The report states that extending majority voting is essential for more efficient and effective operation of the Union, which threatens to become unmanageable once it is enlarged to 25 or 30 Member States. The United Kingdom announces that it will not accept any extension of majority voting in the EU Council of Ministers.

The Benelux heads of state and government agree to the German proposal that the European currency be called the "euro".

15-16 December           European Council in Madrid which finally decides on the introduction of EMU and the *single currency* which will be called the "euro". Stage Three of EMU starts on 1 January 1999 when the rates for conversion between the currencies of the EMU countries themselves and between them and the euro are irrevocably fixed. From that date on, monetary and exchange rate policy will be conducted in Euros. By 1 January 2002 at the latest, euro notes and coins will be placed in circulation alongside the national coins and banknotes. After a maximum of six months the national currencies in all participating Member States will be entirely replaced by the euro and the introduction will be complete.

According to the introduction scenario, the European Council will decide as early as possible in 1998 which Member States satisfy the requirements for transition to the single currency. The ECB must be set up in time to complete the preparations and commence its activities on 1 January 1999. At the beginning of 1998, reliable figures for 1997 will be used to decide which countries meet the convergence criteria. As soon as possible after the decision on who will join, the ECB Board will be appointed. Together with the governors of the national central banks it will form the ECB Governing Council, the principal decision-making body of the ECB. Once the Governing Council has taken office, final decisions can be taken on a number of matters such as the range of monetary instruments. Member States not joining EMU on 1 January 1999 ("pre-ins") will have "derogation" status, i.e. they will join EMU as soon as they meet the convergence criteria. The scenario is said to ensure transparency and acceptability, enhance credibility and reinforce the irreversibility of the process. It is also decided to start the Intergovernmental Conference on 29 March 1996 in order to create the political and institutional conditions required if the European Union is to be adapted to future needs, especially with a view to later enlargement.

31 December     The *Customs Union* between Turkey and the EU enters into force.

1996

1 January     Italy takes over the *Presidency* of the EU.

A *customs union* is established between Turkey and the EU Member States in which all trade barriers are abolished except for the levies on agricultural products and steel.

12 February     According to the French Prime Minister A. Juppé it is in many people's interests that EMU should not be formed. He rejects suggestions by the former President Giscard d'Estaing for a broader interpretation of the *convergence criteria* in view of the recession.

13 February

At a conference in Frankfurt *Bundesbank* Governor Tietmeyer speaks of a possible *Terminverspätung* [postponement] of the entry into effect of EMU. He also sees the euro as a kind of lever for political integration. The single European currency offers valuable opportunities. It can give Europe greater economic strength, and it can encourage Europe to proceed with further political integration. But it will not achieve any of that unless it is stable.[130]

29 March

The European Council meets in Turin where the *Intergovernmental Conference* is opened at the same time, the latter's principal purpose being the revision of the Treaties of Rome. The Council wants to focus mainly on the following matters: a Union which is closer to its citizens, the institutions of a more democratic and efficient Union and widening the scope for external action by the Union.

2 April

The annual report of the EMI calls *budgetary policy* the key to convergence and to satisfactory economic performance in the Community in general. It also gives an account of the EMI's activities regarding the harmonisation of payment systems, supervision of banking activities, management of the EMS mechanisms and monitoring of compliance with the prohibition on governments being financed by their central banks.

12 April

The European Statistical Office *(Eurostat)*, established in Luxembourg, announces that *unemployment* in the EU has risen to 11% (18.3 million unemployed).

13-14 April

The EU Council of Ministers in Verona reaches agreement on (a) an *exchange rate system* between EMU and non-EMU countries. For this purpose the EMS must be expanded and made more flexible. The

---

[130]  H. Tietmeyer, "Die Wirtschafts- und Währungsunion als Stabilitätsgemeinschaft" [The Economic and Monetary Union as a Community of Stability], Deutsche Bundesbank, 1996, *Auszüge aus Presseartikeln*, no. 10, p. 5.

United Kingdom is against new agreements on the EMS, Finland and Sweden also waver; (b) drafting a *stability pact* with sanctions for countries which revert to bad ways with a budget deficit of more than 3% of GDP. The ECB must have its own role in realignments but the ultimate decision rests with the European ministers.

1996

29 April

The six German independent research institutes advocate a flexible interpretation of the *budget deficit and government debt criteria* so as to secure a place in EMU for countries such as Belgium and the Netherlands. Minister Waigel immediately rejects this proposal, saying that any speculation over the interpretation of the criteria or the timetable is damaging.

30 April

According to *Bundesbank* director P. Schmidhuber the new European exchange rate system should have a fluctuation margin of ±6%. He expects that once the decision has been taken at the beginning of 1998 on who is eligible to join Stage Three of EMU, a *two-speed phase* will start.

15 May

The *Nederlandsche Bank* Governor Duisenberg is unanimously nominated by the EMI Council for the post of *President of the EMI* with effect from 1 July 1997. The formal appointment is expected to be made following the European Council meeting in Dublin in December 1996. The appointment is made at the level of heads of state and government, after consulting the European Parliament and the European finance ministers.

In its half-yearly report on the *economic and financial outlook* the Commission is optimistic that EMU can be achieved. It expects economic growth to pick up from the second half of 1996, bringing the budget deficits of seven countries down to 3% of GDP or less. The margin for the Federal Republic of Germany, France and the Netherlands is small. The other four, namely Denmark, Finland, Ireland and

Luxembourg, have plenty of leeway to come well within the limit. No-one mentions the size of the German government debt ratio, which is expected to rise from 58.1% of GDP in 1995 to 61.5% in 1996 and 62.4% in 1997.

**16 May**

Commission opinion on *excessive budget deficits* in Germany. The opinion is accompanied by a recommendation for a Council decision. This means that Germany, like Austria, Belgium, Denmark, Finland, France, Greece, Italy, the Netherlands, Portugal, Spain, Sweden and the United Kingdom is now among the countries to which the EU Council of Ministers has addressed a recommendation that they put an end to their excessive budget deficits.

**3 June**

At the EU Council of Ministers meeting, Denmark is discharged from the *excessive deficit procedure*. The country has managed to reduce its budget deficit to 1.5% of GDP while the debt ratio has fallen from 80% of GDP in 1993 to 71.9% in 1995.

**21-22 June**

European Council meeting in Florence. This is to focus on tackling unemployment in the EU. To that end, Commission President Santer has drawn up a *confidence pact* asking for around ECU 1 billion to help finance the trans-European networks (high-speed railways and telecommunications). Santer's policy on employment gets a cool reception. The financial details are to be worked out at the meeting of finance ministers scheduled for 8 July. The conference is overshadowed by the *British blockade* on European decisions, which has persisted for more than four weeks over the issue of "mad cow disease", which has given Europeans so much to think about in the preceding months. Although the question is resolved at the start of the summit conference, it still leaves its mark. To prevent a repeat of the United Kingdom's policy of obstruction in the future, the summit's concluding statement makes the point that the Intergovernmental Conference will have to consider the subject of "the application of voting by a

qualified majority". The Intergovernmental Conference which began in Turin on 29 March is still in an
"exploratory phase". Italy has compiled a report on
the subjects to be discussed and on the various points
of view. The heads of state and government now want
to proceed with genuine negotiations. A special
summit will be held in Dublin in October 1996 for
that purpose. Finally, the Commission has formally
accepted Waigel's *stability pact* as is evident from its
working paper which the heads of state and
government will discuss. Ireland undertakes to
prepare a draft text by the beginning of November
1996 on the results of the Intergovernmental
Conference.

25 June

The Italian lira reaches a 22 month peak against the
German mark. The Finance Minister and former
Prime Minister C. Ciampi says that Rome aims to
start negotiations as soon as possible on re-entry of
the lira into the *ERM*. However, the subject was only
touched on in Florence.

1 July

Ireland takes over the *Presidency* of the EU.

3 September

In the Netherlands F. Bolkestein, Member of the
Dutch Parliament, argues for strict compliance with
the *EMU criteria*. He warns against a flexible
interpretation by the Dutch central bank and
considers that the Netherlands cannot submit in
advance to a political deal between the Federal
Republic of Germany and France.

9 September

The informal EU Council of Ministers meeting
decides to convene a special European summit in
Dublin in October to monitor the progress of the
Intergovernmental Conference. The greatest obstacle
is the United Kingdom's reservation on every issue,
the main one being the abandonment of the *unanimity
rule* for decisions on the common foreign policy and
the European justice policy.

9-10 September

The Monetary Committee considers the *stability pact*

without arriving at any definite, new recommendations.

16 September

A British opinion poll shows that 30% of those asked
want the British government to rule out immediate
*participation in the euro.* On the other hand, 60%
want to keep that option open.

17 September

Six-monthly *Franco-German Summit* in Bavaria,
where the Finance Ministers, Arthuis and Waigel,
stress that they are persisting in their efforts to bring
the budget deficit down to 3% of GDP in 1997.

18 September

In his "state of the union" speech, Commission
President Santer criticises the Intergovernmental
Conference for creeping forward at snail's pace. He
highlights the need to break through the impasse over
the *unanimity rule* in European decision-making
procedures. The right of veto applies to the common
foreign and security policy, justice policy and some
elements of the Maastricht Treaty, such as the fiscal
chapter.

19 September

50th Anniversary of Churchill's speech in Zurich in
which he advocated the *United States of Europe.* On
that occasion, the British Foreign Secretary, M.
Rifkind, warns that the introduction of EMU will lead
to growing divisions in Europe.

20-21 September

Informal EU Council of Ministers meeting in Dublin
on the technical preparations for EMU. The ministers
are unanimously in favour of a *stability pact.*
Everyone agrees with the principle that a country
with an excessive deficit (over 3% of GDP) should
maintain a non-interest-bearing deposit, presumably
with the ECB. If the country does not mend its ways,
after one year that amount will be converted to a fine
and the country will lose its money. No firm
agreements have yet been concluded on the scope of
the sanction and the speed of its imposition. Prior to
this discussion, the Federal Republic of Germany and
France have already agreed the general outline of the

stability pact which is "vital to the success of EMU" according to the French Finance Minister Arthuis. At the meeting decisions are also taken on EMS II. The euro is the linchpin of the new system and the band width will be ±15 % (i.e. a maximum of 30%). The ECB must not engage in unlimited intervention, but may also initiate the devaluation of a weak currency belonging to one of the "pre-ins". There is some confusion over the date on which the exchange rates will be irrevocably locked. The Belgian Finance Minister Ph. Maystadt and EMI President Lamfallusy, believe that this can take place when the participants are selected in 1998. The Dutch monetary authorities reject this. The exchange rates must be locked, as scheduled, on 31 December 1998 "at five minutes to midnight" says Duisenberg of the *Nederlandsche Bank*.[131]

23 September       The Italian Prime Minister R. Prodi says that he does not want to postpone membership of EMU but warns that it will be disastrous for his country if Italy is left out: "There is no doubt that on Friday the Italian government will present a budget that will bring back *Italy into Europe*. I will not be the Prime Minister who keeps Italy out of the European Union", says Prodi.[132]

4 October          After talking to the French President Chirac, Prodi says that Italy will return to the *EMS* as soon as possible.

7 October          In a speech in Frankfurt, *Bundesbank* Governor Tietmeyer warns the German parliament that it must give the *convergence criteria* a strict interpretation if it is asked to approve Germany's membership of EMU.

---

[131] P. de Graaf, "Euro-ministers eens over contouren EMU" [Euro ministers agree on the contours of EMU], *De Volkskrant*, 23 September 1996.
[132] M. Leijendekker, "Prodi wenst snel toetreden Italië tot EMU" [Prodi wants Italy to join EMU soon], *De Volkskrant*, 24 September 1996.

| | |
|---|---|
| 7-8 October | Informal Council meeting in Dublin where the heads state and government press for a reduction in the size of the agenda for the *Intergovernmental Conference* so as to be ready in time under the Dutch Presidency. |
| 8 October | The German government announces extra *economy measures* totalling DM 3 billion. Chancellor Kohl says that this will bring the 1997 budget in line with the requirements for joining EMU. |
| 14 October | The Finnish mark joins the *ERM* (ECU central rate of the FIM: 5.80661).[133] |
| 4 November | Commission report proposing that the *integrated mechanism for medium-term financial support for the balances of payments* of the Member States be extended to the end of 1998. The reason is that, despite the progress towards convergence, balance of payments problems may still arise during the transition to EMU. |
| 7 November | According to the Commission report on *economic convergence* in the EU, twelve of the fifteen Member States will have a budget deficit of 3% of GDP or less in 1997. They therefore satisfy an important criterion for joining EMU. Only Greece, Italy and the United Kingdom still have excessive deficits. The Commission also draws attention to a significant downward trend in the debt ratios of most Member States. This optimism is not shared by the EMI, which harps on the importance of a budget which is sound in the long term: that cannot be guaranteed by a single cut. |
| | In a speech in Düsseldorf, the Governor of the *Nederlandsche Bank* Duisenberg announces that he is not worried about the ECB's lack of a track record. The *independence of the ECB*, the ultimate aim of price stability and agreements under the stability pact |

---

[133] Pursuant to the decision of the EU Council of Ministers and the Committee of Governors of the Central Banks of the EU Member States dated 12 October.

offer the necessary guarantees for a stable euro. The stability of the euro is said to be a crucial factor for the success of monetary union.

1996

8 November

In the weekly publication *Die Zeit* the former German Chancellor Schmidt addresses an open letter to *Bundesbank* Governor Tietmeyer vehemently accusing him of being the strongest opponent of EMU on account of his persistent advocacy of strict compliance with the *convergence criteria*. The former Chancellor says that the *Bundesbank* is behaving like a "state within a state" and Germany's neighbours do not want to dance to the tune of the German guardian of the currency. In his reply Tietmeyer refers to the importance of a stable currency union. If countries make cosmetic improvements to their economy to qualify for membership, then he calls that *"window dressing"*. Political and economic conflicts will then loom on the horizon, eventually putting Europe in a worse position than it is now, says the Governor.[134]

11 November

The EU Council of Ministers meeting fails to reach agreement on the implementation of the *stability pact*. There is no clear-cut, quantifiable definition for deciding when a Member State may under "temporary and exceptional" circumstances have a budget deficit in excess of the limit of 3% of GDP. However, several Member States press for firm political embodiment of the stability pact, which should be added to the new European Treaty. It is also announced that the final design of the euro note will be presented in Dublin in mid December. Finally, the Council recommends the European Council to issue formal confirmation that Stage Three of EMU will not start in 1997 since a majority of the Member States still do not satisfy the requirements. The Council also proposes that the list of those who will be the first to join the single

---

[134] M. de Waard, "De 'eik' Hans Tietmeyer doorstaat alle stromen" [Hans Tietmeyer stands fast against all onslaughts], *NRC Handelsblad*, 15 November 1996.

currency on 1 January 1999 should be drawn up as soon as possible in 1998.

19 November

The Italian government reaches agreement with the three largest trade unions regarding the *euro tax*. This comprises a number of tax measures and is meant to ensure that Italy qualifies to join EMU in 1999. Prodi says that the tax is the last piece in the puzzle and after a four-year gap the lira can return to the EMS.

22 November

In the French weekly *L'Expresse* former president Giscard d'Estaing argues against the current *parity* between the French franc and the German mark and regrets the obstinacy with which that exchange rate is being defended. In his opinion, this is the real reason for the problems facing the French economy. In a joint press release the German Chancellor Kohl and the French Prime Minister Juppé announce that the two countries will proceed with EMU in accordance with the timetable and convergence criteria agreed in the Maastricht Treaty.

25 November

After a hectic Monetary Committee meeting followed by a discussion by the finance ministers and the governors of the central banks of the EU countries, the lire returns to the *EMS* (ECU central rate: 1,906.48 lire per ECU) with a fluctuation margin of ±15%.

2 December

At its regular meeting the EU Council of Ministers fails to reach agreement on the *stability pact*. Germany wants this pact to be linked to agreements on the legal status of the euro and the new exchange rate mechanism between the future euro countries and the currencies of the EU Member States remaining outside EMU.

6 December

The Irish government presents a draft text on the revision of the *Maastricht Treaty*. One of the proposals concerns the inclusion of a separate chapter on employment policy in the new treaty. It also advocates formulating sustained growth as an explicit objective of EU policy and incorporating the Social Protocol into "Maastricht II".

13-14 December

In Dublin the European Council discusses the report by the EU Council of Ministers on the preparations for Stage Three of EMU and a report by the EMI. This sets out the principles for an exchange rate mechanism in Stage Three and the main elements of the *stability pact*. The latter eliminates an important obstacle on the road to the euro. It is decided that when EMU takes effect, an automatic fine will be imposed on any Member State where failure to comply with the EMU budget rule is accompanied by a decline of at least 0.75% per annum in the rate of economic growth. If the decline is between 0.75 and 2% the Member State may obtain exemption from the fine by invoking "temporary and exceptional circumstances". The EU Council of Ministers will decide on the recommendation of the Commission. It is also formally decided to appoint the Governor of the *Nederlandsche Bank* Duisenberg as the *President of the EMI* for the period from 1 January 1997 until the establishment of the European Central Bank. During the Summit the euro bank notes are presented simultaneously in Dublin and Frankfurt.

19 December

The three Scandinavian members of the EU – Denmark, Finland and Sweden – accede to the *Schengen Agreement.* Iceland and Norway, which are not members of the EU, have simultaneously concluded an agreement (they become associate members) on co-operation with the now much larger group of Schengen countries.

1997

1 January

The Netherlands take over the *Presidency* of the EU.

6 January

The Norwegian government considers another attempt at *EU membership*. In 1992 and 1994 the Norwegians voted against joining.

21 January

Governor L. Lindsey of the American Federal Reserve Bank (Richmond, Virginia) cannot readily understand the *historical and political motives* behind the single currency in Europe: "Generally speaking, in the history of the world, political union has preceded monetary union. It strikes me, as an outsider, that in Europe's case the currency union is being used as a means of bringing about political union." Lindsey is convinced that it will prove impossible to pursue a joint monetary policy in Europe while at the same time continuing to regulate economic and budgetary policy at national level. "That is not a defect of the architecture of Europe's currency union. It is a logical accompaniment, certainly without migration of labour as an alternative stability factor."[135]

28 January

In its report *"The Passage to the Euro"* the Centre for European Policy Studies (CEPS) considers the future exchange rate of the euro: "The best way to avoid legal challenges to the value of the single currency would ... be to take the market rates at the end of 1998."[136] With that in mind, the EMI should adopt a band width of 2 to 3% for the parity of the EMU currencies vis-à-vis the euro well before the start of EMU.

In the French daily *Le Monde* J. Boissonnat, former member of the board of the French central bank, warns that EMU could collapse without a strong European *economic authority*.

29 January

The German State Secretary of Finance J. Stark makes it clear that his country feels there is little to be gained by having in a large number of countries join the *EU* immediately.

---

[135] M. Schinkel, 1997, "Amerikaanse deelstaten zullen soevereiner zijn dan EU-lidstaten" [America's federal states will have greater sovereign status than EU Member States], *NRC Handelsblad*, 21 January 1997.
[136] A. Fisher, "Right rate for euro is fraught with difficulty", *Financial Times*, 4 February 1997 and Deutsche Bundesbank, *Auszüge aus Presseartikeln*, no. 8, 10 February 1997, p. 9.

30 January

The French government's idea is that its proposed *Stability Council* will be a consultation partner of the ECB. It stresses that the ECB's independence will be respected. The EU Council of Ministers will still retain the actual decision-making powers.

3 February

*Eurostat* approves a large number of *accounting measures* whereby the Member States aim to reduce their budget deficits and government debt this year. The decision on Italy's euro tax is suspended until the end of February.

5 February

The British *Financial Times* reports that monetary circles in Brussels are talking about a *compromise proposal*: Italy is not to be allowed to join EMU immediately on 1 January 1999 but will be given a guarantee that it can still join one or two years later. The Italian government firmly rejects this. Prodi repeats that Italy is resolved to meet the EMU criteria by the deadline.

6 February

The Dutch Finance Minister Zalm is sympathetic towards parliament's request that, once EMU is launched, the *euro and the guilder* should circulate side by side for less than the agreed six months. It is also announced that, according to the latest information, the Dutch government deficit for 1996 will be 1.9% of GDP as opposed to an earlier estimate of 2.1% (2.6% when the budget was presented in the autumn of 1996).

Commission President Santer considers it impossible to refuse Italy's entry to EMU if the country satisfies the convergence criteria. Santer also says that France must stop the pressure regarding *political influence over the ECB*. He dismisses out of hand the plan by EU Commissioner Van den Broek to give the larger Member States more votes and a veto in the Council of Ministers on common foreign policy.

7 February

The German Chancellor Kohl tells his Italian colleague Prodi that there is no secret plan for

1997

keeping Italy out of *EMU*. Kohl declares that no-one should expect a change of attitude with the approach of the German parliamentary elections in 1998. At the same time, he warns that the Federal Republic of Germany risks failing to satisfy the EMU criteria if something is not soon done about rising unemployment in that country (12.2% of the active population).

11 February

The Dutch politician Bolkestein says that the Netherlands ought to stay outside EMU if countries join with a budget deficit of more than 3% of GDP. Even if the Federal Republic of Germany and France go ahead with EMU, the Netherlands should not take part under such conditions. He considers that postponing *EMU* is conceivable and "no calamity".

12 February

In a joint statement a group of seventy worried Dutch economists claim that the current *EMU plan* is inappropriate to the Europe of the future. Quite apart from anything else, the Union still offers no prospect of any improvement in the lot of the EU's 20 million unemployed and 50 million poor.

The French State Secretary of European Affairs M. Barnier considers the Netherlands insufficiently ambitious as the President of the EU. If the harmonisation of *justice and internal security policy* is not achieved at the summit in June, then the Federal Republic of Germany and France will proceed jointly on that matter.

16 February

In Portugal, the two main political parties (the ruling socialists and the centre-liberal opposition) unite to give firm backing to the government's claim to be among the *first wave* of EMU members. In an interview the Spanish Prime Minister J. Aznar also dismisses any doubts over whether his country will be among the first wave of EMU as well.

27 February

At a meeting with French members of parliament EU Commissioner De Silguy announces that the decision on which countries qualify to join *EMU* will be taken at the end of April 1998.

28 February

In the Netherlands the Council of Ministers approves the amendment of the Dutch *Bank Act 1948* abolishing the right of the finance minister to issue instructions. This amendment is necessary for Stage Three of EMU.

12 March

At the end of the six-monthly Franco-German talks it emerges that the Federal Republic of Germany and France have agreed on the creation of an *informal stability council* by the countries introducing the euro in 1999. In this council the finance ministers of the participating countries will hold periodic discussions on the economic situation and budgetary discipline in the EU. However, the ministers will have absolutely no say over the ECB's monetary policy.

5 April

At the informal EU Council of Ministers meeting in Noordwijk it is once again expressly confirmed that EMU will start on 1 January 1999. Agreement is reached on the details of the stability pact (sanction rules), the procedure to be followed in 1998 for selecting the countries taking part and on the structure of *ERM II* (fluctuation margins of ±15% for the currencies of EU countries which do not take part in EMU).

17 April

*Bundesbank* Governor Tietmeyer, referring to strict compliance with the *convergence criteria*, leaves open the possibility that EMU, scheduled to start on 1 January 1999, may be postponed for a short time.

France is heading for a budget deficit of 3.8% of GDP in 1997. To bring that figure down to the prescribed maximum of 3% will require stringent *economic measures*.

The French President Chirac calls *early elections* (25 May and 1 June) to prevent the necessary economic measures from damaging the coalition's chances if the elections were held on the due date.

2 May

The Netherlands yields to Chirac's insistence that the additional summit meeting of 23 May should be held in Noordwijk rather than Maastricht, owing to the latter's negative *connotations* for French public opinion.

The British *elections* put Labour into power with T. Blair as the new Prime Minister.

6 May

The new British Chancellor of the Exchequer G. Brown has given the Bank of England freedom to conduct an independent *interest rate policy*. Responsibility for monetary policy is assigned to a committee consisting of nine members headed by the Bank's Governor with four experts brought in from outside.

12 May

On the recommendation of the Commission, the EU Council of Ministers warns Italy that the measures to put *public finances* in order are insufficient to be eligible to join EMU in 1999. However, the budget plans of two other southern European countries, Portugal and Spain, are approved. This establishes a compromise between Germany's reluctance to throw in its lot with the southern countries and the French desire that they should be included in the monetary union at an early date. Finland and the Netherlands are taken off the list of countries with an "excessive budget deficit" (Denmark, Ireland and Luxembourg had already been removed earlier). The EU Council of Ministers addresses "recommendations" on a sound financial and economic policy to nine countries. Only the United Kingdom is granted extra time because the Commission's opinion is still based on the Major administration's budget.

13 May

The Italian Prime Minister Prodi threatens *reprisals* if Italy is not allowed to join EMU. Although his country has managed to reduce the budget deficit to somewhere in the region of 4% of GDP by one-off measures such as early collection of taxes and a non-recurring additional levy, structural reforms are necessary (particularly in relation to pensions and public health) to secure lasting compliance with the budget criterion.

15 May
The German government considers revaluation of its *gold reserves* in order to meet the debt criterion of 60% of GDP. The *Bundesbank* currently has about 3 million kilos of gold, valued at DM 13.7 billion. Revaluation at market value would yield an extra DM 40 billion. Another idea under consideration is to float another block of *Deutsche Telekom* shares, the proceeds from which could be used to reduce the public debt. *Bundesbank* Governor Tietmeyer is adamantly opposed to plans for revaluation of the gold reserves, wishing to leave that until after EMU is set up in 1999. In the days that follow Minister Waigel faces a barrage of criticism from people who believe that he has damaged the independence of the *Bundesbank* and unnecessarily impaired the credibility of German monetary policy.

23 May
The additional European Council meeting in Noordwijk discusses the *common foreign and security policy* and relations between the EU and the WEU.

27 May
Commemoration of the *Marshall Plan* (5 June 1947) in The Hague. The Dutch Prime Minister W. Kok points out that Marshall's vision of a united Europe was reflected by that of Adenauer, Schuman and Spaak, saying that it was their ideas on this that gave rise to the European Community.

30 May
The former Dutch central bank director A. Szász calls for relaxation of the requirements for joining *EMU*. A budget deficit of just over 3% of GDP should not be any impediment if it is clear that the country in question will put its public finances in order within a few years.

1 June

In France – contrary to expectations – the left-wing opposition scores a major victory in the second round of the early *parliamentary elections* called by President Chirac. The leader of the socialist party, L. Jospin, becomes Prime Minister: "The tug of war between the jobs pledge and the budgetary austerity of Maastricht will be the greatest challenge facing the Jospin administration over the next few years", says the Dutch daily *Het Financieele Dagblad* of 6 June 1997.

3 June

The German Minister Waigel and *Bundesbank* Governor Tietmeyer reach a compromise over the *revaluation* of the German gold reserves. They will be revalued this year but the book profit will not be paid over to the state until after 1998. This means that funds totalling DM 15 billion will still need to be found for the 1998 budget. Tietmeyer's response is to announce that, at most, the parties have reached agreement on the formulation to the effect that they will work out a compromise. He assumes that the gold can be revalued without parliamentary pressure. In the press the Governor states that the compromise can only be called a compromise once the central bank board has approved it. That in turn depends on what Mr. Waigel does with the forthcoming legislative proposal which would oblige the *Bundesbank* to revalue its gold reserves.

In Sweden the social-democratic government of Prime Minister G. Persson announces that Sweden will not join *EMU* in 1999, though reserving the option of joining at a later date.

5 June

An *opinion poll* reveals that over 71% of the German electorate want to postpone the EMU launch date of 1 January 1999.

6 June

According to *Eurostat, consumer prices* in the fifteen EU countries showed a 1.5% increase in April against the same month in 1996. This is the lowest rate of inflation ever measured in the EU.

9 June

At the EU Council of Ministers the French government asks for more time to study the *stability pact* agreed in Dublin. France wants the passages on economic policy to put greater emphasis on job creation and maintenance of the social system. The EU Council President Zalm considers that the answer to France's problem is for greater attention to be paid to employment and social issues in the EU. A Dutch proposal is on the table for including in the stability pact a chapter in which the Member States promise to co-operate to a greater extent on economic growth and employment. Agreement is reached on the appearance and composition of the euro coins to be introduced in 2002. The *Nederlandsche Bank* president A. Wellink puts the costs of introducing the single currency at around 6 billion guilders for banks and businesses; against this there is a direct saving of 2.3 billion guilders per annum.

10 June

A spate of articles on EMU appears in the Dutch press owing to the impending *Amsterdam Summit*. They describe the starting position of the EU which is based on three unequal pillars. The first comprises the existing treaties of the European Community: ECSC, Euratom, EEC and EMU. The Commission has the right to initiate legislation here and is responsible for implementation and control. The European ministers decide by a qualified majority in many areas of policy. In Amsterdam they will have to decide on the revision of the voting ratio and the composition of the Commission if the current fifteen member countries are increased to at least twenty. It is also proposed to introduce the practice of qualified majority voting in twenty-five areas of policy where decisions still have to be unanimous. Taxation is an important exception. As regards the European Parliament, it is proposed that the number of decision-making procedures – totalling over thirty – should be reduced to three: approval, consultation and joint decision. The second pillar regards the common foreign and security policy. The third pillar concerns co-operation on the policy on home affairs and justice. The European institutions (Commission, Parliament, Court of Justice) have virtually no role in any of these policies belonging to the second and third pillar. The Commission is just one of the initiators, the Parliament only an adviser. Decisions are taken on an intergovernmental basis. In Amsterdam there will be discussion on majority decisions being taken in the sphere of immigration, visa and asylum policy and on some aspects covered by the second pillar. It will also be proposed that the intergovernmental Schengen Agreement which is not yet administered by Brussels should be removed from the third pillar and incorporated in the first pillar to complete the internal market. After a three-year transitional period, decisions in this sphere should be taken by a qualified majority. The United Kingdom insists on retaining sovereignty in almost all respects. France indicates its opposition as regards foreign policy.

13 June

The Governor of the *Nederlandsche Bank* Duisenberg announces that the *budget rule* for countries wishing to join EMU in 1999 should not be applied too rigidly: he says that "forming EMU on the basis of a deficit of 3.2% 'is not a disaster' ".[137]

In Poitiers the German Chancellor Kohl and the French President Chirac talk about getting the Federal Republic of Germany and France to agree at the *Amsterdam summit*.

16-17 June

The European Council in Amsterdam reaches agreement on a revision of the EU Treaty laid down in the *Treaty of Amsterdam*. The Treaty contains a resolution on compliance with the Stability and Growth Pact, supplemented by a resolution on the promotion of economic growth and employment, intended to supplement a separate chapter on employment in the Treaty. Although promoting

---

[137]"VVD: Duisenbergs heldere blik vertroebeld" [VVD: Duisenberg's clear vision becomes blurred], *Het Financieele Dagblad* (editorial staff), 17 June 1997.

employment is now explicitly mentioned, no extra resources will be made available for the purpose, nor will the EU be given greater powers in the sphere of employment. Under Luxembourg's Presidency, a special summit will be held on employment in October 1997. This agreement has also resolved some of the problems over EMS II and the legal basis of the euro. The main other provisions in the new treaty are :

− The Commission will be streamlined when the first new countries join. The five major countries will then give up one of their two EU Commissioners. In exchange they will receive more votes in the EU Council of Ministers.

− The multi-speed Europe becomes possible. If a number of countries decide that they want to go further in a particular direction, the others cannot stop them.

− The Schengen Agreement will form part of the new treaty, resulting in democratic control. Exceptions have been devised for Denmark, Ireland and the United Kingdom.

− More financial and human resources are allocated for Europol in order to promote closer co-operation in the spheres of police and justice.

− The United Kingdom will sign the social chapter in the new treaty.

19 June

The press describes the *Treaty of Amsterdam* as weak compared with the Treaty of Maastricht. The main element of the new treaty concerns the − unforeseen − securing of the Stability and Growth Pact which opens the way to EMU: "Upgrading the democratic content of the European Parliament, a chapter on employment and more safeguards for the environment and for consumers are all very fine but essentially just trimmings" says the Dutch daily *Het Financieele Dagblad* of 19 June.

1 July

Luxembourg takes over the *Presidency* of the EU.

The *Nederlandsche Bank* Governor Duisenberg becomes President of the *EMI Council* in Frankfurt.

In Italy the *Schengen Agreement* becomes operative by a decision of the Executive Committee.

7 July
The EU Council of Ministers decides to defer temporarily the final decision on the Italian government's plans to cut the *budget deficit* well below 3% of GDP in the next few years. When the meeting is over the Dutch Finance Minister Zalm announces that he rejects an exchange rate for the euro ("the exchange rate is not an interesting economic argument").[138]

11 July
After the cabinet meeting the German Finance Minister Waigel announces that the *budget deficit* of the Federal Republic of Germany will be "considerably" less than 3% of GDP in 1998. A few days earlier *Bundesbank* Governor Tietmeyer has said that the "discussion over the 3%" is diverting attention from other subjects which are important in selecting the EMU candidate countries.

14 July
In New York the *US dollar* reaches a five-year peak at 2.02 guilders.

16 July
In *Agenda 2000* the Commission unveils its plans for the future of the EU. As regards enlargement, a favourable opinion is given for five of the ten would-be members (the Czech Republic, Estonia, Hungary, Poland and Slovenia). Accession negotiations with these countries plus Cyprus will start at the beginning of 1998. Proposals are also submitted for the reform of the agricultural policy, the structural funds and the financing of the EU from 1999 to 2006.

21 July
The French Finance Minister D. Strauss-Kahn wants to impose higher taxes on the profits of large

---

[138] "Zalm wijst wisselkoersbeleid voor euro af" [Zalm rejects exchange rate policy for the euro], *Het Financieele Dagblad* (editorial staff), 8 July 1997.

companies so that the 1997 *budget deficit*, which will be between 3.5% and 3.7% of GDP, can be reduced by 0.4%. This would bring France close to meeting the criterion, and with a bit of luck it might even stay below the maximum. The fact that the French government does meet the criterion of 3% GDP with a supplementary budget opens the way for Italy, Spain and Portugal to join.

19 August

According to the report on the German economy published by the OECD, the Federal Republic of Germany will probably meet the criteria for joining *EMU*. The deficit of 3.25% of GDP predicted for 1997 is within the normal statistical variation. The deficit could fall to 2.7% of GDP in 1998.

25 August

An opinion poll in Denmark finds that 40% of those asked are in favour of the *Treaty of Amsterdam* (at the beginning of the month it was 32%). In Amsterdam it is agreed that matters concerning Danish sovereignty will be put before the electorate.

2 September

The Italian Foreign Affairs Minister Dini talks about the possibility of *postponing introduction of the euro*. EU Commissioner De Silguy responds by stating that postponement is incompatible with the Maastricht Treaty.

4 September

In the journal *Die Woche*, *Bundesbank* Governor Tietmeyer says that postponing the introduction of the *euro* would be neither an economic nor a political disaster. The German government immediately distances itself from this remark: "There is no reason at all for discussing postponement."[139]

5 September

The Dutch politician Bolkestein also feels that it would not be a disaster for *EMU* to be postponed "for a few years".

---

[139] "EMU carousel draait op Duitse verkiezingsprikkels" [EMU carousel driven on by German elections], *Het Financieele Dagblad* (editorial staff), 5 September 1997.

| | |
|---|---|
| 8 September | According to the country report published by the OECD, Greece still has several years of hard work ahead of it before it can join *EMU*. There have been clear improvements in the financial and economic situation, but there is still a huge gap with the other EU countries. The OECD expects a budget deficit of 5.2% of GDP in 1997, which could fall to 4% in 1998. |
| 10 September | According to Commission President Santer, the advent of *EMU* is irreversible. It is not legally tenable to postpone the euro. |
| | At a meeting at the European Summer Institute in Berlin, the Governor of the *Nederlandsche Bank* Wellink criticises the adverse effects of an active *exchange rate policy* after 1 January 1999. He believes that there are people who want the EU Council of Ministers to formulate a regular exchange rate target. This would permit political influence over the ECB's interest rate policy via the back door. |
| 13 September | Informal EU Council of Ministers meeting in Mondorf, Luxembourg. It is agreed that at the *Jumbo Summit* next spring the European heads of state and government will not only decide which countries are to join EMU, but the exchange rates of the participating currencies will also be pegged to one another. In effect EMU would then actually start eight months before 1 January 1999. |
| 17 September | According to Szász, former director of the *Nederlandsche Bank*, it should be possible to discuss postponing *EMU*. The risk that public finances are not yet convincingly under control impairs the credibility of EMU and has negative implications for the financial markets and political confidence. |
| | Belgium, France and Italy insist that *institutional changes* are necessary before the EU can be enlarged. They have drawn up a declaration to that effect for attaching to the Treaty of Amsterdam. |

19 September

At the 70th Franco-German Summit the two countries have failed to arrive at a definite joint proposal for the *European Summit on Employment* to be held in Luxembourg in November. The Federal Republic of Germany considers that promoting employment can best be left to the market. France is aiming at a European initiative to combat unemployment for which Brussels can pay the bill.

21 September

There are rumours that Italy, as well as France, is hesitant about appointing Duisenberg as *President of the ECB*. The Italian Prime Minister Prodi denies this after his visit to the French President Chirac.

24 September

The EMI has decided that the *convergence report* scheduled for publication in November will be postponed until March or April 1998 since it is desirable to have the complete figures for 1997.

28 September

The Italian government approves the 1998 budget in which the *Italian budget deficit* will be cut by about 25 billion lire (ECU 15 billion) to 2.8% of GDP.

The *Spanish budget* for 1998 expects a deficit of 2.4% of GDP (assuming a growth rate of 3.4%).

The *tax reform* planned by the German government has been dropped and will not be on the agenda until the next cabinet (elections are held on 27 September). However, the government does want to reduce the solidarity surcharge on its own initiative from 7.5% to 5.55%, though it is not yet clear how the resulting loss of DM 7 billion in revenue is to be offset.

30 September

In the British press there are rumours that the government will take a "more positive attitude" towards *British participation* in EMU. Financial analysts are convinced that the United Kingdom will join sooner than was thought.

1997

2 October

The foreign affairs ministers of the European Union countries sign the *Treaty of Amsterdam.*

6 October

The Belgian government approves the 1998 budget which shows a deficit of 2.3% of GDP with a predicted economic growth rate of 2.5% (the deficit is 2.8% of GDP in 1997 and 3.2% in 1996). The *government debt* will come to 122.3% of GDP against 125.1% in 1997.

9 October

Finland will evidently have no trouble meeting the *criteria* of the Maastricht Treaty. The 1997 budget deficit is around 1.3% of GDP and is expected to decline by 0.1% of GDP in 1998. The government debt is less than 60% of GDP. In October 1996 the Finnish mark joined the ERM. According to the strictest interpretation, this may be considered too late. The 15% unemployment among the working population is cause for concern (inflation is forecast at 1% in 1997).

*The Bundesbank* initiates a new spate of *interest rate* hikes in Europe by raising its main money market rates.

13 October

Four German professors (including W. Nölling, former member of the *Bundesbank* management board) argue in favour of postponing the euro and want to involve the *German constitutional court.* They consider that not only the Federal Republic of Germany but other EU countries, too, can see ways of meeting the convergence criteria for joining EMU by manipulating the figures.

The European Commission rejects the German proposal for paying around DM 7 billion less in to the *EU budget* from 2000 onwards (current contribution around DM 22 billion).

EMI President Duisenberg expects a large group of Member States to qualify for *Stage Three* of EMU in May 1998. "On 12 January 1999 'ten or eleven'

Member States could be starting EMU", according to Duisenberg.[140]

1997

14 October

At their bilateral summit meeting, the Federal Republic of Germany and France agree on the co-ordination of economic policy in EMU. The intention is that the finance ministers should meet for an informal meeting (known as *Euro X Council*) at the start of Stage Three, prior to the regular meeting of all EU finance ministers. The German Finance Minister Minister Waigel proclaims a "very significant" step forwards, his colleague Strauss-Kahn says he is "delighted" that the Federal Republic of Germany and France have reached agreement.

18 October

In an interview in the British *Financial Times* the Chancellor of the Exchequer Brown repeats the view that the United Kingdom is "most unlikely" to join *EMU* on 1 January 1999. The Chancellor's advisers hint that Britain is equally unlikely to join soon after that date.

26 October

Italy genuinely accedes to *"Schengen"*.

27 October

The press contains reports that during the first three days of May 1998 the decision will be taken on which countries qualify for *EMU* on 1 January 1999. The final decision will be taken on 3 May.

The British Prime Minister Blair announces that the United Kingdom will not exchange *sterling* for the euro before the turn of the century. If re-elected, the earliest that the Labour government will decide whether to join Stage Three of EMU will be after the next general election (which must be held within five years), and there will have to be a referendum.

29 October

The European Parliament wants six *euro coins* rather than eight (the two and twenty cent coins ought to be

---

[140] "Duisenberg ziet EMU starten met brede kopgroep" [Duisenberg sees EMU starting with a broad first wave], *Het Financieele Dagblad* (editorial staff), 14 October 1997.

scrapped). Also, no EU country must be allowed to place a national symbol on one side of the coins. The finance ministers can deny this request but they will need to be unanimous.

4 November

France proposes Governor J.C. Trichet of the *Banque de France* as a candidate for the presidency of the ECB. According to the *Nederlandsche Bank* the candidacy gives the "wrong signal" on EMU.

5 November

At an informal EU Council of Ministers meeting there is a strong disagreement on whether target figures should be set for a European co-ordinated *policy on employment*. The Federal Republic of Germany and Spain are against it, but France as well as Luxembourg, which holds the EU Presidency, do think it a good idea. Unemployment in the EU currently stands at around 19.5 million. The forthcoming "Jumbo Summit" will discuss how unemployment running at 11% of the working population can be reduced to 7% over five years, which will mean creating 12 million jobs.

The Dutch Finance Minister Zalm continues to support Duisenberg as a candidate for the *presidency of the ECB*. The former German Chancellor Schmidt suggest satisfying France by appointing Giscard d'Estaing as President and Duisenberg as Vice President. President Chirac and the German Chancellor Kohl agree to maintain contact on the question in the immediate future. The names of two other candidates are now circulating in Brussels: Governor L. Rojo of the *Banco de España* and the Belgian Finance Minister Maystadt.

9 November

Following the bilateral talks between France and the United Kingdom the French Prime Minister Jospin announces that the United Kingdom should be given a seat on the board of the *ECB* as soon as the country decides to join the euro. This statement is a variant of the German view that the EMU countries should keep a place "warm" on the ECB board.

| | |
|---|---|
| 10 November | According to the Dutch Foreign Affairs Minister H. van Mierlo his government does not rule out a compromise in the *battle for Duisenberg*. The minister cannot confirm whether the Federal Republic of Germany will support the Netherlands. |
| 11 November | The Italian Prime Minister Prodi explicitly opposes *Duisenberg's candidacy*. He prefers the central bank governor Trichet (France) or Tietmeyer (Germany). |
| 13 November | The Greek government continues its strenuous efforts to bring its economy in line with *EMU and the euro*. To do this the government aims to reduce the budget deficit from 4.2% of GDP in 1997 to 2.5% in 1998. |
| 16 November | France wants the EU Member States to arrive at *convergence criteria* for combating unemployment which are "global, quantified and assessable". These requirements should ultimately be equal in importance to the monetary and financial criteria laid down in the Maastricht Treaty. |
| | According to the German *Sachverständigenrat* (panel of five wise men)[141] the Federal Republic of Germany will just fall short of the *budget criterion*. The 1997 budget deficit is estimated at 3.1% of GDP. The deficit predicted for 1998 is 2.6% of GDP. The panel therefore does not see why Germany should not be eligible to join EMU. |
| 17 November | At the EU Council of Ministers meeting it is decided that the *euro* will be placed in circulation on 1 January 2002. In practice this means that the single currency will come into use on 5 January 2002. Although under the Madrid agreement of 1995 the euro and national currencies can be in circulation simultaneously until 1 July 2002, it is expected that this period will be reduced to a maximum of one or |

[141] The *Sachverständigenrat zur Begutachtung der gesamten wirtschaftlichen Entwicklung* is an independent panel of advisers to the German government, set up by the law of 14 August 1963.

two months. Moreover, the establishment of the *Euro X Council* is opposed by Denmark, Greece and Sweden. These Member States which are unwilling (or in Greece's case unable) to join EMU are afraid that the finance ministers will hold preliminary discussions in that council on decisions which will affect the internal market.

21-22 November    At the employment summit in Luxembourg the EU heads of state and government take a first step towards a more co-ordinated employment policy. It is decided that the ministers of social affairs will shortly start devising individual employment plans. On the same lines as the EMU convergence criteria, *social convergence criteria* are to be formulated for employment and used to assess national employment plans. The European Council will evaluate the progress of the plans once a year, in December.

24 November    After the employment summit the German Chancellor Kohl states that his country is aiming at a "sensible compromise" in the contest between Duisenberg and Trichet for the future *presidency of the ECB*. Shortly afterwards the Governor of the Bank of England E. George announces that he supports Duisenberg's candidacy and the Belgian Prime Minister J.L. Dehaene says that he will not be putting up a candidate of his own, ending the speculation that the Belgian Minister Maystadt might be in the race.

1 December    The EU Council of Ministers agrees to eliminate the main differences in *business taxes* (corporation tax and tax on profits) within five years. There is doubt about whether eleven countries will launch EMU. It could be one or two fewer because they do not satisfy the criteria. There is disagreement over the establishment of a *Euro X Council*.

In Austria and Greece the *Schengen Agreement* becomes operative by a decision of the Executive Committee. This means that eight European countries have eliminated all border checks for people: the five original Schengen countries (Benelux, France and Germany) plus Austria, Greece and Italy. [142]

13-14 December

The European Council in Luxembourg agrees to the establishment of the *Euro X Council* in which the members will be the ten countries adopting the euro in 1999. The agenda of this consultative body will be forwarded to EU countries not joining EMU so that they can state any items on which they would like to be invited to attend (this is not an entitlement). It is also agreed that at the end of March the European Union will start the process of enlargement with ten East European countries plus Cyprus. After that, negotiations on joining the Union will in practice only be conducted with six countries (the Czech Republic, Cyprus, Estonia, Hungary, Poland and Slovenia). The other four candidates (Bulgaria, Lithuania, Romania and Slovakia) can conduct "preparatory negotiations" with the EU. Turkey has also applied for membership but has not yet made sufficient progress to be considered eligible. To demonstrate that all eleven candidate countries are involved in the enlargement process, a meeting of the ten foreign affairs ministers will probably be held once a year. A compromise is in sight on the appointment of Duisenberg as the first President of the ECB. It means introducing an age limit of, say, 67 years. After that the French candidate Trichet would take over the reins.

## 1998

1 January

The United Kingdom takes over the *Presidency* of the EU from Luxembourg.

2 January

The *Italian budget deficit* for 1997 comes to 2.7% of GDP, as against 6.8% in 1996.

---

[142] Although Denmark, Finland and Sweden have signed the Act of Accession to the Schengen Application Convention, this Act has not entered into force.

In France the constitution has to be amended so that the Treaty of Amsterdam can be approved. This treaty makes it possible to pass decisions by a majority vote on immigration and cross-border traffic. The *French constitution* regards both subjects as a matter of national sovereignty.

8 January

In Germany four professors consider that EMU should be postponed because the conditions required for the currency union are not met. They plan to lodge a complaint against the euro with the *Constitutional Court* in Karlsruhe.

In Belgium, provisional figures put the 1997 *budget deficit* at 2.4% of GDP (1996: 3.2% of GDP). A deficit of 3.3% of GDP is forecasted for Germany in 1997.

EU Commissioner De Silguy suggests that Duisenberg should take on the *Presidency of the ECB* for the first four years, after which Trichet can take over.

12 January

The four German economists submit the document *Der Kampf um den Euro* [The battle over the euro] to the Constitutional Court in Karlsruhe with the aim of securing an interim injunction preventing the German government from agreeing to adopt the euro on 1 January 1999.

14 January

The foreign exchange market is in turmoil over the Dutch view on *Italy's membership* of EMU. According to reports in the Dutch press, Finance Minister Zalm has threatened to resign if Italy is allowed in. The Monetary Committee has now approved the Italian budget for 1998. Through the chairman of the government council of economic advisers Germany says that, for political reasons, it is "inevitable" that Italy will join EMU in 1999. In Spain, the State Secretary C. Montoro has publicly declared that there is no longer any doubt over whether *Spain* will be among the first wave of EMU.

21 January

In the European Parliament the managing director of the IMF M. Camdessus calls Italy a credible *candidate* for EMU.

The press announces an impending compromise between the German Chancellor Kohl, the Dutch Prime Minister Kok and the French head of state, Chirac, on the *appointment of Duisenberg* as President of the ECB. Duisenberg is to be appointed for a period of eight years but under a "gentlemen's agreement" Trichet will take over as President after four years. There are objections to this draft compromise. If Duisenberg is appointed for a scheduled term of eight years but after four years hands over the presidency to Trichet who, according to the rules, is appointed for four years, Trichet would then have to be appointed for a further eight-year term according to the treaty. In this way the ECB would have a French President for twelve years.

27 January

*Eurostat* criticises the way in which the Italian government recorded the proceeds from a disputed *gold transaction* in 1997. In July 1997 the Italian foreign exchange agency sold off all its gold stocks to the Banca d'Italia. The resulting book profit of 8.8 billion guilders was handed over as tax to the Italian state. In his reply to parliamentary questions, Minister Zalm states that this type of transaction does not make a lasting contribution to reducing the budget deficit and therefore does not count towards the deficit according to the wording of the Maastricht Treaty. Prime Minister Prodi dismisses the Dutch doubts about Italy's membership of EMU. According to him, "internal political games"[143] are irrelevant to the final assessment.

5 February

During his visit to Bonn the Dutch State Secretary of Foreign Affairs Patijn hears that the German government supports the *appointment of Duisenberg*

1998

---

[143] "Prodi: 'Italië doet gewoon mee aan de euro' " [Prodi: "Italy will join the euro as expected"], *De Telegraaf* (editorial staff), 29 January 1998.

as the first ECB President for an eight-year term. Insiders are nevertheless still reckoning on a "gentlemen's agreement".

6 February

According to R. Jochimsen, member of the *Bundesbank* board, only five small Member States (Denmark, Finland, Ireland, Luxembourg and the Netherlands) qualify for EMU on the basis of the *criteria* of the Maastricht Treaty. He considers that the European leaders are too eager to create a single European currency with the set criteria and procedures. He calls the establishment of EMU a process of "closing our eyes and hoping for the best".

In the Netherlands, Minister Zalm has asked the *Nederlandsche Bank* for an opinion on the creation of *EMU* in which it will express its views on the convergence of the EU Member States. The German Chancellor Kohl has asked for the *Bundesbank*'s opinion on the EMU conditions. The EMI is also preparing a report which examines whether the Member States have achieved sufficient economic and monetary convergence to join EMU. The European Commission will issue an opinion as well. At the end of March the opinions of the *Nederlandsche Bank*, the EMI and the Commission will be forwarded to the Dutch parliament and will form the basis of the *debate on EMU* to be conducted in April. Over the weekend of 2 May the European heads of state and government will decide which countries can join EMU.

11 February

In 1997, the *French budget deficit* came to between 3.0 and 3.1% of GDP, putting it just above the criterion for joining EMU.

The European Commission is in favour of reducing the length of time during which the *euro and national currencies* can circulate side by side from six months to between two and six weeks. The Netherlands wants to accomplish the switch from the guilder to the euro within six to eight weeks.

Germany is considering an even faster switch from the DM to the euro.

16 February

The *Belgian budget deficit* for 1997 comes to 2.1% of GDP. The deficit is expected to fall below 2% of GDP in 1998. The *Spanish budget deficit* is forecast to be below 2.8% of GDP.

27 February

The final figures presented to the EU Commission by the fifteen Member States reveal that eleven countries more or less satisfy the *convergence criteria* for joining EMU. Denmark, Sweden and the United Kingdom would also qualify according to the figures, but would rather wait before deciding. Only Greece fails to qualify.

2 March

According to the German news magazine *Focus* the French President Chirac would not mind if Duisenberg were appointed as *President of the ECB* for a full eight years. The information comes from anonymous sources in the German coalition.

9 March

At the meeting of the EU Council of Ministers in Brussels, Italy and Belgium put forward new measures which will permit a further reduction in their high *government debt* after 1 January 1999. The Italian debt ratio is 121.6% of GDP, the Belgian is 122%. The ministers agree that after 1 January 2002 all EMU countries can decide for themselves how soon to replace the national currency with the euro as the only legal tender.

The Dutch Prime Minister Kok considers that the European Member States should step up their co-operation in the political sphere now that monetary union is approaching completion. "EMU can become a cornerstone of Europe's continuing *political integration*" says Kok.[144]

---

[144] "Kok: 'EMU kan leiden tot politieke integratie' " [Kok: "EMU may lead to political integration"], *De Volkskrant* (editorial staff), 10 March 1998.

| | |
|---|---|
| 10 March | German Chancellor Kohl sees no point in dividing the first term of the future *ECB President*: "I don't understand where these rumours come from, and anyone spreading them has not read the Treaty."[145] |
| 14 March | Following a 13.8% devaluation the Greek drachma joins the *ERM* at a central rate of 357.68 drachmas per ECU. The fluctuation margin is ±15% (only Denmark, Sweden and the United Kingdom remain outside the ERM). On the same day the Irish pound is revalued, increasing its central rate by 3% against the ERM currencies. Both measures take effect on 16 March. |
| 16 March | During the visit by the French Foreign Affairs Minister H. Védrine to The Hague it emerges that France and the Netherlands are still at loggerheads over the *Duisenberg question*. Védrine has made it clear that France is standing by its rival candidate, Trichet. |
| 17 March | The former director of the *Nederlandsche Bank* Szász is concerned about the way in which *EMU* is being created: "The question is to what extent the criteria for joining EMU are watered down in May." EMU is being created for political reasons. Szász asserts that if EMU does not work well it will encourage divisions rather than a bond.[146] |
| | Following the example of the United States, the *European Shadow Financial Regulatory Committee (ESFRC)* will evaluate the policy on supervision of financial institutions in the EU as determined by the EU directives, national legislation and the recommendations of international bodies (the Basle Committee and the Group of 30). The ESFRC comprises economists from eleven European |

[145] "Kohl noemt opsplitsen ECB-termijn 'onzin' " [Kohl calls it "nonsense" to split the ECB term of office], *Het Financieele Dagblad* (editorial staff), 11 March 1998.
[146] "Monetaire expert Szász ongerust over start EMU" [Monetary expert Szász worried about the start of EMU], *Het Financieele Dagblad* (editorial staff), 18 March 1998.

countries and is chaired by H. Benink of Maastricht University.

18 March

In *Agenda 2000* the EU Commission publishes its final budget plans for the years 2000 to 2006. This shows that the enlargement in Eastern Europe can be achieved without additional cost, i.e. it can be paid for out of the 2.5% economic growth which the Commission predicts for the years ahead. Although the long-term plan was intended to include reform of the common agricultural policy and rationalisation of the structural funds, the Commission continues on the same course as before and does not explain how both forms of policy should help the East European candidates to develop and adjust to European legislation.

19 March

Press reports reveal that the National Bank of Belgium has sold 299 tonnes of *gold* (half its total gold reserves) in recent months to five central banks elsewhere in the world. The profits totalling over ECU 2.5 billion will not be used to reduce the budget deficit.

21 March

The six-monthly informal EU Council of Ministers meeting in York is devoted to the contributions to the *EU budget*. In terms of wealth, the Netherlands is in eighth position in the euro area but it is the largest net contributor. The Netherlands wants to pay less, along with Austria, Germany and Sweden. The Duisenberg question is in deadlock, and no solution has yet been found to the question of allocating the six seats on the *ECB Board*. France assumes that it will automatically get a seat alongside Germany and Italy, but the Netherlands is against that because it feels that the small countries would then risk being dealt a weak hand. In any case, no place will be reserved for the United Kingdom until it joins EMU.

25 March

According to the *convergence reports* by the Commission, the EMI and the *Nederlandsche Bank*, eleven countries (Austria, Belgium, the Federal

Republic of Germany, France, Finland, Ireland, Italy, Luxembourg, the Netherlands, Portugal and Spain) are eligible to join EMU. The United Kingdom, Sweden and Denmark also meet the criteria but do not wish to be among the founding members of EMU. However, both the EMI and the Dutch central bank severely criticise the high government debt in Belgium and Italy. As far as the Netherlands is concerned, the EMI and the Bank conclude that the 1999 budget deficit should be eliminated altogether in order to bring the government debt down to 60% of GDP "within an appropriate period of time". The EMI report offers a technical appraisal of the degree to which the EU countries have met the convergence criteria, while the Commission issues a formal recommendation to the European finance ministers. In four candidate countries (Austria, France, Luxembourg and Spain) the status of the central bank still does not meet the EMU requirements. Amendments to the law have been announced which should enable these countries to comply with the rules in time.

27 March

In its recommendation to the government the *Bundesbank* approves the introduction of the *euro* in eleven countries on schedule on 1 January 1999: "in the light of the progress made in many EU Member States and after assessment of the outstanding problems and risks, membership of the monetary union seems defendable in terms of stability policy".[147] However, the bank does say that the extremely high level of government debt in Belgium and Italy is "a mortgage and a risk" for currency union.

The Dutch cabinet approves the Netherlands' membership of an *EMU* of eleven countries. It also agrees to Italy's membership if its plans for accelerated re-organisation of government finance,

---

[147] "Bundesbank: Italië en België blijven risico's" [Bundesbank: Italy and Belgium still represent risks], *NRC Handelsblad* (editorial staff), 28 March 1998.

submitted earlier to the Commission, can count on adequate political support in Italy.

31 March

The EU opens formal negotiations on *accession* by Cyprus. The British Minister and EU President R. Cook says that efforts to find a solution to the division of the island are continuing.

3 April

The *Constitutional Court* in Karlsruhe declares the actions against the introduction of the euro, submitted by the four German professors, to be "obviously unfounded" and therefore inadmissible. The Court's judgement is based on the fact that the *Bundestag* and the *Bundesrat* had already approved the Maastricht Treaty in 1992. This provided a sound constitutional foundation for EMU, according to the court.

Italy's spending cuts for 1999 are less than was promised. Owing to additional revenue, the reduction in the *Italian budget deficit* will be 12,000 billion lire (around ECU 6.2 billion), against an earlier estimate of 14,500 billion lire (ECU 7.5 billion), bringing the deficit to 2.6% of GDP.

6 April

The Danish Supreme Court dismisses an action by euro-sceptics against the *Maastricht Treaty*. The verdict comes in a case brought against the Rasmussen administration in 1993.

8 April

In France the National Assembly approves by a large majority a law transferring the *sovereignty* of the *Banque de France* to the future ECB. According to the Finance Minister Strauss-Kahn, the ECB "will be no more independent of the French finance minister than the *Banque de France* is now".[148]

15 April

In the *Dutch parliament* there is a large majority vote in favour of the cabinet's intention to confirm on the

---

[148] "Voor Parijs is tekortverlaging niet heilig" [Reducing the deficit is not sacred for Paris], *Het Financieele Dagblad* (editorial staff), 10 April 1998.

first weekend in May that the Netherlands will join EMU.

The press responds by announcing that 16 March at 16.07 hrs marked the beginning of the end for the Dutch guilder (the abolition of the *Dutch guilder* by the Upper House on 20 April is merely a formality). Finance Minister Zalm reiterates that the Netherlands will insist that the President of the ECB should be appointed for the full eight years in accordance with the Maastricht Treaty. The next day the French President Chirac announces that he will continue to support Trichet as a candidate.

17 April

The *Finnish parliament* votes by a large majority in favour of Finland joining EMU on 1 January 1999.

21 April

The French Prime Minister Jospin demands *democratic control* over the ECB. In the French parliament he argues in favour of giving both the European Parliament and the national parliaments power to invite members of the ECB to attend hearings.

22 April

The *French parliament* votes by a large majority in favour of introducing the euro on 1 January 1999. According to the French Prime Minister, the euro is only the first step. In the next stage Europe should become more democratic and more welfare-minded, with the emphasis on economic growth and employment.

23 April

The German *Bundestag* votes by a large majority in favour of introducing the euro on 1 January 1999. The political message communicated by the euro, according to the former Minister Genscher, is this: "the euro is Europe's answer to a long history of fraternal feuds and two devastating World Wars, opening the way to a new era of a united Europe in which Germany will live in permanent peace with all its neighbours. Germany does not want to divide Europe but to gather all nine neighbouring countries

around it, neighbours without whom we cannot live.
We must continue to make use of this trust that our
neighbours placed in us so soon after Hitler's reign of
terror ... The euro is the key to the future. Stories that
France insisted on the abolition of the German mark
as a precondition for German unification are not only
totally untrue, they put a curse on European unity.
Ever since 1988, over a year before the collapse of
the Wall, practical work has been in progress at
European level on the much older idea of a single
currency." Genscher says it is "arrogant, stupid and
pedantic"[149] to blame Italy for non-compliance of the
convergence criteria.

26 April

The *Belgian parliament* approves the introduction of
the euro by a narrow majority. 58% of the population
still wants a referendum on the euro.

The *Bundesbank* considers withdrawing its
recommendation on introduction of the euro if the
first *President of the ECB* is not appointed for an
eight-year term. The bank considers the period of
office to be one of the principal institutional
guarantees of the stability of the euro and the
independence of the ECB. It feels it would be an
infringement of the Maastricht Treaty to split that
period as proposed by France. The German
Chancellor Kohl and Finance Minister Waigel are
fully behind the *Bundesbank* on this point. The Dutch
Prime Minister Kok also considers it unacceptable to
split the period of office and threatens a veto in the
European Council (of heads of state and
government).

1-2 May

European Summit in Brussels. After an eleven-hour
meeting in an atmosphere of crisis, the heads of state
and government of the EU countries reach a
compromise on the *appointment of Duisenberg* as the

---

[149] W. Beusekamp, "Genscher noemt kritiek op Italië arrogant en dom, Duitse Bondsdag neemt afscheid van de D-mark" [Genscher says it is arrogant and stupid to criticise Italy, German Bundestag says goodbye to the D-mark], *De Volkskrant*, 24 April 1998.

first President of the ECB. Duisenberg is appointed for an eight-year term but states that he will retire "totally voluntarily" before that "in view of my age",[150] whereupon France is entitled to put forward a successor. France also proposes the Vice President of the ECB. In his response the Dutch Prime Minister Kok declares that the decision is "good for the credibility of the euro".[151] Apart from Duisenberg, the council of the ECB will comprise the Vice President Ch. Noyer (France, chairman of the Club of Paris) and four directors, namely: O. Issing (Germany, member of the Bundesbank board) for economic policy, T. Padoa Schioppa (Italy, president of the Italian stock exchange supervision committee and member of the EMI council) for the European payments system, bank supervision and the management of international relations, E.D. Solans (Spain, member of the board of the Spanish national bank) and S. Hämäläinen (Finland, governor of the central bank) for daily routine. Next, it is officially decided that the *euro* will be introduced in eleven countries from 1 January 1999. From that date on, the national currencies will cease to exist in Austria, Belgium, Germany, Finland, France, Ireland, Italy, Luxembourg, the Netherlands, Portugal and Spain. It is also finally decided that the current bilateral central rates in the ERM will be used to calculate the final exchange rates of the official ECU to be fixed on 1 January 1999 as the *irrevocable conversion rates* for the euro.

3 May
The Dutch press criticises the *compromise* over the appointment of the first ECB President. The American Newspaper *New York Times* refers to "an inauspicious start for a project that is meant to

---

[150] "Duisenberg maar vier jaar baas eurobank" [Duisenberg head of the euro bank for just four years], *De Volkskrant* (editorial staff), 4 May 1998.
[151] Idem.

demonstrate Europe's political will to become an economic super-power like the US".[152]

The Dutch Finance Minister Zalm interprets the compromise as "a minimum of four years". He claims that the *President of the ECB* has said that he will stay "at least" until the national currencies are totally replaced by the euro in 2002, a process which is to be completed by no later than 1 July 2002. "So if he wants, he can stay longer" says Zalm.[153] Through K.D. Kühbacher, a member of the board, the *Bundesbank* questions the validity of the compromise achieved: "Kohl has let himself be used. He allowed himself to be drawn into the negotiations whereas he could just have said: Germany cannot and will not agree to this."[154]

11 May

The European Parliament's economic and monetary committee overwhelmingly approves Duisenberg as the first *ECB President*. The Parliament issues its recommendation to the European Council (of heads of state and government) which has yet to take a formal decision on the appointment.

13 May

According to Commission President Santer, all fifteen EU Member States have submitted *national action programmes* to combat unemployment. Social Affairs Commissioner P. Flynn criticises the action plans of Greece, Italy and Portugal which contain hardly any measures to overcome long-term unemployment. The Commission is also somewhat sceptical about the French and Italian plans for shorter working hours introducing a 35-hour working week.

---

[152] "Amerikanen vinden ECB-compromis 'wankele start' " [Americans consider the ECB compromise to be a "shaky start"], *Het Financieele Dagblad* (foreign correspondent), 4 May 1998.

[153] M. Ackermans, "Duisenberg kan langer dan vier jaar blijven" [Duisenberg can stay longer than four years], *De Volkskrant*, 5 May 1998.

[154] "Bundesbank betwijfelt geldigheid van compromis Europese Centrale Bank" [Bundesbank doubts validity of European Central Bank compromise], *Het Financieele Dagblad* (editorial staff), 5 May 1998.

14 May

The Belgian Finance Minister Maystadt announces that the profit on the sale of part of the *gold stocks* of the Belgian national bank will be used to reduce the government debt, cutting it by 88 billion Belgian francs.

The *profit* made by the *Bundesbank* in 1997 of over DM 24 billion came mainly from the revaluation of its foreign exchange reserves. The profit is used to reduce the debt burden of the former GDR.

18 May

According to *Eurostat*, the *current account surplus* in the euro area totalled ECU 83.5 billion in 1996, corresponding to an increase of 134% over 1995. However, the EU is still trading mainly with itself. The surplus with the US fell by 44% to ECU 3.8 billion. In March unemployment in the EU was 10.3%, putting it below the 11.4% for the eleven countries joining EMU.

26 May

Europe's heads of state and government give their formal approval to the appointment of Duisenberg as the *President of the ECB* and to the appointment of the other five members of the board. As a result, the ECB can be officially launched on 1 June.

28 May

According to the latest *EMI annual report* for 1997, though the European economies are gaining strength, large-scale unemployment and the rather high budget deficits which still persist in many countries give cause for concern. EMI President Duisenberg draws attention to the need for a number of would-be members of EMU to endeavour to bring their deficit down to near zero, or even to achieve a surplus. As regards convergence, the report concludes that by the end of the year all eleven countries will have interest rates which are sufficiently similar to guarantee price stability throughout the euro area.

In a referendum the Danish people vote convincingly in favour of the *Treaty of Amsterdam* concluded in

1997, though the turn-out is called remarkably low at 75.6%.

1 June

In Frankfurt the *European Central Bank* is established with the abolition of the European Monetary Institute. This means that, at least in monetary respects, the plea which Churchill made in Zurich in September 1946 for establishing a kind of "United States of Europe" is fulfilled almost fifty-two years later.

In an interview with the Dutch journal *Management Team* the Governor of the *Nederlandsche Bank* Wellink says that certain aspects of EMU are "second best". He has faith in the stability pact, "... but at the same time I think that this system is untenable in the long term. We must move towards a *European Ministry of Finance* which can issue directives on budgetary policy. Then you are really talking about European political union".[155]

4 June

First meeting of the *Euro 11 Council*. From now on the Council will meet before the regular Ecofin Council meeting.

8 June

The German Chancellor Kohl and the French President Chirac of France consider that the principle of subsidiarity should be brought "closer to the people". In a joint letter to the British Prime Minister Blair they argue for an effective EMU. According to both politicians, it was never the intention of European policy to establish a *central state of Europe*. For the forthcoming European Summit in Cardiff they suggest drawing up a short list of subjects on which Europe or the Member States will decide.

9 June

First meeting of the seventeen-member *ECB Council* comprising the Executive Board of the ECB and the

[155] F. Bieckmann, "De EMU is 'second best' " [The EMU is "second best"], *Management Team*, 5 June 1998.

governors of the central banks of the eleven EU countries taking part.

**15-16 June**

In the opinion of the ECB President Duisenberg, the euro will be just as important as the dollar within ten years. Many countries already plan to hold part of their currency reserves in euros. Also, the United States should not expect to carry on having its trade deficits financed in dollars by other countries. Duisenberg firmly rejects any accusation that the *ECB's independence* and its power of decision might be affected by "political instruments" such as the Euro 11 Council: "The ministers have practically no instruments for influencing exchange rates. There are only two options: intervention or use of the interest rate weapon, and both those powers rest with the ECB"[156] says Duisenberg.

On the occasion of the Dutch City Lunch in London, the Governor of the *Nederlandsche Bank* Wellink indicates that he is very much in favour the United Kingdom's joining EMU at an early date. He says that the British are hesitant about participating in *European integration*, but that has always been so in the past. The United Kingdom's membership would add 16% to the EU's national product and might also to some extent counter-balance the pressure from France and Italy to cut the working week to 35 hours.

The main theme of the European Council in Cardiff is *Agenda 2000* containing a package of measures to get Europe ready for enlargement when a number of East European countries join. The financing problem in the EU is discussed. It has come about because Austria, the Federal Republic of Germany, the Netherlands, and Sweden want a reduction in the compulsory contributions, causing other countries to fear that they will have to pay more. Apart from that,

---

[156] "Duisenberg: euro wordt net zo belangrijk als de dollar" [Duisenberg: the euro will be just as important as the dollar], *De Telegraaf*, 15 June 1998 following an interview with Duisenberg in the German weekly magazine, *Der Spiegel*, on 15 June 1998.

Commission President Santer has the support of six Member States (including France and the Netherlands) advocating more stringent compliance with the general economic guidelines laid down by the Commission. In this connection the Belgian Minister for Finance Maystadt believes that the Ecofin Council should continue to deal with economic policy in the future, that being a field in which consensus is not always sought.

20 June    The Federal Republic of Germany commemorates the 50th anniversary of the *German mark*. In a speech, J. Gaddum, Vice Governor of the *Bundesbank*, referring to the introduction of the euro, sees no reason "why we should not be confident that a policy based on the same principles will produce the same success. That is the D-mark's birthday message to the European currency of the future". According to the German Chancellor Kohl, introduction of the euro will "advance the process of Europe's political unification".[157]

23 June    According to the leader of the German socialist party G. Schröder, the euro can ultimately succeed only if the single currency is combined with greater *political integration*. Harmonisation of financial and economic policy and tax systems should be the next step in the process of European integration: "The euro can only succeed if there is greater political union. Merely co-ordinating monetary policy is not enough," the politician says. He does not expect the single currency to compete with the dollar: "It will be a long while yet before the euro can play the same role on the world stage as the dollar currently does."[158]

27 June    In an interview with the Dutch daily *NRC*

---

[157] Deutsche Bundesbank, *Festakt Fünfzig Jahre Deutsche Mark* [Festschrift Fifty Years German Mark], p. 7, 28 June 1998.
[158] "Schröder pleit voor meer politieke integratie in EU" [Schröder wants more political integration in the EU], *Het Financieele Dagblad* (foreign correspondent), 24 June 1998.

*Handelsblad,* ECB President Duisenberg talks about his *appointment.* Speaking of France's President Chirac, he comments: "I had one discussion with him in Brussels at the invitation of the British Prime Minister Blair, who chaired the meeting. Three days later Blair was in the House of Commons where he was asked: "If Mr. Duisenberg chooses to serve the full eight-year term, can he do that?" Blair answered "Yes". Chirac responds by saying "I understand that President Duisenberg of the European Central Bank wishes to retain the initiative regarding his departure from the ECB 'for reasons of principle'." Referring to his earlier statement to the BBC, that Duisenberg had given him his word as a gentleman that he would leave voluntarily after four years, Chirac says "... I have no doubt at all that Duisenberg will keep his word".[159]

29 June

The EU Council of Ministers (for foreign affairs) agrees to the new policy on development co-operation. Under this policy the Union maintains a special relationship with the former colonies in Africa and the Caribbean as laid down in the *Lomé Convention,*[160] which has already applied for forty years. These countries will continue to enjoy preferential treatment in their trade with Europe in the next century.

In an interview with the Greek journal *Eleftherotypia,* ECB President Duisenberg says that Greece can join the *euro area* in 2001 so long as the government goes ahead with the current programme of economic reforms.

---

[159] "Geloofwaardigheid krijg je niet in een dag" [Credibility is not built in a day], *NRC Handelsblad,* 27 June 1998.
[160] The Lomé Convention of 28 February 1975 governs relations between EU Member States and their former African, Caribbean and Pacific colonies, known as the ACP countries. The Netherlands considers that European aid should benefit the very poorest developing countries, in particular. The EU Member States have promised that from 2000 onwards they will gradually open up their market to the poorest countries which are not former colonies. That means that some 48 countries will be able to import almost all products into the EU free of customs duties by about 2005.

| | |
|---|---|
| 30 June | The *ECB* is officially inaugurated at the *Frankfurter Oper* in the presence of the central bank governors of the fifteen EU Member States and seven European heads of state and government (France is represented by its Finance Minister, Strauss-Kahn). |
| 6 July | At the meeting of the Euro 11 Council the Commission President Santer warns against the danger of *laissez-faire budgetary policy*. The countries should do more to eliminate structural budget deficits. The ministers agree with the Commission proposal for leaving the parity between the CFA franc[161] and the French franc unchanged when the euro is introduced. The meeting also approves a number of changes to the 10 and 50 cent euro coins. |
| 9 July | Ratification of the *Treaty of Amsterdam* by the Belgian Chamber of Deputies. On 4 June of the same year, the Senate approved the Treaty. |
| 30 July | *Eurostat* announces that in the euro area *consumer prices* were 1.4% higher in June against June 1997. |
| 10-11 August | The Danish government announces that Denmark will hold a *referendum* on the Treaty of Amsterdam after March 1999. According to an opinion poll 32% of Danes are in favour of the treaty and 31% against. |
| | Results of a poll by the British research agency, MORI, indicate a steady decline in the number of Britons who object to joining EMU. According to the pollsters it is still too early to hold a *referendum* on joining EMU, but the change of attitude implies that the United Kingdom will join monetary union between 2001 and 2003. |
| 17 August | In its August monthly report the *Bundesbank* states |

1998

---

[161] This currency is used as a unit of account in the 14 French-speaking African countries which together form the *Coopération Française en Afrique*.

that, according to its own method of accounting, the *harmonised money supply* (M3) has grown by 5.5% since January compared to 4.5% in the corresponding period last year. Italy and Ireland were largely responsible for that growth, while the money supply in France also showed an above-average increase. In the report the bank warns of growing inflationary pressure and says that it attaches great importance to the precise assessment of M3 in EMU. For a rough estimate of the European money supply, the bank considers that an average of all European harmonised M3s is an excellent instrument, but this method is not sufficiently accurate for determining the money supply once EMU starts. Non-one has yet thought of a way of measuring it.

*Financial crisis* in Russia, where a temporary cessation of foreign debt payments is announced and the band within which the rouble is linked to the dollar is widened by 50%. Foreign-held Russian bonds total an estimated 30 billion roubles. The national debt is also compulsorily restructured.[162]

24 August

ECB President Duisenberg does not think that the crisis in Russia presents any major threat to the European economy as yet. During a speech in Munich, Duisenberg says that the ECB will guarantee a stable euro, as safe as the German mark. He goes on to say that the ECB is on the brink of agreeing the strategy to be pursued in order to ensure *price stability*. It will probably combine keeping an eye on the growth of the money supply with monitoring the monthly inflation figures. On 11 September the ECB Council will take a final decision on this.

---

[162] The crisis in Russia came on top of the crisis in Asia which began in Thailand in July 1997 and spread to South Korea and Indonesia. This placed heavy demands on IMF resources. In the past financial year this institution lent a record figure of almost 26 billion dollars to members with financial problems, including 22 billion dollars to Asia. At the end of April 1998 the total outstanding IMF loans came to roughly 75 billion dollars excluding the aid promised to Russia totalling over 22 billion dollars.

25 August

*Consumer prices* in western Germany dropped by 0.1% in August against July. Over twelve months prices have risen by 0.7%, the smallest increase for eleven years.

11 September

A meeting of the ECB Board and the governors of the eleven central banks taking part fails to reach a decision on *European monetary policy*. "I had hoped that we would be able to present our tactics today, but it is a complicated subject. There is certainly no question of disunity between the countries," says ECB President Duisenberg after the meeting. He stresses that the strong economic growth in Europe has not ended yet. Inflation is still low and unemployment is falling, but he criticises the fiscal policy "of a small number" of the eleven European members of EMU: "Given the current strong economic growth, we expect more effort to bring down the budget deficit. But some governments are adopting a lax fiscal stance."[163] Referring to the financial crises in Russia and Asia, Duisenberg remarks that though this is putting the dampers on economic growth in the euro zone, the impact should not be exaggerated.

18 September

The ECB announces that its first *refinancing operations* for merchant banks will begin on 4 January 1999. The market is expecting the interest rate charged to be between 3.3 and 3.5% (repo rate). This arrangement enables the merchant banks to call on the ECB by pledging securities. The term of the loan may range from two weeks to three months.

26 September

At a meeting of the EU Council of Ministers in Vienna, Greece and Denmark indicate that they will take part in the new European exchange rate mechanism, the *EMS II*. Denmark will let the crown fluctuate by a maximum of 2.25% against the euro. The band width for the drachma will be ±15%.

---

[163] "Duisenberg: crisis dempt groei van economie Europa" [Duisenberg: crisis puts the dampers on Europe's economic growth], *NRC Handelsblad* (editorial staff), 12 September 1998.

Sweden and the United Kingdom do not join EMS II for the moment. The Treaty of Maastricht stipulates that countries wishing to join EMU in the future must first take part in the EMS for two years. But that system is now being replaced by EMS II and nothing was agreed on that in the treaty. This time, Denmark, Greece, Sweden and the United Kingdom also attended the informal Euro 11 Council on account of the current crises in Asia and Russia. The Finance Ministers agree to decide by 1 January 1999 how the EU will be represented in other international bodies (Mr. Euro). According to the Dutch Finance Minister Zalm, the spokesman for the euro area should be either the President of the EU (Ecofin Council) or the President of the Euro 11 Council. His French colleague favours having the euro area represented by the large countries such as France, Germany and Italy.

27 September

In the *elections* in the Federal Republic of Germany, the Chancellor in office, Kohl, is defeated. The socialist party (SPD) becomes the largest party which, together with the Greens, will form a coalition in which the Social Democrat G. Schröder becomes the next chancellor. The new Finance Minister is his party colleague, O. Lafontaine.

30 September

During his visit to France's President Chirac, the future German Chancellor gives an assurance that the *Franco-German friendship* will continue unimpeded though he would like the United Kingdom to play a greater part in the EU. Schröder supports the French proposal for a "new Bretton Woods" to control international capital movements.

1 October

In the Dutch lower house there is a large majority in favour of exchanging the guilder for the euro in a *big bang* on a single day in 2002. Finance Minister Zalm has indicated that he is aiming at the shortest possible transitional period, which might last a few weeks. The banks are also in favour, but small and medium-sized firms, in particular, are fiercely opposed to a transitional period.

5 October

*Bundesbank* Governor Tietmeyer no longer rules out a cut in *interest rates* if the international financial situation continues to worsen. At the G-7 meeting he declared that he saw no reason at all why the European countries should cut their rates any further.

8 October

Ratification of the *Treaty of Amsterdam* by the Spanish Chamber of Deputies. On 24 November the Senate approved the Treaty.

9 October

In Italy, the Prodi administration loses a vote of confidence in the Lower House. The *government crisis* came about because the orthodox communists withdrew their support to the government. On 22 October the new centre-left government takes office, headed by the former communist M. D'Alema.

13 October

The ECB announces that its *monetary policy* will initially be geared to the trend in the European money supply and inflation, though other economic indicators will also be monitored. According to the ECB President Duisenberg the policy will be based on two pillars, with the growth of the money supply playing a "prominent role" and the rate of inflation being assigned "an important role". Other indicators are the euro exchange rate, wage costs and employment.

22 October

The French Finance Minister Strauss-Kahn and his future German colleague Lafontaine announce that a "joint document" will be presented in November on the reform of the *international monetary system*, the aim being to limit fluctuations in the dollar exchange rate. The two politicians are thinking of a band within which currencies are free to move. European policy must also be co-ordinated to combat unemployment, and there needs to be a European policy on promoting economic growth. Lafontaine wants a "European economic government" to co-ordinate the budgets, taxation and social policy of the eleven EMU countries. That is essentially what the French put forward in Amsterdam as a "political counter-weight" to the ECB.

24 October

Informal European Summit in Portschächt (Austria) where it is agreed that Europe must put more effort into a joint economic policy now that monetary union is becoming reality. In his introductory speech, the Dutch Prime Minister Kok argues in favour of greater *economic co-ordination*: "We have Economic and Monetary Union: EMU. It is not MU – just Monetary Union."[164] The finance ministers are asked to define their positions in areas where more co-ordination is possible. They must report by no later than December to the heads of state and government who will then decide how to put the co-operation into effect. In view of the presence of the new German Chancellor Schröder[165] (who has not yet been sworn in) and the new Italian Prime Minister D'Alema, the Dutch press talks of "the most left-wing European summit" ever held. On the same day, at the Foreign Exchange Congress in Maastricht the Governor of the *Nederlandsche Bank* Wellink says that he expects European interest rates to be around 3.2 to 3.3% by the end of the year, the lowest level that Germany and France have already reached.

26 October

With the euro on the horizon, the Italian central bank lowers its *interest rates*, thereby following the example of Portugal, Spain and Ireland which had already cut their rates in October.

31 October

In a speech in Duisburg, the German Chancellor Schröder says that the *Bundesbank* is responsible not

---

[164] G.J. Bogaerts, "EU wil meer lijn in economisch beleid brengen" [EU wants more consistency in economic policy], *De Volkskrant*, 26 October 1998.

[165] The new German government was installed on 27 October 1998. The change of government marked the end of the post-war period in the Federal Republic, which began with Adenauer and culminated under Kohl in the reunification of Germany as a sovereign state in the heart of Europe. The handing over of power also heralds the new Berlin Republic as the successor to the old Bonn Republic.

only for a *hard currency* but also for economic growth and employment: "I do not want war with the *Bundesbank*, but I do want all the available instruments to be used to stimulate growth."[166] Although he does not mention the word "interest", the media interpret this as pressure on the *Bundesbank* to cut interest rates.

3 November    ECB President Duisenberg ignores all political demands for a cut in *interest rates*. He considers it perfectly normal for politicians to fly kites of that sort from time to time, "but it would be abnormal for us to take any notice".[167] Duisenberg is convinced that monetary policy cannot solve the structural problems with which Europe is wrestling.

4 November    At a meeting with the Dutch Prime Minister Kok the German Chancellor Schröder states that he respects the *independence of the ECB* but adds that its independence is not absolute. Jospin, head of the French government, announces in a meeting with Kok on the same day that he does not intend to use monetary policy to combat unemployment. Kok stresses that the European governments should create lasting jobs via a strong economic policy. That requires more co-ordination. He says that the ECB will not operate in a vacuum but in a political context.

12 November    The system of European central banks will not encourage the euro's role as an *international key currency*, but neither will it obstruct that, says the ECB President Duisenberg in a talk at the Economic Club in New York. The markets should decide for themselves and the ECB will not pursue any explicit policy of trying to outdo the dollar with the euro.

---

[166] "Duitse regering kampt met grote tegenvallers elders" [German government battles with great setbacks elsewhere], *De Telegraaf* (editorial staff), 2 November 1998.
[167] "Duisenberg immuun voor Duits politiek steekspel" [Duisenberg immune to German political jousting], *De Telegraaf* (foreign correspondent), 4 November 1998.

But if prices are stable in the euro area, the euro will become more desirable as an international currency.

13 November

According to the French Finance Minister Strauss-Kahn the euro is an essential element of *political integration* in Europe. The countries joining EMU will not lose their sovereignty, but will conquer it. It gives them mastery of the progressively global economy. The minister considers that the Social Democrats' victory in Germany signalled the go-ahead for a common European policy geared to employment, economic growth and harmonisation of tax legislation.

In the British newspaper *Financial Times* the Italian Finance Minister C. Ciampi advocates a flexible interpretation of the *stability pact*. In so doing he is taking his cue from the repeated appeals by the Prime Minister, D'Alema, who wants to keep the Italian government's expenditure on infrastructure outside the pact. The Prime Minister claims that Italy has been "good" and therefore deserves a "reward".

15 November

The British Sunday paper, *The Observer*, states that at their next meeting the finance ministers of the eleven future EMU countries will jointly request the ECB Council to be candid and be held politically accountable for policy. A few days earlier, as President of the EU, the Austrian Chancellor V. Klima has already asked the ECB to publish the minutes of the policy meeting without delay. According to Wellink, Governor of the *Nederlandsche Bank*, pressure by politicians on ECB policy is a complicating factor: "Influencing, or attempting to influence, monetary policy may be counter-productive. Financial markets can render an interest rate cut ineffective if they have the impression that the central bankers prescribed the medicine under political pressure."[168] The issue of

---

[168] "Jacht op notulen ECB in volle gang" [ECB under pressure to publish minutes], *Het Financieele Dagblad* (editorial staff), 18 November 1998.

the openness of *ECB policy* has been under discussion ever since ECB President Duisenberg commented in the European Parliament that the ECB's minutes will remain secret for sixteen years.

| | |
|---|---|
| 16 November | In Königswinter the finance ministers and central bank governors of France and Germany agree to step up their *financial and economic co-operation*. In so doing they aim to play the part of pioneers in the euro area. Nothing was decided on the plan by Minister Lafontaine for a more stable euro/dollar parity. Both ministers stress that they do not want to argue about the stability pact. *Bundesbank* Governor Tietmeyer announces that on 22 December the ECB will decide on the level of interest rates in the euro countries, though the ECB does not confirm this. |
| 23 November | The meeting of the Euro 11 Council is dominated by the issue of *EMU's external representation*. EU Commissioner De Silguy finds that he himself is a candidate. The Dutch Finance Minister Zalm suggests delegating the task to the President of the Euro 11 Council. No decision is taken. |
| 24 November | At the traditional annual opening of parliament Britain's Queen Elizabeth declares that the United Kingdom does not plan to increase its *contribution to the EU* (currently around ECU 3 billion), but will insist on maintaining the reduction in the British contribution to the EU budget which the then Prime Minister Thatcher had managed to extract in 1984. The Netherlands and Sweden are also trying to get their EU contributions reduced. Both countries want the current EU budget frozen for 2000-2006. |
| 26 November | The European Union will not take a decision on the *accession* of new Member States before the year 2000. Accession negotiations began earlier in November with Cyprus, the Czech Republic, Estonia, Hungary, Poland and Slovakia. |
| 28 November | At a symposium in London, ECB President |

Duisenberg appears rather more amenable to an *expansionary policy* in EMU. In his opinion, under certain circumstances, if output, inflation and employment are at a low level, an expansionary monetary policy may help to boost employment, but its role is very limited. The main thing is to encourage greater flexibility in labour markets paralysed by excessive regulation. Unemployment in the urban areas of the EU still varies greatly in fact, ranging from 2.8% of the working population in Luxembourg to 30.5% in Andalusia, Spain.

1 December

The ECB announces its *monetary target* for 1999. The money supply in the eleven euro Member States is allowed to expand by 4.5%. This target is regarded as appropriate in the light of the forecast economic growth of 2 to 2.5% with inflation averaging well under 2%.

Meeting of the ministers for finance, economic affairs and social affairs in the *"Jumbo Council"* on employment in the European Union. This debate is a continuation of earlier meetings in late November at which a number of Commission reports on employment were discussed. Views differ on how to tackle unemployment. The German Minister Lafontaine supported by his French and Italian colleagues favours an active, co-ordinated budgetary policy. The United Kingdom and Spain reject incentive measures and launch an initiative for greater liberalisation of labour markets.

The *72nd Franco-German summit* is held in Potsdam (the first meeting was the signing of the Elysee Treaty in 1963 between Adenauer and De Gaulle). The two couintries declare that they want to deepen the process of European unification and give it a new stimulus. The German Chancellor favours more meetings on specific topics.

3 December

The Dutch daily *NRC Handelsblad* announces that "European monetary union started at 2 a.m. on

Thursday, 3 December 1998".[169] Contrary to expectations, the countries joining EMU on 1 January decide on a *uniform official interest rate* of 3.0%. In formal terms the eleven euro countries have reduced their interest rates on their own initiative, but in fact this action was co-ordinated by the ECB. This means that the way is almost clear for EMU to start on 1 January with a short-term interest rate of 3%.

4 December

In an interview with the Dutch daily *de Volkskrant* the Governor of the *Nederlandsche Bank* Wellink assumes that Duisenberg will remain as *ECB President* for longer than four years. "In May there was a major battle over Duisenberg's appointment, in which he claimed and obtained total freedom of action." To demonstrate that, Duisenberg will stay longer, according to Wellink.[170]

8 December

*Big Bang scenario* for introducing the euro (in a single day at the beginning of 2002) is legally possible and economically desirable, ECB President Duisenberg says. He takes the opportunity to tell the euro countries that they are taking too long over reducing their budget deficits. Between 1993 and 1997 their deficits declined by an average of 1% per annum to 2.5% of GDP. At the end of this year the figure will be 2.2%, and only 0.3% lower at 1.9% of GDP by the end of next year.

9 December

A survey by NSS Research & Consultancy reveals that the average Dutch person is well below standard in *knowledge of the euro*. One third of consumers think that the euro will be introduced as a coin straightaway next year. Over two-thirds do not even know how much the new currency will be worth. More than half say that they will only use euros when they can no longer pay in guilders.

---

[169] "ECB geslaagd" [ECB successful], *NRC Handelsblad* (editorial staff), 4 December 1998.
[170] F. Haan, "Wellink: 'Duisenberg gaat niet na vier jaar weg' " [Wellink: "Duisenberg will not go away after 4 years"], *De Volkskrant*, 5 December 1998.

11-12 December

At the European Council in Vienna the heads of state and government agree to conclude a pact against unemployment. They talk about a *Viennese strategy for Europe* though no real decisions are taken. The pact contains little more than the previous agreements made on employment policy. Apart from that, it was agreed that the euro countries should be represented in the G-7 by the chairman of the Euro 11 Council (this proposal has yet to be approved by the non-European members of the Group, namely Canada, Japan and the United States). By far the most important subject is *Agenda 2000*, the programme intended to make the EU ready for enlargement by the addition of eleven countries from East and South-East Europe. The heads of state and government agree on a few principles which are to form the guideline for the negotiations. In any event, agreement must be reached on the financing of the EU before an additional summit meeting to be held in Brussels on 24 and 25 March 1999. During the next year decisions are also expected on the reform of the European institutions, co-ordination of economic policy and a common defence policy, and a start will be made on drafting a new "constitution" for the Union.

14 December

The ECB publishes its *first review of the money supply* in the EU countries which will use the euro from 1 January 1999. This review shows that the money supply grew by 4.8% on an annual basis in October. While that is higher than the September figure of 4.3%, the increase was due purely to technical factors. The average for August, September and October was 4.5%.

17 December

In a supplement to the Economic Outlook, the OECD concludes that the *budgetary policy* of most EMU countries is inadequate. If economic growth is poor, there is a danger of the budget deficit exceeding 3% of GDP in eight of the eleven euro countries (it does not say which ones). In that case, those countries will no longer adhere to the stability pact concluded in

Dublin in 1996. The OECD urges the EMU countries to replace their current budget deficit targets with agreements whereby they will aim at a balanced budget by about 2002

21 December

According to *Eurostat*, the eleven countries which will take part in Stage Three of EMU had a *trade surplus* of ECU 5.2 billion in September. That is ECU 2.2 billion less than in the same month in 1997. The decline is due to a 4% fall in the growth of exports. The trade balance of all fifteen EU countries together actually shows a deficit of ECU 2.1 billion against a surplus of ECU 3.3 billion in September the year before.

22 December

The ECB announces that it will keep the *official interest rates* within a narrow corridor of 50 basis points for the first three weeks of 1999. After that the band width will be extended to 250 points. The three-week transitional period is intended to provide operators with a smoother introduction to the integrated euro money market. The deposit interest rate will be 2.75% until 21 January and 2% thereafter. In the money market the ceiling will be set at 3.25% for the first three weeks. After that the top rate will rise to 4%. At 3%, the lending rate is in the lower half of the wide 2% to 4% corridor.

29 December

The *Banco de España* adjusts two important *interest rates.* This concerns the marginal lending facility, on which the rate is cut from 3.50% to 3.25%, and the deposit rate (interest which commercial banks receive on surplus cash which they voluntarily place with the central bank) is raised from 2.50% to 2.75%. With this adjustment, Spain has brought its rates in line with those of the ECB.

31 December

The *euro* is born. By a few strokes of the pen the European ministers for finance put their seal on what is perhaps the most historic moment that Europe has ever known. Eleven European currencies are

*History of the European Union*

irrevocably locked together at fixed exchange rates, and are replaced by the euro.

Contrary to the euro banknotes, each country will have eight different coins in circulation in 2002 with one common side and one national side. Altogether, there will be 88 different national euro coins. The euro banknotes are uniform. With the launch of the euro, the EU moves on to the next phase, political union, according to the European Commission President Santer. The French EU Commissioner De Silguy points out that this is the first time that Europe has had a single currency and also the first time that such a thing has been achieved without a war.

The value of 1 euro is fixed as follows:

| | |
|---|---|
| 13.7603 | Austrian schillings |
| 40.3399 | Belgian francs |
| 2.20371 | Dutch guilders. |
| 5.94573 | Finnish marks |
| 6.55957 | French francs |
| 1.95583 | German marks |
| 0.787564 | Irish pounds |
| 1,936.27 | Italian lire |
| 40.3399 | Luxembourg francs |
| 200.482 | Portuguese escudos |
| 166.386 | Spanish pesetas. |

According to ECB President Duisenberg, a new chapter in European economic history will be opened on 1 January 1999. After years of intense and thorough preparation, the launch of the single currency in Europe has been accomplished successfully. Looking ahead, the introduction of the euro and a stability-oriented monetary policy to be conducted by the ECB will contribute significantly to the creation of the conditions necessary for improved growth and employment prospects, says Mr. Duisenberg.

1999

| | |
|---|---|
| 1 January | Germany takes over the EU Presidency. |

*ERM II* is launched with the Danish krone and the Greek drachma participating. Their central rates have been fixed at DKR 7.46038 and GDR 353.109 to the euro, on a par with their rates in the Exchange Rate Mechanism (ERM I) under the EMS. The drachma will fluctuate within a ±15% margin; concerning the krone, a ±2.25% margin has been agreed. New accessors could have been the United Kingdom and Sweden, but they have opted out for the time being.

An *opinion poll* held in Denmark shows that 48% of respondents is now in favour of Denmark's EMU membership. For the first time, those in favour outnumber those against. A similar survey in Britain shows that the public still has little interest in the euro. Less than 50% of respondents know that the name of the new currency is going to be "euro".

The *euro* is off to a strong start on the international exchange markets. Trading begins in Sydney, where it is quoted at $1.1747. In London, the first quotation is $1.1847.

| | |
|---|---|
| 7 January | The Portuguese parliament ratifies the *Amsterdam Treaty*. |
| 18 January | A large majority of the joint Houses of the French parliament votes (758 against 111) in favour of a constitutional amendment clearing the way for the ratification of the *Amsterdam Treaty*. |
| 21 January | The ECB Governing Council decides to set the *interest rates* for its marginal lending facility and its deposit facility at 4.5% and 2.0%, respectively. The main refinancing operations will be settled as fixed-rate tenders at a 3.0% interest rate. |
| 27 January | The German Finance Minister Lafontaine renounces |

his plan to establish *fixed bandwidths* for the exchanges rates of the euro, the US dollar and the yen. He expresses his support for the ECB's policy on this issue. In Mr. Lafontaine's view, the ECB has sufficient room to reduce its official interest rates, provided the restraint in wage and inflation developments is continued.

1 February

The *euro* reaches its lowest point against the dollar since its introduction on 1 January, at $1.1299. The main causes cited are the declining growth of the European economy and the related continuing speculations about a cut in interest rates.

4 February

The Governing Council of the ECB decides that for the main refinancing operations to be settled on 10 and 17 February 1999, the same conditions will apply as for the first such operations settled earlier in the year (*interest rate* at a level of 3%). In addition, it decides that the interest rates on the marginal lending facility and on the deposit facility continue to be 4.5% and 2% respectively.

The Commission criticises the *Italian stability programme* detailing financial policy up to 2002, arguing that the economic growth estimates of the Italian Cabinet are overly optimistic. The public debt ratio in 1998 stood at 120% of GDP. The stability programme has the public debt ratio come down to 107% in 2001.

12 February

The French Finance Minister Strauss-Kahn warns that the EMU could be damaged if the ECB pursues a monetary policy which is at odds with the wishes of the national governments. Whatever the ECB would gain in *profile and credibility*, it would lose in legitimacy and the European economy would be bound to suffer in the end, Mr. Strauss-Kahn says.

16 February

The ECB, in its *Monthly Bulletin* for February, announces it expects the euro to remain undervalued against the dollar for the foreseeable future. The

European economy has taken a downturn, but how profound it will be is yet "uncertain". According to ECB estimates, the euro's exchange rate will, in the medium term, turn out "somewhat below" its long-term average. The ECB ascribes the euro's decline largely to the strength of the dollar which benefits from the unexpectedly strong growth and low inflation in the US.

The Commission criticises the German and French *stability programmes.* EU Monetary Affairs Commissioner De Silguy says that both member states are lacking ambition in reducing their budget deficits. The German proposals, according to Mr. De Silguy, constitute a "minimum position" whose safety margin is insufficient to allow for economic growth undershoots. Added to this, the budget deficit will remain at 2% of GDP for too long: the German government does not expect the deficit to come down to 1.5% of GDP before 2001, after which it will decrease further to 1% of GDP in 2002. Regarding the French plans the Commission says that they, too, contain margins that are too narrow to initiate new policies or to absorb adverse deviations from expected growth or pension spending.

18 February

The ECB Governing Council decides to leave its *interest rates* unchanged at 3.0% for the main refinancing facility; 4.5% for the marginal lending facility and 2.0% for the deposit facility. It declares an interest rate cut not necessary "on examination of the monetary and economic situation".

The Greek Parliament ratifies the *Amsterdam Treaty* with a majority of 246 votes.

20-21 February

During the G-7 meeting in Bonn, agreement is reached on a proposal by *Bundesbank* President Tietmeyer to establish a *stability forum* to monitor global monetary order. The new forum is led by BIS President A. Crockett and includes members delegated by the central banks and finance ministries of the seven big industrial nations, representatives of the IMF and the World Bank and of (stock exchange) supervisory bodies. Twice yearly, they are to pool their expertise in order to pinpoint weak spots in the international financial system.

The US authorities have opposed ideas about the establishment, in the long term, of *target zones* for the exchange rates of the euro, yen and US dollar. The Americans think there is only one way to keep the exchange rates balanced, and that is an equally solid monetary and budgetary policy on both sides of the Atlantic. On February 8, ECB President Duisenberg categorically ruled out the setting of target zones for the exchange rate between the euro and other major currencies.

22 February

According to ECB President Duisenberg, the weakness of the euro is the result not only of strong economic growth in the US, but also of the political pressure exerted on the ECB to reduce interest rates. This *political pressure*, especially from German Finance Minister Lafontaine, is translated into a lower euro exchange rate as the market anticipates a lowering of the interest rates by the ECB.

23 February

The German Finance Minister Lafontaine makes another appeal to the ECB to lower *interest rates*. He sees danger of a deflation spiral setting in if the interest rates do not come down quickly to stimulate economic growth.

British Prime Minister Blair announces to the House of Commons the practical manner of *participation in the EMU*. Three months after the British government gives the green light, a *referendum* could take place. A positive result would mark the beginning of a 3.5 year transition period, ending in the introduction of the euro and, three months after that, the withdrawal of the pound sterling.

24 February

The British Prime Minister reiterates his government's stance that Britain will not rejoin the *ERM*, from which it was rejected in 1992, or shadow the European single currency prior to possibly joining the euro after the next general election.

26 February

During an informal meeting in Bonn, European leaders fail to make progress in their discussions about the *reform of the EU*.

3 March

EU Commissioner De Silguy calls on member states to incorporate more safety margins in their national budgets. All fifteen member states have, for the first time, put a *stability programme* before the Commission and the EU Council of Ministers. In their programmes, governments indicate how they will structure their national budgets for the current and three subsequent years and on what economic indicators they have based their plans.

4 March

The *euro* reaches a new low point at $1.0866. ECB President Duisenberg appears not to be worried, claiming that what "we see is not so much a weak euro as a strong dollar". Rumours to the effect that the ECB has already intervened he dismisses out of hand as pure figments.

8 March

In 1998 the euro-zone countries had a combined *budget deficit* of 2.1% of GDP, down from 2.5% of GDP in 1997. The fifteen nation EU had a deficit of 1.5%, down from 2.3% in 1997. The euro-zone's public debt declined to 73.8% of GDP from 74.6%. Aggregate EU debt shrank to 69.5% of GDP from 71.7%.

11 March

German Finance Minister Lafontaine resigns unexpectedly. He also gives up his chairmanship of the Social Democratic Party. The euro gains 2% in a matter of minutes, rising to $1.1027. On the financial markets, expectations are that Mr. Lafontaine's resignation paves the way for the ECB to reduce interest rates. Mr. Lafontaine is succeeded by the Prime Minister of Hessen, Hans Eichel.

The Italian budget deficit for 1999 is estimated at 2.3% to 2.5% of GDP. This estimate is significantly higher than the target of 2% of GDP quoted by the government in Rome.

14 March

Amid disappointing figures on economic growth in the euro-zone, the *euro* declines to $1.0942.

15 March

A *critical investigation* into the conduct of the Commission ends in the publication of a report saying that the Commission has lost control of the administrative system. After almost three hours of hectic consultations, the entire Commission steps down.

24-25 March

At the special Summit of the European Council in Berlin, the former Italian Prime Minister Prodi is elected as the new President of the Commission. An agreement also seems to be in the offing on *Agenda 2000*, the comprehensive reform package including the EU's common agricultural policy. The purpose of Agenda 2000 is to equip the EU with a more effective policy in the spirit of solidarity, taking care at the same time that an equally stringent budgetary policy is maintained both at the European and national level. Concerning structural and cohesion policy, the Council reserves €213 billion, of which €18 billion go to the Cohesion Fund and €195 billion to the structural funds. As for the agricultural policy restructuring, the agreement envisions the creation of a financial framework stabilising around the €40.5 billion level, plus loans for rural development and veterinary measures.

ECB Governing Council member Issing voices severe criticism of the EMU Member States' *budgetary policy*. He says that most governments are still far from drawing up a balanced budget, let alone objectives aiming at a budgetary surplus. The budget deficits came down slightly in 1998, while in 1997 they declined by 1.5% on average.

In its first *report on the euro-zone*, the OECD hints broadly that the ECB should loosen its monetary policy. The report focuses on the worsening economic outlook for Europe since the euro was launched and the implications this would have for the policies of national governments. On fiscal policy, the OECD says many governments in the euro-zone would have to make "considerable progress" pruning budget deficits to respect the limits in the Stability and Growth Pact.

29 March

As a result of war threatening to break out in former Yugoslavia, the *euro* declines by 8.4% against the dollar to a new low of $1.0708, unprecedented since its introduction on 1 January 1999.

30 March

As the last of the EU countries, France ratifies the *Amsterdam Treaty* which will be effective as of 1 May 1999. The ratification process has taken over eighteen months.

8 April

For the first time since the introduction of the euro, the ECB cuts its *interest rates*. The interest on the main refinancing operations will be lowered by a 0.50 percentage point to 2.5%. The rates on the marginal lending facility and on the deposit facility are reduced by 1 and 0.50 percentage point to 3.5% and 1.5% respectively. ECB President Duisenberg makes it clear that the decision has been taken in a forward-looking perspective, focusing on the medium-term trends in inflation and the compatibility of these trends with the eurosystem's definition of price stability. He urges government leaders to keep the agreements on the maximum budget and financial deficits made when the euro was introduced, and to commit themselves to convincing structural reforms of the economy.

In the euro-zone countries *unemployment* remains stable at 10.5% of the workforce. After Luxembourg, where 2.8% of the workforce is unemployed, the Netherlands comes out second best at 3.4%.

1999

13 April

The *euro* slips back to $1.0750 as dealers react to the apparent deterioration of the crisis over Kosovo and the impasse between Russia and the US after the Defence Minister's Summit in Oslo.

14 April

The new German Finance Minister Eichel announces a change in German *fiscal and budgetary policy* and warns that, if necessary, he will use emergency legislation to intervene in existing spending patterns. In conformity with the Stability and Growth Pact, the general government deficit in 2000 must not be greater than DM 45 billion, necessitating budget cuts totalling DM 30 billion.

16 April

During an informal French-German meeting in Dresden, French Finance Minister Strauss-Kahn proposes to transform the *Euro 11 Council* into a genuine European government. The German Minister Eichel regards this proposal as "an interesting contribution to the discussion about improved co-ordination of economic and financial policy in the euro area". Both politicians emphasise that the reduction in interest rates has shown that the ECB, like the Euro 11, can work in total independence towards the same goal of economic growth and employment.

19 April

The euro falls to its lowest level yet ($1.0622) with concern that funding the war in Kosovo will swell Europe's budget deficits, slow economic growth and deter investors from buying euro assets. ECB President Duisenberg says he is not concerned about the *euro's 9% decline* against the dollar and that the bank is not planning to buy euros to boost Europe's single currency.

In its *Monthly Bulletin* the ECB shows that the eleven euro countries have put their budgetary house in better order than had been presumed. For the euro area as a whole, the *budget deficit* in 1998 declined to 2.1% of GDP, while the debt-to-GDP ratio decreased by 1.8 percentage points to 73.6%. Nevertheless, the

ECB persists in its opinion that the average deficit-to-GDP ratio in the euro area is still too close to the 3% ceiling and should come down to close to the equilibrium level.

22 April  Italy brings down its *budget deficit* by a 0.3 percentage point through a financial manoeuvre. It issues bonds for an amount of over €4 billion. The interest rate depends on the collection of overdue insurance premiums.

26 April  The ECB launches an *offensive against critics* of the euro, saying the new currency's weakness against the dollar does not mean that its long-term stability is in doubt. Mrs. S. Hämäläinen of Finland, a member of the ECB's six-strong executive board, says in San Francisco the euro's 10% fall since its launch largely reflects the US economy's strength and concern about the Kosovo war rather than any fundamental problems with the euro.

28 April  Swedish support for adopting the euro has risen to 38% in April, according to a *poll* commissioned by news agency Direkt. In the last survey, 34% supported a Swedish membership. Opposition remained unchanged at 47%.

1 May  The *Treaty of Amsterdam* comes into force.

4 May  The *euro's 9% fall* against the dollar is not a concern, although the ECB may intervene in currency markets should the decline be extended, says President Duisenberg. In his view, war in the Balkans has not had a "significant" impact on economic growth of the euro-zone. The fact that the ECB has not set an explicit exchange rate target does not mean that the ECB is indifferent to the external value of the euro or even neglects it, Mr. Duisenberg says.

10 May  The EU Council of Ministers back market-oriented reforms to stimulate growth and cut unemployment. In a preliminary discussion, it accepts with few

reservations a draft of the *"broad economic policy guidelines"* for 1999 put forward by the Commission. The guidelines serve as the basis for policy co-ordination among the fifteen member states.

11 May

In Germany, the Social Democrat Ernst Welteke, is appointed *President of the Bundesbank*. President Tietmeyer will retire on 1 September. Mr. Welteke was Finance Minister of Hessen when Mr. Eichel was the state's prime minister. He is to become the seventh *Bundesbank* President.

17 May

At the meeting of the European Foreign Ministers, it becomes clear that the EU's *institutional reforms* will be limited in scope. It is unlikely that the broad approach advocated by the Netherlands will be adopted, which would involve a comprehensive review of institutional agreements on the composition and operation of institutions.

18 May

In its *Monthly Bulletin*, the ECB accuses the euro-zone countries of allowing themselves an overly *minimalist approach* to budgetary policy. On the basis of current medium-term programmes, only Belgium and Spain envision a longer term budget balance. Germany, France, Italy, the Netherlands, Austria and Portugal act on the implicit assumption that a deficit of 1% of GDP in 2001 or 2002 may serve as the end for their fiscal consolidation efforts.

24 May

The EU Council of Ministers agrees that Italy, despite lower than expected growth, will not allow its 1999 *budget deficit* to run higher than 2.4% of GDP, which serves to confirm that Italy will not achieve the deficit estimated earlier, of 2% of GDP.

28 May

The *euro* reaches a new record low of $1.0399. The reason for the decline is said to be increasing concerns that European countries will ease their budgetary discipline.

ECB President Duisenberg describes the *euro* as

"stable" against the dollar. The euro's decline in external value is, he says, "not unnatural and not unexpected". He points out that the US economy has been growing for nine years, while Europe now is in its first year of a temporary downturn.

2 June

In his biweekly press conference, ECB President Duisenberg maintains his optimism about the *euro*, saying that the principal objective, that of guarding price stability in the euro area, is still being met. The euro comes under renewed pressure and on 3 June it sinks to a level of $1.0304.

3-4 June

At the European Summit in Cologne member states approve an *Employment Pact* which has the makings of a "grand design". This Pact still does not contain any concrete recommendations. It endorses the previously recorded processes of Luxembourg and Cardiff, where the EU member states agreed to inform each other about their employment policies and to reform their products and labour markets. Apart from that, the EU leaders fail to see eye-to-eye on the need for a collective statement to bolster the euro, even as the currency is hovering near record lows against the dollar. Dutch Finance Minister Zalm complains that leaders gathered at a two-day summit are unable to speak with a *"unanimous" voice* on the currency.

Pursuant to the Amsterdam Treaty, the European Council appoints Mr. Javier Solana to the newly created office of *Secretary General* of the Council and High Representative for the EU's common foreign and security policy.

10 June

In Germany, the *"Stability Pact"* for South-Eastern Europe is signed. Besides former Yugoslavia, this region includes Albania, Bulgaria, Romania and Moldavia. The Pact creates a framework for the implementation of a plan drafted by the Centre for European Policy Studies in Brussels. The plan is centred on the following measures:

1. Participating countries must integrate their customs services, starting with the countries of South-Eastern Europe, followed by those of the single European market.
2. The EU will compensate countries from its own budget for the loss in customs revenues. This compensation is wholly dependent on progress made in establishing conditions for the creation of an open society.
3. The countries involved, supported by the EU, should use the euro or, until it is introduced, the *Deutsche* mark.

11 June    News of the end to the Kosovo war and the suspension of the NATO bombings has a positive *impact on the euro*, which rises to over $1.05.

12 June    At their preparatory meeting for the Cologne Summit in Frankfurt, the Finance Ministers of the G-7 agree to cancel $50 billion in debts owed by the world's poorest 36 (mostly sub-Saharan) nations. They also reach a *compromise* on the issue of how the euro area should be represented in the G-7. They agree that when monetary matters and the world economy are discussed, the ECB President may participate fully in the G-7 deliberations, and so may the acting chairman and vice-chairman of the Euro 11 Council.

17 June    In the *Financial Times*, economist W. Buiter, appointed in 1997 as independent member of the Bank of England's monetary policy committee, advocates Britain's speedy accession to EMU. The argument that first the economies of the euro area and the UK must converge sufficiently is shot full of holes by Mr. Buiter. He also sharply criticises the *decision-making process of the ECB*, which he calls opaque and secretive. Mr. Buiter favours the British model, requiring the Bank of England to comply with a published inflationary target and to publish its minutes six weeks after each meeting.

18 June    In an effort to rein in the rising yen and shore up the

struggling European single currency, the ECB has bought euros for yen on behalf of the Bank of Japan. This is the first *intervention in the currency markets* by the ECB since the euro was introduced.

1999

19-20 June

At the *G-7 meeting* in Cologne, the agreement made earlier, about the debt relief for the poorest nations, is endorsed. It is also decided to admit Russia as a member, so that in future, they will refer to themselves as the G-8 or the "G-7 plus Russia". Another matter agreed on is the decision to merge the West European Union into the EU.

21 June

Commission President Prodi warns against *Italian inflation* running too high, pointing out that the average inflation rate in the euro area is no more than 1% and warns that Italy might drop out of EMU. In a shocked response by the financial markets, the euro falls to $1.0332.

The EC Council of Ministers gives as its opinion that the present assets and liabilities of the ECSC, when the *ECSC Treaty* expires in 2002, should go to the remaining Communities and be used to create a special fund to finance research activities on behalf of the steel and coal sectors. The Council requests the Commission to submit a draft decision including the necessary measures for implementing the substance of the resolution.

25 June

German Chancellor Schröder announces large-scale *austerity measures*, cutting spending by DM 30 billion. This way, the government wishes to begin reducing its national debt of DM 1,500 billion most of which is the result of German unification.

1 July

Finland takes over the *EU Presidency* from Germany.

6 July

The *euro's exchange rate* falls to $1.0250 after ECB Board member Noyer has announced that actions to interrupt the euro's glide are not forthcoming.

| | |
|---|---|
| 8 July | Another drop in the *euro's exchange rate*, to $1.011, brings it close to parity after German Finance Minister Eichel has declared he cares little about the low exchange rate. |
| 15 July | According to Polish EU negotiator Mr. Kulakowski, Poland will not accede to the EU on 1 January 2003 if Brussels is unwilling to fully include Poland's agriculture in its common agricultural policy. Inclusion would entail that from *Poland's accession* in 2003, Polish farmers would lay claim to direct income support that would take up two thirds of total EU agricultural subsidies. The EU has refused this. |
| | The *euro* slips against the dollar, erasing earlier gains as traders focus on Europe's slow growth, betting that the single currency will soon reach parity with the dollar. Traders brush aside upbeat comments from Mr. Duisenberg, who said he was optimistic about the region's growth prospects and hinted the bank would raise interest rates if growth improves. |
| 27 July | A *"miracle resurrection"* of the euro seems to have taken place. In a single week, the currency has soared by 6% against the dollar, to $1.0703. Reports point at the first signs of German economic recovery and a tendency towards weakening growth in the US. The upward movement is checked abruptly when incoming *Bundesbank* President Welteke, who will be taking office in a few weeks time, signals that the German central bank would not like the euro to become too strong "because that would hurt our export position". |
| 29 July | The ECB leaves its full set of interest rates unchanged before breaking for a four-week summer vacation. A decision to stick to a fixed, rather than variable, tender also comes as no surprise. Central bank officials, including chief economist Issing, say a *variable rate tender* will be a more efficient way of lending money. A fixed rate encourages oversized |

bids from banks that want to be sure to get the financing they need.

18 August

*Bundesbank* President Tietmeyer sees no immediate inflationary dangers ahead and thinks there is a good chance that *consumer price rises* will remain within a 2% limit both this year and the next. Yet Mr. Tietmeyer is convinced that both monetary and budgetary policies should remain watchful.

25 August

In his valedictory speech as *Bundesbank* President, Mr. Tietmeyer warns that many Europeans are still unaware of what lies in store for them. The *euro* will toughen competition. Businesses will use wages as their primary competitive weapon, while member states will undercut each others' taxes in order to allure businesses. He argues against a rise in the cost of social insurance and for limited wage rises, for more flexible working hours and for cutting back the regulatory forest that is impeding investments.

In July, according to ECB figures, annualised *money growth* (M3) rose by 5.6%, compared to 5.3% in the previous month. This implies that M3 is moving away from the 4.5% growth objective which the ECB has set itself for 1999.

Although inflation shows no signs of acceleration, some economists point to the danger of rising *oil prices*. Current levels would indicate that for 1999 as a whole, a rise as high as 140% should be expected, the sharpest rise in twenty years.

9 September

ECB President Duisenberg is expecting *inflation* to pick up slightly in the coming period, mainly as a result of risen oil prices. But the maximum acceptable inflation rate of 2% set by the ECB is not yet in danger of being crossed, except in the case of excessive wage rises. A few days earlier, Mr. Duisenberg himself urged again the eleven participating euro countries to speed up their necessary structural reforms, including the deregulation of the labour market. The participating countries have yet to become fully aware of the fact that they are now all in the same euro boat and hence should harmonise their economic policies. Failure to do this will have a detrimental effect on the euro, Mr. Duisenberg says.

11 September        Most of the eleven euro-zone countries agree to reduce the *double circulation period* in which their currencies will be used alongside the euro when it goes into circulation on January 1, 2002. The double circulation period earlier had been set at six months, but many of the members decided such a lengthy period would breed confusion among consumers. The reduced period will now be from four to eight weeks, with discretion given to individual countries.

15 September        Romano Prodi is officially elected *President of the European Commission* by the European Parliament. In an address held in Strasbourg he emphasises that countries which have made adequate preparations for accession to the EU will be informed before the end of 1999 about the date on which they may join.

In Britain, *inflation* falls to its lowest level since July 1963: 1.1%. The underlying inflation rate (excluding mortgage interest) is, at 2.1%, also lower than expected by analysts.

In its *Monthly Bulletin*, the ECB concludes that the euro will not be accepted as a *commercial currency* until it has reached equal status with the US dollar in the currency market. Internationally, the euro is the second most used currency after "king dollar", but still the gap seems almost unbridgeable.

20 September        In a lecture on the occasion of the 50th anniversary of the *Frankfurter Allgemeine Zeitung*, ECB chief economist Issing speaks about the relationship between the euro and the political union. "A Europe which ventures to monetary union cannot avoid making a decision over the shape of the political

union", Mr. Issing concluded in 1996. Admitting that this is still valid, he now wonders whether a pragmatic, *step-by-step progress* would not be a more promising approach. Calls for a social union to complement or correct monetary union go in the wrong direction. If one were to concede such demands, rising unemployment and mounting tensions between countries and regions would be the consequence. Apart from that, the chances of success for monetary union increase to the extent that each country tackles its own reform challenges. Mr. Issing warns about the danger of any inappropriate form of "Europeanisation". If tasks are delegeted to the European level, without having established an efficient supranational institution with the relevant competencies responsibilities become blurred and home-grown deficiencies are relegated to the background. The psychological damage which this would imply for the process of European integration cannot be overstated. "Considering the risks to the public good that can arise from any premature commitments, we need not necessarily regret, as far as economic and monetary affairs are concerned, that the Maastricht Treaty did not initially go further in terms of political integration."[171]

26 September

According to American Citibank Chairman, Mr. O. Ruding, the *euro*, despite its decline, is still a success in the US. According to Mr. Ruding, the euro will continue to fluctuate, but within the year, he expects it to rebound to $1.15.

From Washington, where the World Bank and the IMF are holding their annual meeting, ECB President Duisenberg announces that in the longer term, *supervision of commercial banks* may have to be moved to the ECB. In the present situation it may be defensible to leave banking supervision to the

---

[171] O. Issing, "Europe: common money-political union?", *Economic Affairs*, Volume 20, No.1, March 2000.

national central banks. "A truly European financial services market has yet to develop. But in the coming years, we will have to see whether it is possible to continue supervision on a national level," says Mr. Duisenberg.[172]

The fifteen central banks in the ESCB, in the interest of clarifying their intentions with respect to their *gold holdings*, make the following statement:

1. Gold will remain an important element of global monetary reserves.
2. The undersigned institutions will not enter the market as sellers, with the exception of already decided sales.
3. The gold sales already decided will be achieved through a concerted programme of sales over the next five years. Annual sales will not exceed approximately 400 tons and total sales over this period will not exceed 2,000 tons.
4. The signatories to this agreement have agreed not to expand their gold leasings and their use of gold futures and options over this period.
5. This agreement will be reviewed after five years.

28 September    The Committee of Three Wise Men (Belgian former Prime Minister L. Dehaene, German former President R. von Weizsäcker and Lord Simon from Britain) which is to advise the Commission on a new organisational design for the EU, submits a plan involving a *"Two-speed Europe"*. A core Union should be created including eight or nine countries. Around the core, two groups would converge of countries having closer and less close relations to the core countries. As a minimum, the core should include France, Germany, the Benelux countries, Italy and Austria. These countries will be fully integrated in many respects. Not only will they have

[172] "Toezicht banken wellicht naar ECB" [Banking supervision may move to ECB], *Algemeen Dagblad*, 28 September 1999.

the euro as a common currency, but they will also pursue common defence, foreign, justice and police policies. The first shell around the core should include Spain, Portugal, Ireland and Denmark. Some of these share the euro with the core Union, but in other areas they will co-operate less closely. The second shell consists of the present candidate member states, most of which are in Eastern Europe.

7 October

The Commission recommends opening negotiations with all twelve countries which have submitted an *application to join the EU*. Currently, the Union is negotiating with only six countries (Cyprus, Poland, Hungary, the Czech Republic, Slovenia and Estonia), while the other six (Malta, Bulgaria, Romania, Latvia, Lithuania and Slovakia) have been put on hold. On 15 October, in Tampere, Finland, the heads of government will agree informally to the proposal. The official decision will be made during the European Summit in December 1999.

The *British pound* continues its strong advance on the euro. Since the beginning of the year, sterling has risen by 8%. Investors act on the assumption that a rise of interest rates will come sooner or be sharper in Britain than in the euro area.

8 October

In Switzerland, the House of Representatives and the Senate have approved the seven *bilateral treaties* between Switzerland and the EU which the Swiss government has signed in June. The treaties are the result of four years of negotiations which were needed after Switzerland had declined, in a referendum in late 1992, to join the EEA (the other EFTA countries – Norway, Iceland and Liechtenstein – had joined and been granted economic access to the single market.) The seven treaties now have to be finally endorsed by a referendum.

15-16 October

The European Summit in Tampere, Finland, states with renewed emphasis that the EU must become an *area of freedom, safety and justice*, with full utilisation of the new possibilities offered by the Amsterdam Treaty.

The *euro* rises to over $1.0850, the highest rate since the end of March 1999. Prompting the rise is an address by Federal Reserve President Alan Greenspan in which he advises the commercial banks to reserve additional assets in case there is a landslide adjustment of the US stock market.

22 October
On the basis of a report prepared by the British Liberal Mr. Ch. Huhme, members of the European Parliament say the ECB should be required to publish the *minutes of Board meetings* relating to interest rate policy. They also wish to be able to interrogate the ECB President after every decision to change the interest rate.

26 October
ECB President Duisenberg points out to the European Parliament that publication of summarised ECB Board meeting *minutes* would bring confusion rather than clarity. The monthly press conference, the *Monthly Bulletins* and other publications closely approximate the summarised minutes published by other central banks such as the US Federal Reserve and the Bank of England.

27 October
By a 397 vote majority, European Parliament rejects a move to publish the *voting behaviour* of ECB Board members on proposed interest rate changes. There is approval for the promise made earlier by ECB President Duisenberg that starting next year, the ECB will publish its own macroeconomic forecasts.

The European Parliament discusses the report of the Committee of Three Wise Men proposing changes in the structure of the EU on its expansion. Although the report does not answer the question what the changed EU should look like – a European Union of more than fifteen member states will be heading for paralysis unless dramatic changes are made to the way it is managed – one of the authors, Mr. L.

Dehaene, makes no secret of his support for a *federal Europe* with a European constitution, but with far-reaching regional autonomy, not unlike the German situation.

The report is published nearly simultaneously with a report written by former French politician J. Attali, in a personal capacity, *Europe 2020: pour une Union plurielle* [Europe 2020: the case for a pluralist Union]. The most probable outcome, in Attali's view, is a "vague" Union (*"Union floue"*), growing in waves without any changes to operational rules or negotiating techniques, while neither the weighting of votes nor the composition of the Commission is ever reviewed. Once the European Union numbers over 20 members, compromises become increasingly difficult to achieve so that a "dictatorship of minorities" remains. Europe then becomes a large free-trade area without any political identity and hence without any clout. Mr. Attali distinguishes five types of union: federal, sovereignist, "vague", Atlantic and pluralistic. After the Maastricht Treaty, he sees no further future for a federal Union. Neither, in his view, is it desirable to put deepening of the Union before enlargement, because that would imply leaving half of Europe out in the cold indefinitely, with all the risks this would involve. Nor does he favour the sovereignist type of Union, in which member states increasingly turn back in on themselves. The pluralist Union, although not regarded as the most probable outcome, looks like a multiple-speed Europe. What should be created is an *"à-la-carte Europe"* in which new member states may pick and choose the elements they are ready to join, or in other words, in which they are able to fulfil their duties as well as enjoying the benefits. In such a set-up the shock of accession should be cushioned by a Marshall Plan for which Mr. Attali proposes to budget €1,000 billion.

The Hungarian Finance Minister, Z. Jarai, declares that *Hungary* can join the EU in 2003 and will be ready between 2004 and 2006 to join EMU.

1 November

In the German newspaper *Handelsblatt*, ECB President Duisenberg adds fuel to the rumour that an *interest rate rise* by the ECB is imminent. "Our inclination for higher interest rates has certainly risen somewhat."[173] Never before in the brief existence of the ECB has the President given such a clear hint.

In the first ten months of 1999, Italy has run up a *budget deficit* of 20% below that of the same period in 1998. The new figure (62,100 billion lire) suggests that the government is able to bring down its budget deficit to 2.2% of GDP, i.e. below the upward-adjusted target of 2.4% of GDP.

In connection with a *fraud investigation*, the French Finance Minister Strauss-Kahn resigns. He will be succeeded by the State Secretary for budgetary affairs, Christian Sautter.

4 November

The ECB Governing Council decides to increase the *interest rate* on its main refinancing facility with a 0.50 percentage point to 3.0%, effective 10 November. Similar increases are applied to the marginal lending facility, whose new rate is 4.0%, and to the deposit facility, which comes out at 2.0%. In responding in time to the threat of rising inflation and of the money supply running out of hand, the ECB does, in fact, ensure continuity, President Duisenberg says.

The President of the Halle Economic Research Institute, Mr. R. Pohl, estimates that from 1990, some DM 150 billion have been transferred annually from West Germany to the former GDR (almost 5% of West Germany's GDP). He does not expect the flow of payments to dry up for some time to come. The Kohl administration has negotiated a continuation of the present *financing arrangement* until 2004, but Mr. Pohl thinks it will remain in place even longer.

---

[173] "Duisenberg ziet rente stijgen" [Duisenberg can see interest rates go up], *De Telegraaf*, 1 November 1999.

After nine years of unification, productivity in the eastern *Länder* is still only 60% of that in West Germany.

**8 November**

The EU Council of Ministers agrees to shorten the *transition period* to euro notes and coins after January 1, 2002, with the aim that most cash transactions take place in the new currency after two weeks. The dual period, in which both the national currency and the cash euro are circulating alongside each other, will last between four weeks and two months.

**10 November**

The Commission largely adopts the proposals made by the Committee of Three Wise Men about the *reform of the EU*. This implies that more matters must be dealt with than the Amsterdam Summit of June 1997 was unable to reach compromises on (i.e. composition of the Commission, redistribution of vote weights among member states and the unanimity rule). The Commission wants majority decisions to become the rule. It also proposes to divide the Union Treaty into a basic part of major provisions and an operational part of minor provisions. Changes in the operational part could then be decided by qualified majority vote and without a ratifying procedure in the national parliaments. In addition, member states should be able to co-operate more closely than is currently allowed under the Treaty.

In Prague, EU Commissioner Verheugen, responsible for enlargement, says that the Commission would like to see *new member states* to accede to the EU in early 2005. It is, however, too early yet to say whether the group of newcomers will be small or larger.

Commission President Prodi abandons efforts to end national vetoes on EU tax policies, shying away from a confrontation with the United Kingdom. While calling for major reforms such as handing more power to the Commission and the extension of majority decision-making, Prodi says *unanimity*

1999

should prevail in sensitive areas such as finances and foreign affairs. Concerns about surrendering tax powers to EU institutions have heightened British scepticism toward the common currency with the United Kingdom threatening to wield its veto against a planned interest withholding tax.

12 November      After consultations in Helsinki between the ECB and the central banks of the former Soviet satellite states, the ECB declares that no hard and fast monetary and exchange rate convergence scenario will be agreed for *Eastern European countries* wanting to join the EU. It is determined, however, that newcomers will not have the right to stay out of EMU. Joining the EU, for them, will also mean converting to the euro, albeit with the necessary delay.

17 November      The *euro*, at an exchange rate of $1.0442, shows the strongest recovery in the past five weeks, prompted by rumours in the German press that the ECB will intervene as soon as the exchange rate falls below $1.03. The exchange rate of the euro will average $1.10 next year, a forecast made by Germany's Council of Economic Advisers.

19 November      According to ECB President Duisenberg, the ECB has no ambitions to lay claim to the *supervision of banks in Europe*. International consultation among supervisors is to be preferred to centralisation, Duisenberg says. The ECB can, however, co-ordinate the European stand in the Basle consultations. BIS President Crockett thinks there will never be an international banking supervisor, because governments will never relinquish their control over the banking system. According to him, the future lies in co-operation between different types of supervisors. Speaking about this issue, *Bundesbank* President Welteke warns against the creation of a new bureaucratic organisation in Europe.

During a bankers' conference in Frankfurt, ECB President Duisenberg declares that the statement read during the monthly press conference of the ECB Board meeting provides more insight into the bank's policy than the minutes: "It is our objective to provide clear and structured communications. Publishing detailed records of our meetings would only create confusion."[174]

Dutch report about the myth of *democratic deficiency* is published. It firmly rejects the idea that the EU is suffering from a shortage of democratic substance. The fact that the European ideal has been modelled on the national democracy leads to the misconception that international organisations like the EU are amenable to democratic control. But the popular will is unable by definition to assert itself with any force outside the national borders, and there is no such thing as a European popular will. Despite supra-national institutions such as the Commission and the European Parliament, the EU retains many characteristics of an international community of states making decisions by means of consultative bodies, and this imposes structural limits on democratic control, the report argues.

The *price of crude oil* increases to $25.90 a barrel, the highest level since early 1991, in reaction to an unexpected export stop by Iraq.

25 November        The growing likelihood of a one-to-one *relationship between the euro and the dollar* has prompted quite a few comments in the press. IMF Managing Director M. Camdessus announces that the decline of the euro is no cause for alarm, provided the currency does not continue to wax and wane or accelerate its decline. Experts agree that the effect of interventions by the ECB can only be temporary..

29 November        The EU Council of Ministers is not concerned about the currently low levels of the euro, and sees little

---

[174] "Persconferentie ECB helderder dan notulen" [ECB press conference more transparent than minutes], *Het Financieele Dagblad*, 20 November 1999.

risk of rising oil prices boosting inflation. The Council recognises that Greece no longer has an excessive *budget deficit*. In just a few years, Greece has reduced the deficit from 13.8% to 2.5% of GDP.

2 December

The ECB Governing Council decides to leave the maximum *acceptable growth of the money supply* for the year 2000 unchanged at 4.5%. This decision is taken on the basis of the definition of price stability used by the Eurosystem (a less than 2% annual rise of the harmonised consumer price index for the euro area), a 2% - 2.5% real growth trend and a 0.5 % - 1% slowdown trend in the income velocity of M3. Relatively broad liquidity will help economic recovery in Europe, says ECB President Duisenberg.

7 December

According to former advisor to the US Fed, Alan Blinder, the ECB has created difficulties for itself by embracing its *two-pillar strategy*. The reason why it followed the *Bundesbank* in adopting a money growth objective, Blinder thinks, has been to sell the ECB to the German public. The *Bundesbank* used to deviate frequently from its objective, but it could afford to do so on the strength of its reputation for keeping down inflation. The ECB, as a new organisation, still has to make that reputation for itself. Time after time it will fail its money growth objective, if only because financial innovations and other developments will continue to disrupt the linear relationship between money growth and inflation. The implications may be very painful, especially if there comes a moment when the market loses confidence. A clear objective, in Blinder's opinion, would be an inflation objective. "When you increase interest rates, you tell the world, we're afraid inflation may run too high, so we're clamping down on it. You can't get more clear than that."[175] For that matter, the

---

[175] "Blinder toont ECB de weg" [Blinder shows ECB the way], *Het Financieele Dagblad*, 8 December 1999.

ECB might even overtake the US Fed, which does not have any clear objective, Blinder adds.

ECB Board member Issing calls the *money supply objective* of the ECB a useful instrument. Money supply policy is characterised by simplicity. According to Mr. Issing, money growth has proved stable in Europe, and correlates closely with price developments.

**11-12 December**

European Summit in Helsinki announces the creation of a European military force and *expansion of the EU* by twelve member states. Apart from this, a limited number of issues is placed on the agenda of the intergovernmental conference which begins in February 2000 and has to make administrative preparations for the expansion. The conference should be completed before the end of 2000, with a "Nice Treaty". The administrative reform of the EU involves the following issues:

1. Restriction of the number of EU Commissioners to no more than 27. Those countries which give up a Commissioner should be compensated for by more voting rights in the Council.
2. Review of the voting weights in the EU Council of Ministers.

A two-speed Europe has not been put on the agenda. Also, it is decided to let the issue of tax reform rest for half a year.

**14 December**

In Switzerland, the House of Representatives has consented to end the pegging of the *Swiss franc* to the price of gold. This clears the way to the sale of part of the Swiss central bank's gold reserves. Because the old foreign exchange act fixed the franc to the price of gold at SFR 4,595 a kilogram, it made such a sale impossible. From January 2000, the gold reserve will be valued at market prices, or three times the current valuation. Switzerland is planning to sell some 130 tons of gold in the longer term.

| | |
|---|---|
| 16 December | Berlin sees the first meeting of the *G-20* [176], on which ECB President Duisenberg has a seat next to the IMF and the World Bank. The Canadian Minister of Finance, P. Martin, will chair the G-20 for the next two years. |
| 23 December | Analysts of investment banks expect the yen, the dollar and the *euro* to return to their old reciprocal rates in the year 2000. Most explain the decline of the euro from the immense power radiated by the American economy. The general view is that the euro will gain strength and will return to its introduction level by end-2000. Economists at Morgan Stanley cite the euro as their favourite currency for the next year. The bank has great confidence in the deregulation measures taken in European countries. |

2000

| | |
|---|---|
| 1 January | Portugal takes over the EU *Presidency* from Finland. |
| 3 January [177] | With the start of the new millennium, all *systems of the ECB* and the national central banks of the EU area start smoothly and are functioning correctly. |
| | A *poll* held in Sweden among 75 prominent university professors and economists in the financial sector reveals that 63% of participants think Sweden would benefit by joining EMU. |
| 13 January | In its January *Monthly Bulletin*, the ECB expects that inflation in the euro-zone will peak during the first |

[176] During the G-7 meeting of September 1999, at the urgent request of the US, the G-20 was formed, including the "G-7 plus Russia", Argentina, Australia, Brazil, China, India, Indonesia, Mexico, Saudi Arabia, South Africa, South Korea and Turkey. Participants are the Ministers of Finance of these 19 countries plus representatives of the BIS, ECB, EU, IMF and World Bank.

[177] On January 3, 2000, US President Clinton appointed the 73-year-old banker Alan Greenspan for a fourth term as Chairman of the Federal Reserve System. Over the past twelve years, Greenspan built up an almost unassailable reputation as a battler against inflation. After succeeding Paul Volcker to the post in August 1987, he was highly praised for the manner in which he handled the consequences of the stock market crash of that year. A succession of interest rate cuts between 1988 and 1992 ended the recession and laid the foundation for the longest period of economic growth in the history of the United States.

few months of this year. Assuming that oil prices do
not rise any further, the effect of earlier oil price rises
on the annualised calculation of the inflation rate will
taper off in the course of the year, the report says.

15 January

*Revaluation* by 3.5% of the Greek drachma in the
ERM II. The new central rate is 340.75 drachmas to
the euro.

17 January

A poll held in Denmark reveals that in a *referendum*,
53% of voters would vote in favour of joining the
euro and 43% would vote against.

18 January

Former Commission President Delors, criticises the
*expansion plans* of Mr. Prodi. In Delors' view,
expansion of the EU from the present fifteen to
twenty seven member states will endanger economic
integration in Europe. "I do not believe such a
Europe of 27 members, or even 30 or 32, if peace
returns to the Balkans, can entertain such broad
ambitions as are laid down in the Maastricht Treaty,"
Mr. Delors says.

The EU and Mexico have concluded a *free trade
agreement* which offers the EU the same or more
benefits than the US and Canada under the NAFTA
agreement concluded earlier with Mexico. In 2007,
all import duties on industrial products will have been
lifted.

20 January

In Britain, *unemployment* has fallen to 4%, the lowest
level in twenty years. The pound sterling scores
another record at €1.6414. The IMF has calculated
that if the United Kingdom were to introduce the euro
at this moment, it would do so with a pound that
would in fact be 20% overvalued.

25 January

The *euro* falls below parity with the dollar as
international investors continue to be lured by the
prospect of rich returns from US asset markets. The
currency briefly dipped to $0.9988. The ECB reports
that in the first ten months of 1999, 151 billion euros

1999/2000

worth of direct investment left the euro-zone, compared with 53 billion dollars that entered.

26 January

Chief economist Issing of the ECB says that the ECB will only attempt to stop the euro from falling against the dollar if its weakening threatens to push up *inflation* in the euro area. He points out that a stable exchange rate of the euro is not in itself an objective of the ECB's monetary policy.

The Commission presents its advice on the *reform of the EU*. Commission President Prodi says that one third of the member states should be able to decide on closer co-operation among themselves, even though the majority will not go along. The Schengen Treaty, Prodi says, has shown it can be done. The Dutch government fears the concept of a core Union will strengthen the position of the big countries, because they will have less need of the smaller countries' help in reaching decisions.

31 January

ECB President Duisenberg is still satisfied with the *euro's performance*. The euro may have fallen by 14% against the US dollar since its introduction on 1 January 1999. But compared to two years before, the euro has lost only 5% to 6% of its value. Duisenberg also says that Britain will not be ready to join the euro for some years to come. British Foreign Minister Cook admits that "technically speaking", Mr. Duisenberg is right. He also announces that the British government is not going to conduct a referendum on the euro before the next general elections (expected to be held in May 2001).

The *euro* reaches its lowest exchange rate against the dollar so far: $0.9682. The Finance Ministers of the euro-zone insist the euro's tumble to record lows against the dollar is only temporary.

2 February

In Austria, businesses panic amid *threats* by the other EU member states to freeze contacts with the country if the radical right-wing party *Freiheitliche Partei*

*Österreichs (FPÖ)* is invited to join the Government coalition.

| | |
|---|---|
| 3 February | The ECB Governing Council decides to raise the *interest rate* on the Eurosystem's main refinancing operations by a 0.25 percentage point to 3.25%. Simultaneously, the Council decides to raise the interest rates on both the marginal lending facility and the deposit facility by a 0.25% percentage point to 4.25% and 2.25% respectively. According to ECB President Duisenberg, the decision should not be seen as a panic reaction. It was "pure coincidence" that the US Federal Reserve and the ECB raised rates in the same week.[178] |
| 4 February | In Austria, the new coalition government is sworn in, made up of Conservatives and the *FPÖ. Sanctions* are imposed by the other EU member states. |
| 10 February | In its *Monthly Bulletin*, the ECB states that *consumer prices* in the euro area will come under upward pressure later this year, as a result of oil price rises during the past three quarters. The price of a barrel of Brent crude has risen by 80% since March 1999, to reach $27.37. |
| | ECB President Duisenberg says that the bank will do "nothing directly" to halt the fall of the *euro*, insisting that the currency will rise without intervention. The euro continues its fall with one euro worth $0.9864 in late London trading. |
| 14 February | In the Portugese city of Oporto, the *Intergovernmental Conference* starts. In the coming months the EU's Ministers of Foreign Affairs hope to reach agreement on the institutional reform of the EU and its decision making processes. |

[178] On 2 February, 2002, the US Fed increased its target for the federal funds rate to 5.75% from 5.50%. It raised also its discount rate by a 0.25 percentage point to 5.25%.

15 February          Germany and Italy are warned by the Commission to
                     hold the line on *public spending* in order to keep the
                     economy in the euro-zone on the growth track. Apart
                     from Germany, which intends to cut taxes in 2001 by
                     DM 30 billion, France, the Netherlands and Belgium
                     have also planned sharp tax cuts. The Commission
                     agrees with the budget plans of non-euro member
                     states Britain and Denmark. According to responsible
                     EU Commissioner Solbes, no euro country runs the
                     risk at this point of exceeding the established
                     maximum deficit of 3% of GDP.

23 February          Canadian Nobel Prize winner, R. Mundell, would
                     appreciate it if central banks succeeded in keeping the
                     *exchange rate of the euro* at about $1. Exchange rate
                     fluctuations between large currency zones with stable
                     internal prices serve no purpose, he says. The "hedge
                     funds" are the only ones to benefit. The central banks
                     should form a consortium which keeps the exchange
                     rates stable. The only way this can be done is by
                     having a common monetary policy and a common
                     inflation target. Once this has been agreed on, interest
                     rates would also move to the same level. The result
                     would amount to a global currency. Mr. Mundell's
                     prediction is that by 2010, the euro-zone will be as
                     large as the dollar area.

                     The United Kingdom and Belgium present a plan to
                     transform the EU into an "active welfare society", in
                     preparation for a special European Summit in Lisbon
                     (on 23 and 24 March 2000). The plan follows similar
                     documents produced by Spain and a plan by French,
                     Italian and Belgian Social Affairs and Employment
                     Ministers. The Commission contemplates asking EU
                     government leaders to commit themselves to concrete
                     *unemployment targets*, e.g. 6% in 2005 and around
                     3% in 2010 (current unemployment is 9%).

28 February          The *euro* falls to a new low of $0.9390. The
                     immediate cause is an earlier statement by ECB
                     Board member Noyer, to the effect that the next ECB
                     Board meeting will probably not raise interest rates.

9 March

Greece submits its official application *to join the euro* by 1 January 2001. According to Finance Minister, I. Papantoniou, his country meets the Maastricht convergence criteria. Inflation has fallen to 2.1% and the fiscal deficit to 1.9% of GDP. Public debt stands at 103.5% of GDP, which although officially too high, is lower than that of Italy and Belgium.

16 March

The ECB Governing Council decides to raise the *interest rate* on the Eurosystem's main refinancing operations by a 0.25 percentage point to 3.25%. Simultaneously, the Council decides to raise the interest rate on both the marginal lending facility and the deposit facility by a 0.25 percentage point to 4.25% and 2.25% respectively. The move was widely anticipated.

23-24 March

Special European Summit in Lisbon on employment, economic reform and social coherence. Government leaders agree to publish *quantitative EU targets* for key economic variables: an average annual economic growth target of 3%; an unemployment rate of no more than 4% in 2010; and a 70% participation rate of the labour force (now 60%). The fifteen government leaders emphasise that increased European competitive power should be balanced by "social cohesion".

13 April

EU Commissioner F. Bolkestein lashes out at the largest EU member states which lack the leadership the EU needs. According to Bolkestein, the problem is not the Commission, but the impotence of the governments of the major EU member states. He foresees a development in which *further integration* is hampered as every country pursues its own interests. Little is to be expected from France because "that country wants to use the EU for the realisation of its own ambitions". The Germans are "too absorbed by their domestic problems". Now that the Franco-German axis has evaporated, France and some other countries are inclined to enter into ad-hoc coalitions.

**17 April**

In its *Annual Report*, the *Bundesbank* calls the sharp decline of the euro against the dollar and the yen "surprising and unexpected". The bank is convinced the ECB will act vigorously against *inflationary threats* in Europe.

The Austrian Minister of Finance, K.H. Grasser, does not exclude the possibility that his country will thwart *EU decision making* if the fourteen other EU countries continue their boycott against fellow Member State Austria. If Austria uses the possibility of vetoing decisions, the Union will grind to a halt, according to Mr. Grasser.

**19 April**

The exchange rate of the *euro* falls to $0.9359. According to *Bundesbank* President Welteke, the ECB has no intention of shoring up the euro.

**20 April**

French Foreign Minister H. Védrine says that within the context of the EU, different groupings of Member States should take the lead in solving a number of controversial issues. He thinks that neither the Franco-German axis nor the eleven euro countries are capable of leading the EU now that it is preparing for a considerable expansion. The larger Member States can no longer accept that a small number of Member States representing only a small part of the Union's population, should be able to block decision making on several issues. The EU, Védrine says, should adopt a system of *qualified majority voting* on social and fiscal matters.

Former politicians Giscard d'Estaing and Schmidt – co-chairmen of the Committee on Economic and Monetary Union in Europe – present their views on *the future of the EU*, according to which an extended Europe of twenty seven nations will, in the next two to five decades, develop along three separate lines.

1. Development of the European economy and free trade in coherence with political integration limited to the present level. Priority must then be given to institutional reform if the system is to remain workable. What must be avoided at all costs is that the inability to reform should be veiled in a mist of empty compromises. Within the European space each country, Germany and France included, will accept only what it holds to be in its own interest, except for an appropriate degree of solidarity. Each will wish to go on handling all those affairs which do not require common solutions and regulations. The subsidiarity principle should at last be made enforceable.

2. Organisation of a common European defence force. If such a force is to become operational, member states of considerable military power should commit themselves to its creation, while the public should be willing to accept a swift decision making process.

3. Complete integration is not a realistic goal for twenty seven countries with large differences in political traditions, culture and economic development. The only realistic option is for those countries which possess the political will and whose economic and social circumstances are nearly identical, to work for further integration. All countries in this category lie within the euro-zone.

Both politicians wonder whether these countries try to integrate part of their political powers on the basis of a federative structure. Such an approach will require at least an initiative by the constituent countries France, Germany, Italy and the Benelux countries, plus some other willing and determined candidates. Also, new institutions will be required: a Council, a parliamentary structure with operational ties to the national parliaments, but probably not a Commission. In practice, these might be "institutions within the existing institutions" of the EU. The only

2000

restriction which the non-participating countries could impose on the new group would be that the latter will respect all obligations which the EU as a whole enters into, and that the new institutions must not enter into competition with the European ones. Under certain reservations one might say that the new grouping would be a political entity on the larger European continent, just as the United States of America is an independent political entity on the North American continent.

27 April

The ECB Governing Council decides to raise the *interest rate* on the Eurosystem's main refinancing operations by a 0.25 percentage point to 3.75%. Simultaneously, the Council decides to raise the interest rates on both the marginal lending facility and the deposit facility by a 0.25 percentage point to 4.75% and 2.75% respectively.

3 May

In its *Convergence Report*, the Commission proposes to allow *Greece* to accede to the euro-zone on 1 January 2001. Greece meets all economic conditions for joining EMU. The ECB does see "upward risks" for inflation and the budget deficit, and thinks the Greek government should make "credible" structural adjustments in the labour and goods markets.

4 May

The *euro* falls to $0.8846. A rebound in the European economy and four ECB interest rate increases in the past six months have failed to halt the currency's descent.

In an *open letter* to the citizens of Europe, ECB President Duisenberg tries to reassure them as regards the development of the euro. He emphasises that the ECB has so far realised price stability and will continue to do so. Hence, the future looks sunny: a strong euro, based on price stability and the strength of the European economy, the ECB President says.

8 May

The EU Council of Ministers first expresses openly its concern about the falling exchange rate of the euro. The Council agrees to give the ECB the green light to double its capital and reserves to, respectively, €10 billion and almost €100 billion.

**9 May**

The Dutch Finance Minister Zalm announces that Dutch *public debt* has for the first time fallen below the EU debt criterion. Favourable economic development has caused it to drop to 59.6% of GDP, just below the 60% agreed within EMU.

Celebration of the 50th anniversary of the *Schuman Declaration*. In his memorial speech for the French National Assembly, Prime Minister Jospin speaks of an ambitious but pragmatic programme, geared towards a Europe "which aspires towards growth and full employment, which is closer to the citizen and which functions more effectively." On the issue of a two-speed Europe, Jospin describes as "quintessential" that some countries integrate faster while others are given the opportunity to join in later. He dismisses the idea of ex-Commission chairman Delors to form a "hard core" of countries willing to integrate to a far greater extent.

**10 May**

The exchange rate of the *euro* scrambles back up ($0.9118) amid a spate of rumours among currency traders that the ECB has intervened and begun to buy euros. The bank, however, cloaks itself in silence and will neither confirm nor deny the rumours.

French Prime Minister Jospin indicates he wishes to strengthen the role of the *Euro 11 Council*. The Council is without a status under the EU Treaty but has been created on the initiative of France, which wanted to install a political counterweight to the ECB. Although initially, a majority of member states saw little in the idea, that scepticism has now gone. According to the Dutch Finance Minister Zalm, the Euro 11 forum offers ministers an opportunity for a more profound discussion of the economic situation, inflation and employment policy than is possible in the EU Council of Ministers (Ecofin). Besides, the

Euro 11 Council, on which there are only two seats per country plus one for a Commission representative, is much more informal in character.

During the celebrations on the 150th anniversary of the National Bank of Belgium, Prime Minister Verhofstadt, calls for reinforcement of the *political identity of the euro-zone*, through strengthening the Euro 11 Council. He calls EMU a powerful engine driving EU integration, but expresses his worries about the institutional shortcomings of the euro-zone. "Especially the supervision and monitoring of financial institutions and markets is still fragmented while the political level offers the spectacle of an informal club of Finance ministers"[179] says Belgian Finance Minister Reynders.

12 May

German Foreign Minister Joschka Fischer, speaking at the Humboldt University in Berlin, revitalises the idea of a *European federation*. The formation of a European Government and a European Parliament and the framing of a European Constitution are the only way if a future twenty seven-member EU is to make any meaningful decisions, Mr. Fischer says. However this does not imply that member states must give up their entire sovereignty. Apart from a representative assembly, the federation should have a European constitution which must delineate exactly the borderline between the powers of Brussels on the one hand and the national governments on the other. Mr. Fischer would also like to see a "gravitational centre" of a limited group of member states setting an example and possibly taking on board all other member states on the road to federation. The Minister has founded his ideas on the close consultations France and Germany held over the past year, about the future of Europe. Although Fischer's ideas are not new, there is a huge difference in comparison to the

---

[179] "Roep om versterking Euro-11 wordt steeds luider" [Ever louders calls for strengthening of Euro 11], *Het Financieele Dagblad*, 16 May 2000.

debates of the early 1990s led by Europe-minded politicians such as Helmut Kohl, François Mitterrand and Jacques Delors. They, too, envisioned a European federation, but one involving a much more comprehensive transfer of powers to a central authority. This time, the subject is the delineation of powers between the national governments and that of Europe. The fundamental concept of Member States' sovereignty is not under discussion now. In that respect, Chirac has determined exactly the difference compared to ten years ago: then the debate was about the United States of Europe; now, it is about the *united Europe of the states*. In December, a Nice Treaty must be agreed. The dominant opinion in Brussels is that while Nice is extremely important, it can be no more than a first step toward the much more profound changes which Mr. Fischer and Mr. Chirac think the Union will face in the longer term. Nice may come too early. The Union is like a pressure cooker: it reaches decisions only when there is high pressure. The pressure, in this case, is the threat of ungovernability if the Union is expanded. But that expansion is not expected to happen until 2005. Therefore plans are circulating in Germany to organise another round of reform consultations in 2004. Then the time will be ripe for both EU expansion and for the more radical plans presented here in embryonic form. In a first response, French Foreign Minister Védrine declares he finds Mr. Fischer's proposals interesting and regards them as an important contribution to the debate.

15 May
Commission President Prodi receives a study by the Schuman Institute of Florence containing a blueprint of a new, much simplified *EU Treaty*. According to some observers, the study could serve as a basis for the "constitution" mentioned by Mr. Fischer.

16 May
Former *Bundesbank* President Tietmeyer is of the opinion that lack of clarity about the EU's further integration plans is instrumental in creating the weakness of the euro. He thinks Europe needs clarity

about competencies and decision making processes
which have become increasingly opaque, and have
thereby made the EU ever more rigid. In order to
speed up the *political integration process*, he
advocates a model of concentric circles in which
groups of countries agree on varying degrees of co-
operation. He is surprised by Minister Fischer's
proposals: "For many years, things like that were
unthinkable at the German Foreign Ministry,"[180]
Tietmeyer says.

Former Dutch central bank Director Szász comments
on Tietmeyer's vision, pointing out that EMU cannot
be sustainable without *political union*. "The euro will
not be a really common currency until we accept that
we Europeans are, in a monetary and financial sense,
each other's fellow-countrymen."[181] In this connection, he calls the stretching of EMU fiscal criteria
on behalf of Greece's accession a bad example.

21 May                In a *referendum* in Switzerland, 67.2% of the
                      population has expressed support for seven important
                      bilateral agreements with the EU made by the Swiss
                      Government on 8 October 1999.

3 June                French Finance Minister L. Fabius emphasises that
                      the strengthening of the *Euro 11 Council's role* will
                      be one of the spearheads of the upcoming French
                      chairmanship. He emphatically presents his ideas as a
                      proposal under which both France and Germany will
                      give shape and substance to the wish of both to
                      deepen European integration. The Dutch Finance
                      Minister Zalm dismisses the proposal; he fears an
                      undesirable split in the Union when it comes to
                      determining economic policy.

5 June                The EU Council of Ministers fails to make any
                      progress towards *uniform taxation* on all savings

---

[180] "Tietmeyer: 'zwakke euro heeft politieke oorzaak' ", [Tietmeyer: 'weak euro has political
cause'.], *Het Financieele Dagblad*, 16 May 2000.
[181] Ibid.

interest in the EU. There have been talks for years on means to counter cross-border tax evasion. The result was a compromise under which two systems, one of withholding taxes and one of information-sharing by tax collectors, would coexist for some time. Ten out of fifteen member states support this plan, but Britain wants the EU to adopt an information-sharing system within five years. Here it finds Austria, Luxembourg, Greece and Belgium in its way, these countries are against setting any term, because that would imply lifting their bank secrecy laws within five years.

7 June

The *euro* rises to its highest level against the dollar in seven weeks amid expectations that the ECB will raise its benchmark short-term interest rate. In trading, the euro comes to $96.19 rising by  more than 7.5% since it closed at a record low at $0.8846 on May 4.

8 June

The ECB Governing Council decides to raise the *interest rate* on the Eurosystem's main refinancing operations by a 0.50 percentage point to 4.25%. Simultaneously, the Council decides to raise the interest rates on both the marginal lending facility and the deposit facility by a 0.50 percentage point to 5.25% and 3.25% respectively. According to ECB President Duisenberg, medium-term inflationary risks in the euro-zone are so alarming that firm action must now be taken. To blame are robust money growth, very strong increases in lending, sharply-risen oil prices and a weak euro.

9 June

Franco-German Summit in Mainz, Germany, to discuss plans the French government has for the upcoming French presidency of the EU. France wants to draw up a *"social agenda"* and to draft a new European treaty, to be finalised at the concluding EU Summit in Nice, next December, which should prepare the EU for the expansion with twelve new Member States.

13 June

In Spain and Ireland, *inflation* threatens to run

berserk. In May, prices in Ireland were up 5.2% and in Spain 3.2% compared to a year before. But the Netherlands, and Finland also saw inflation rise in May, to 2.4% and 2.9%, respectively. Rising energy prices gave inflation in Europe an unprecedented impulse, threatening to send inflation for the euro-zone crashing through the 2% limit set by the ECB.

**15 June**

The government of Portugal produces a bulky report presenting the state of affairs in the debate about a *new European Treaty* needed to prepare the governing bodies of the Union for the upcoming expansion with another twelve Member States. The four main subjects are: (a) reduction of the number of EU Commissioners; (b) a review of the Member States' relative voting weights; (c) extending the range of subjects to which qualified majority voting applies; and (d) the so-termed "enhanced co-operation" allowing small groups of Member States to co-operate more closely, in principle on the expectation that the others will join them later. Intentions are to start real negotiations on these issues under the upcoming French presidency, in the run-up to the Nice Summit in December. Since the address by German Foreign Minister Fischer, who envisions a "federal Europe" as the final objective, negotiations about the new Treaty can no longer be separated from the issue of Europe's future. The bridge to be built between the new EU Treaty and the debate on Europe's "final objective" should be a better definition of "enhanced co-operation", say both Portuguese Secretary of State, F. Seixas da Costa and French Foreign Minister Védrine. As an option, it is already included in the current Treaty, but it has never been realised.

The EU Council of Ministers agrees on the principles of a *EU savings tax*. Within ten years, these principles should lead to a uniform system of information sharing about the interest paid on individuals' savings. Luxembourg and Austria are given special status. A crucial point in the agreement is that third countries such as Switzerland and the US will also share information.

19-20 June

EU Summit in Feira, Portugal. Under Article 122 of the Treaty establishing the European Community, the Council of Ministers decides that Greece meets the necessary requirement to be allowed to join the euro-zone by 1 January 2001. At this moment, Greek public debt stands at 104% of GDP. The Government hopes to achieve the 60% limit in 2010. Greece's participation brings the number of euro Member States up to twelve.

27 June

In an address before the German Parliament French President Chirac presents a *new French vision on Europe*. Mr. Chirac closely echoes the views of German Minister Fischer, who on 12 May spoke of a core Europe "Those countries wishing to pursue integration should be allowed to do this on a voluntary basis and in specific areas, without hindrance from those who wish – as they have every right to do – to move forward less rapidly. Together with Germany and France, they might form a group of pioneer states which, if necessary, will enter into co-operation agreements outside and in addition to the European Treaty, without impairing the coherence of the Union," Mr. Chirac says.[182]

1 July

France takes over the EU *presidency* from Portugal.

11 July

France makes another bid to give *politics* a greater say as regards the euro. Before the European Parliament, Finance Minister Fabius says that he "can imagine how in some years' time the European Finance Ministers, not the Governors of the ECB, will determine how high the inflation rate in the euro-

---

[182] "Nieuwe Franse visie sluit aan bij ideeën van Duitse minister Fischer. Ook Chirac wil snelle Europese integratie" [New French vision echos ideas expressed by German Minister Fischer. Chirac also wants rapid European integration], *De Volkskrant*, 5 July 2000.

zone may be".[183] He also thinks that the Finance Ministers of the euro-zone should elect a single spokesperson.

The French proposal gets support on the part of a former member of the Bank of England's monetary policy committee, W. Buiter, who proposes to have the euro area's inflation targets set, in future, not by the ECB but by politicians, more in particular by the European Council. Mr. Buiter is confident that politicians will opt for a low *target inflation*, simply because inflation is bad for the economy. He also expects to see the Council pursue more predictable policy than the ECB, which he suspects of having a "hidden implicit agenda". Mr. Buiter sees his suggestion partly as a gesture that would make it easier for the United Kingdom to join the euro-zone.

17 July     The French Finance Minister Fabius, backs down on his attempts to enhance the *influence of politics* on ECB policy making. His more modest stance is a reaction to a remark made by the Dutch Finance Minister Zalm, that the ECB is autonomous in all its decisions about monetary matters such as interest rates, exchange rate policy, inflation and money supply. Finance Ministers may have their debates, but it is Duisenberg and the ECB Governing Council who make the final decisions, Mr. Zalm says. Fabius' reading of the matter is that he "was misunderstood" by the European Parliament.

25 July     In June, the *inflation rate* for the euro-zone reaches the highest level in four years, at 2.4%. The German research institute, IFO, predicts that the average inflation rate for the year 2000 in the euro-zone will come out above the 2% limit imposed by the ECB. At the same time, growth is accelerating in the euro area: 3.4% in 2000 as against 2.4% in 1999.

---

[183] "Frankrijk wil opnieuw ECB buiten spel zetten" [France tries again to sidetrack the ECB], *De Telegraaf*, 12 July 2000.

15 August

In London, the *price of oil* soars to a record high of $32.28, topping the earlier peak of $31.95 on 7 March. Only during the 1990 Gulf crisis was more money paid for oil. Hence the ECB, in its *Monthly Bulletin* for August, openly worries about high oil prices which, in addition to the weak euro, are said to be a major reason for the sharpened rise of the inflation rate, now at 2.4%. According to the ECB, consumer prices will in the coming months be influenced by the sharply increased oil price and the low exchange rate of the euro. Eurostat figures point out that inflation in Ireland is highest (5.9%), followed by that in Luxembourg (4.4%). The lowest price rises are observed in Germany, France and Austria: around 2.0%.

31 August

The ECB Governing Council decides to raise the minimum bid rate on the Eurosystem's main refinancing operations by a 0.25 percentage point to 4.5%. Simultaneously, the Council decides to raise the *interest rates* on both the marginal lending facility and the deposit facility by a 0.25 percentage point to 5.5% and 3.5% respectively.

4 September

At a conference in Berlin, German Chancellor Schröder expresses his satisfaction with the level of the *euro's exchange rate*. According to the Chancellor, the relative weakness of the European currency is partly responsible for economic recovery in Germany. "This should be reason for contentment rather than concern," Mr. Schröder says. His words squarely contradict those of French central bank governor Trichet, who says that "the euro is clearly undervalued by most market parties".[184]

8 September

At an informal meeting, the EU Finance Ministers clearly distance themselves from the statement made by German Chancellor Schröder on September 4. In a

---

[184] "Euro naar laagste koers versus yen" [Euro touches bottom against yen], *Het Financieele Dagblad*, 6 September 2000.

joint statement, the Ministers and the ECB express their concern that the current *exchange rate of the euro* does not reflect the strong economic base of the euro area. In spite of this, the euro declines further to $0.866. The currency has lost more than 25% of its value against the dollar since it was launched in January 1999.

12 September

ECB President Duisenberg, in his account before the European Parliament, says that high oil prices and the weak *euro* are a cause for concern because they push up inflation. In his view, the financial markets are wrong because they clearly undervalue the euro. A 3% economic growth for the next two years, with very low inflation by international standards, must at some time bear fruit.

The EU member states end their *sanctions against Austria*. This finally puts to rest, after seven months, the worst political crisis the EU has seen in its entire existence. In their joint statement, the countries declare that "the nature of the FPÖ remains a cause for concern" and express their opinion that "special watchfulness" regarding that party is in order.

14 September

The ECB Governing Council decides to leave the short-term interest rates unchanged. In addition, the ECB announces that cumulative *interest earnings* on foreign exchange reserves (ca. $2.5 billion) are to be sold off in exchange for euros. ECB President Duisenberg does not call this a currency intervention.

15 September

American professor R. Dornbusch says that the new European currency will be a structurally weak currency for some time to come. His statement is a reaction to the *IMF model studies of long-term equilibrium values* of the major currencies. According to the report, the euro is undervalued by 30% against the dollar, and by 18% against the yen. Mr. Dornbusch points out three restrictions underlying such model studies:

1. The scenario by which a country labouring under a persistent current account deficit should prepare for a hard landing of its currency is obsolete. As long as such a country is stable and attractive for investments, a current account deficit will not in itself be sufficient ground for the market to force a sharp downturn.
2. Models are based on the past and do not take account of dramatic changes on the supply side or in the financial world.
3. Europe and Japan thrive on the US trade deficit. If the private funding of these deficits were in doubt, the ECB and the Japanese central bank will buy up all the dollars their private sectors pass up. There is a precedent for this: as soon as the dollar weakens, overseas central banks queue up to offer help.

According to Mr. Dornbusch the euro is bound, at one time, to fight its way into the world, but at present, it does not stand a chance.

21 September    The *euro* hits a record low of $0.8438. *Bundesbank* President Welteke says the currency is clearly under-valued. Yet he declines to call the European currency a fiasco: "I do not understand how anyone can say the euro is a failure. I don't remember anyone saying fifteen years ago: 'Let's throw out the D-mark, it's stopped working.' "[185] Welteke expects the euro to buck up after the US general elections of November.

22 September    The ECB intervenes on the currency market to support the weak euro, spending an estimated 3 to 5 billion dollars. The *intervention* is carried out conjointly with the central banks of the US, Japan, Canada and the United Kingdom.

28 September    A *referendum* held in Denmark results in the

[185] "Voor Welteke is de euro geen fiasco" [For Welteke, the euro is not a fiasco], *Het Financieele Dagblad*, 20 September 2000.

rejection of the euro by a majority of 53% of the voters. Reactions from the EMU front are somewhat matter-of-fact. ECB President Duisenberg response is: "business as usual". EU President Jospin thinks that considering the size of the Danish economy, it is not a problem for a currency "which should be stable at the right level". According to British Prime Minister Blair, Britain will make its own decision and the German Finance Minister Eichel simply says, "Europe moves on".

2 October

A *poll* by the British research bureau, Mori, shows that in a referendum, as many as 70% of the British would vote against joining the euro. Also, 46% say Britain should leave the EU. In Sweden, anti-euro sentiments soar. A Gallup poll reveals that 42% of participants reject the euro, while 31% want to introduce the currency and 27% are undecided. A poll conducted in the Netherlands shows that if given the chance, 53% of the Dutch would vote against participating in EMU.

3 October

Germany looks back on ten years of *reunification*. The Berlin research bureau DIW reports that West Germany has spent almost DM 1,200 billion on the former GDR. About one-third of this amount was spent on social security and unemployment benefits. Unemployment in the eastern *Länder* stood around 17.5% in August 2000, or twice the West German figure.

5 October

The ECB Governing Council decides to raise the minimum bid rate on the Eurosystem's main refinancing operations by a 0.25 percentage point to 4.75%. Simultaneously, the Council decides to raise the *interest rates* on both the marginal lending facility and the deposit facility by a 0.25 percentage point to 5.75% and 3.75% respectively. It is the seventh increase in twelve months. According to ECB President Duisenberg, the interest rate rise aims to prevent the upward pressure of high oil prices and imported inflation on consumer prices from being over-expressed in the monthly inflation figures.

9 October

German Finance Minister Eichel warns that the euro will become a fiasco unless the eleven euro area countries adjust their economic and fiscal policies more closely to one another. The euro requires a completely different degree of *policy co-ordination* between the Finance Ministers, Mr. Eichel says. His statements follow articles by ECB Board members Padoa-Schioppa and Issing in some newspapers about the tension caused by, on the one hand, a monetary policy centralised in Frankfurt and several kinds of national policies on the other hand. In the same spirit, Dutch central bank President Wellink, during the IMF and World Bank annual meeting, points to the asymmetry of having a single currency and eleven governments: "The original idea was to implement both monetary and political integration at the same time. Now all we have, so to speak, is one leg to stand on. The euro has arrived, but politics is trailing behind." [186]

13-14 October

Informal European Summit in Biarritz, preparatory to the Intergovernmental Conference to be held in Nice in December. *Issues debated*, therefore, include qualified majority voting, the composition of the Commission and the voting weights in the Council of Ministers. No official recommendations are made.

ECB President Duisenberg announces that the decline of the euro is at an end. "We will intervene again if we think it is necessary; that goes for the ECB as much as for the G-7"[187], says Mr. Duisenberg, referring to the joint *interventions* by the ECB and the G-7 countries on 20 September, when the dollar

[186] "Duitse minister waarschuwt voor mislukking euro" [German Minister cautions against euro's failure], *Het Financieele Dagblad*, 10 October 2000.
[187] "Duisenberg: 'Daling euro voorbij' " [Duisenberg: 'Euro's decline ends'], *NRC Handelsblad*, 14 October 2000.

exchange rate of the euro fell to its lowest level since the introduction of the euro on 1 January 1999.

16 October

In the London *Times*, ECB President Duisenberg hints that interventions in support of the euro will not take place if the currency comes under external pressure, as from a crisis in the Middle East Currency traders say Mr. Duisenberg commits a *"mortal sin"* by robbing the intervention tool of its best weapon, the element of surprise.

18 October

At a rate of $0.8330, the euro hits a new bottom.

24 October

In the run-up to the European Summit in Nice the Spanish Government rejects the introduction of *qualified majority voting* by the European Council on taxation issues. In such areas as taxation, social security, border control and the distribution of social funds, Spain insists on keeping the veto.

25 October

As no signals emerge from the G-20 meeting in Montreal that another support operation for the euro is on the cards, currency traders sell off the single currency on a massive scale. For the first time since its introduction on 1 January 1999, the euro scores a new record low at $0.8260.

Swedish support for participating in EMU has fallen to its lowest point in twelve months. According to a *poll* by the Swedish daily newspaper, *Dagens Nyheter*, 52% of participants reject the euro. Only 30% are in favour. Experts ascribe this result to the referendum held in late September in Denmark, where 53% voted against joining the euro-zone.

26 October

The *euro* reaches a new low against the dollar, at an exchange rate of $0.8230.

30 October

ECB President Duisenberg fails to see a reason for his *early retirement* in the large amount of criticism levelled at his behaviour as "guardian" of the euro. In an interview with the *International Herald Tribune*,

Mr. Duisenberg acknowledges he had a bad start, because France had stipulated that roughly halfway through his eight year term, he would hand the reins to the Frenchman Trichet, now governor of the *Banque de France*. That provision, however, is not in black and white. According to the German weekly *Der Spiegel*,[188] the agreement with France does exist in black and white, in a telefax sent in early May 1998 by Mr. J. Bitterlich, Foreign Affairs advisor of the then chancellor Kohl. The telefax, however, has disappeared without trace.

3 November

In an unexpected move, the ECB begins to make *supporting purchases* of euros. Similar action is taken on 6 November. After a short, sharp rally to $0.8727, the currency sinks back to $0.8650.

In his reaction to the ECB intervention, French Finance Minister Fabius underlines the importance of adequate co-ordination with the *"Eurogroup"*, a term coined under the French EU presidency to denote the Euro 11 Council. By introducing the new name, France suggests it is willing to accommodate the regular complaints heard elsewhere that the ECB at the present stage of European integration does not have a political counterpart at the specifically European level. ECB President Duisenberg reveals that he has taken up a more positive position towards co-operation with the Eurogroup to which he refers for the first time as a "political partner": "Whilst I may have been sceptical as to the status of such a dialogue, I have come to value it as a golden opportunity to say what we think of them and to hear what they think of us," Mr. Duisenberg says at a press conference.[189]

A *poll* carried out in Germany among a thousand

---

[188] W. Didoleit, R. Leick, C.H. Reiermann and U. Schäfer, "Wer lügt?" [Who's lying?], *Der Spiegel* 44, 30 October 2000.
[189] "Voor Welteke is de euro geen fiasco" [For Welteke, the euro is not a fiasco], *Het Financieele Dagblad*, 20 September 2000.

participants shows that 56% of them would, if possible, reject the euro. Among participants in the eastern provinces, the percentage is as high as 69%.

7 November[190]     The EU Council of Ministers decides that new accessors to the EU will not have to meet *additional criteria* if they want to introduce the euro. However, they will be required to join ERM II, under which the rate of the national currency must remain within a certain bandwidth against the euro.

8 November     A Commission report on the *expansion of the EU* does not propose a rigid time scheme. The twelve candidates meet the political criteria, which means that democracy and respect for human rights have been firmly established in the societies of these countries. Only Turkey, the thirteenth applicant, has some way to go yet. Regarding the economic criteria, the report says that new accessors will have to be "functioning market economies", able to cope with "competitive pressures and market forces" inside the Union. The Commission does not say which countries are ahead in the race, but it does leave room for tentative conclusions. Cyprus and Malta are in the lead (provided Cyprus can solve its problems with Turkey), with Estonia, Hungary and Poland hard on their trail. These countries will join in or shortly after 2005. Membership lies much further away for the other countries.

9 November     The ECB carries out *supporting purchases* to underpin the euro's exchange rate. Although this is the fifth intervention within a week, a clear recovery of the euro has not materialised.

ECB President Duisenberg says he expects *the inflation rate* in the euro area to remain above 2% for

---

[190] The elections in the United States fail to produce a clear winner between the Democratic Al Gore and the Republican George W. Bush. An almost insoluble quandary ensues and the decision is made to recount the votes in the state of Florida. Finally, Mr. Bush wins the elections.

longer than had been foreseen until a short while ago. He refers to the sharply risen energy prices and to the existence of some imported inflation on account of the euro's low exchange rate. "If those are left out, the core inflation rate is far lower. The ECB takes such things into account in setting its interest rate policy," Mr. Duisenberg says.[191]

**16 November**

The ECB announces that as of December, it will for the first time publish its *growth estimates* for the euro-zone. Until now, it has only made qualitative statements on the EU economic prospects.

**23 November**

ECB President Duisenberg, speaking before the European Parliament, warns against rising *public expenditures* in countries where public debt is over 60% of GDP. The list of high public debt countries is headed by Italy, Belgium, Germany and Austria.

**7-9 December**

At the EU Summit in Nice it is decided that in principle, as of 1 January 2005, the EU may be expanded by fifteen to twenty seven Member States at most. Candidates for accession are Poland, Romania, the Czech Republic, Hungary, Bulgaria, Slovakia, Lithuania, Latvia, Slovenia, Estonia, Cyprus and Malta. The vanguard among these will include Poland, the Czech Republic, Hungary, Slovenia, Estonia and Cyprus. The following decisions have been made, to be enacted in the *Nice Treaty*:

1.  Redistribution of the voting weights in the EU Council of Ministers.[192] If Member States wish to follow a Commission advice regarding new policy, at least 255 votes will have to be in favour. If Member States wish to instigate new policy, then 255 votes plus two thirds of the number of Member States must be in favour. In addition, at least 62% of the Union's population

---

[191] "Duisenberg: euro-inflatie voorlopig boven de 2 pct." [Duisenberg: euro inflation rate to stay above 2%], *De Telegraaf*, 11 November 2000.
[192] See: Appendix II.

will have to support every such policy proposal.

2. Abolition of the right of veto on: (a) supporting measures for poverty regions – but only as of 2007; (b) the appointment both of the Commission President and of the High Representative on Foreign Policy; and (c) some areas of trade policy. Partial veto rights will remain on decisions regarding asylum, immigration and visa policy. In fiscal matters, unanimity voting is maintained.

3. The number of MEPs will increase gradually to 728 as more countries join the EU.

4. The size of the European Commission is limited to twenty seven members. That means that as from 2007, each member state will have one EU Commissioner.

5. European defence co-operation is included in the Treaty and is thereby given a basis in international law. The EU is to have a committee of ambassadors which will have political executive powers regarding defence co-operation.

6. In areas where policy agreements for the entire Union cannot be made (taxation, the euro and common border controls), smaller groups of Member States may move to integrate their policies. This enhanced co-operation is open to new members, but they will have to pass muster: a majority within each enhanced co-operation group will have to approve new accessors.

Negotiations in Nice have put the Franco-German relations under pressure, especially the endless tug-of-war over the redistribution of votes. France was fixated on Germany being denied a greater voting weight than itself, despite a considerable difference in population. The international press agrees that in Nice, France once again made European interests subservient to its own national interest, indicating that French attitudes towards a united Europe have been essentially unchanged from the day the EEC was founded in 1957. According to some government leaders, France has used the EU presidency to advance its own interests.

2000

14 December

The ECB Governing Council decides to maintain the *reference value for monetary expansion*, i.e. the maximum acceptable annual growth rate for M3, at 4.5%. The decision is founded on the fact that available figures continue to confirm the assumptions underlying the original calculation of the reference value in December 1998 (and its reaffirmation in December 1999). These assumptions were: a medium-term decline of the income velocity of M3 by 0.5% to 1% annually and a trend-based potential annual growth in production of 2% to 2.5%.

21 December

In its December *Monthly Bulletin* the ECB publishes, for the first time, *economic projections*. The economy of the euro area will, in the next two years, show "robust expansion" at 2.5% to 3.5% annual growth. Declining oil prices will mitigate inflation, although internal pressures on prices will increase. The estimates, whose significance the ECB qualifies by presenting them explicitly as projections prepared by its staff, will be published twice yearly. Besides other financial and economic indicators, the projections will play a role in Pillar II of the ECB's monetary policy strategy. The bank also writes that the generous fiscal policies pursued by several member states threaten to increase upward pressures on prices. The tax cuts intended by many countries will not be fully offset by reduced spending. Although no countries are named, the ECB's criticism clearly includes the taxation plans of the Netherlands, Ireland, Italy and France.

27 December

Greece's central bank lowers its main *interest rate* from 5.75% to 4.75%, an adjustment to the minimum bid rate on the main refinancing facility of the ECB. The adjustment was necessitated by Greece's accession to EMU on 1 January 2001.

2001

1 January                 Sweden takes over the EU presidency.

Greece takes part in EMU and the euro. The
exchange rate of the Greek drachma has been fixed
on 340.75 per euro.

22 January                The EU Council of Ministers approves the Treaty of
Nice. Preparations start for the Intergovernmental
Conference to be held in 2004 about the EU's future.
Germany not only advocates a European federation
but also proposes to define *the final aim of
integration* as well as to boost the role the Commission plays in the decision making process. These
proposals are not in line with the French and British
views. According to the French President Chirac it is
the national state which has to be the reference point
in the European integration process. British Prime
Minister Blair troubles with the Charter of civil rights
approved by the EU leaders in the Nice Treaty.

24 January                The Commission takes the unprecedented step of
telling Ireland to change its economic policies on the
grounds that it's expansionary budget contradicts the
EU's broad economic guidelines. It is the first time
that the Commission uses its powers to *discipline* a
member state over economic policy.

25 January                In Germany, the centre-left government proposes
*radical changes* to the way Germany's markets are
supervised. The reforms are designed to strengthen
the country as a financial centre and to offer a model
for other European nations. According to the Finance
Minister Eichel the government intends to amalgamate the three agencies responsible for supervising
Germany's banking, insurance and securities markets
into a single independent body. It is also planned a
reform of the *Bundesbank*, turning it into a more
centralised institution with a six member executive
board.

27-28 January

At the *World Economic Forum* in Davos Europe's business leaders call for a clearer political road map for the EU ahead of its forthcoming enlargement. Their calls for more institutional reforms, including more majority voting, reflect disappointment with the modest results of the Summit in Nice. Businessmen such as Mr. Breuel, chairman of the board of *Deutsche Bank*, share Chancellor Schröder's view that the 2004 constitutional conference must once and for all clarify the division of power between the regions, national governments and the EU. But with presidential election looming in France next year, President Chirac and Prime Minister Jospin appear constrained in their ability to respond to German demands for clarity on Europe's future.

31 January

Analysts at *Deutsche Bank* see the euro climbing to parity with the dollar in the next three months and to $1.05 in six. Still more economists and strategists see the dollar falling – at least against the euro – over the long run. One reason is the fall in *US interest rates* which gets an extra stimulus by the Federal Reserve's move to cut its key rate a 0.50 percentage point (for the second time in a month) to 5.5% to jump-start the slowing US economy. The ECB keeps the interest rate unchanged because it expects that the twelve nation euro-zone does not face an acceleration of inflation.

Meeting between the German Chancellor Schröder and the French President Chirac. It seems that Germany has moved faster since the Nice Summit than the French expected in pressing for closer *EU political integration* at the expense of co-operation among national governments. Both sides say the meeting is intended to concentrate on the future rather than the past. They assure each other of their determination to keep the Franco-German motor of European integration in good working order and promise to carry on meeting informally every six to eight weeks (these gatherings may become known as the *Sauerkraut Club*). But there is little in these

2001

words to suggest that France and Germany have resolved any of their fundamental differences over policy, and the future direction in the EU.

4 February

The dispute between the Commission and the Dublin Government over *Ireland's 2001 budget* escalates with the Brussels executive rejecting a claim by the Irish Deputy Prime Minister, M. Harney, that the country's economic strategy is in line with the EU's economic policy guidelines. Economic and Monetary Affairs Commissioner Solbes rejects this view because the guidelines for 2000 said Ireland should use budgetary policy to counterbalance overheating in the economy and should gear its 2001 budget to this objective.

12 February

The EU Council of Ministers formally reprimands Ireland for slow progress on cutting inflation. In a final *communiqué* it describes Ireland's budget for 2001 "inconsistent with the broad guidelines of economic policy" and calls on the country to take "countervailing budgetary measures" in 2001. But Ireland rejects the criticism as "unreasonable" and says that it will not change its policy. The *EU's reprimand* cannot be followed by any sanctions.

The Belgian Finance Minister Reynders who is president of the *Eurogroup* predicts an increasingly important role for this group which meets every month to co-ordinate economic policy in the euro-zone. He believes the twelve Member States will want to go further ahead in co-ordinating economic policy than the fifteen simply because they have a single currency.

19 March

Economic Affairs Commissioner Solbes is in favour of more *economic policy co-ordination* among euro-zone governments but that does not mean changing the informal nature of the Eurogroup. He says that he is not calling for centralised "economic governance" for Euroland but adds that co-ordination is needed to achieve the right mix of fiscal and monetary policy.

"Even though the informal character of the Euro-group should be maintained to permit an open debate among the participants, more communication with the public about our analysis and about the agreed concrete commitments would doubtless be of use for the functioning of the system." This comment comes amid controversy sparked by the Belgian Finance Minister Reynders who has recently advocated strengthening the Eurogroups' role.

21 March

The Hungarian government approves a bill establishing a monetary council more along the lines of Western European central banks. The bill will increase the *independence* of the Hungarian central bank and bring it closer to EU norms, the government says.

23-25 March

At the EU Summit in Stockholm, European leaders approve the Lamfalussy Committee's proposals for a new system for EU financial regulation. A special committee will be created (*Securities Markets Regulatory Committee*) that will write most rules for EU financial markets. Market players are hopeful that the new system will bring closer the oft-proclaimed goal of creating a single financial market to match the unified currency zone of the euro. The deal does not cover the substance of financial rules in the EU area, but it radically changes the procedures for adopting them. The basic idea is that the European Parliament and member governments will pass a general framework law and then leave all the detailed regulations to the committee, taking advice from national stock market holders.

At the Summit it is further decided to give the EIB a limited mandate to provide *loans to Russia* for the first time. With the visit of the Russian President Vladimir Putin to Stockholm it is the first time that a Russian leader participates in the EU Summit. The Swedish presidency has stressed the importance of integrating Russia into Europe and encouraging economic reforms. Commissioner Pattern (External

Affairs) says: "We are a continent with Russia and we will share a longer boundary after enlargement. We don't want the boundary to mark a huge gulf in standards of living and crime."[193]

The ECB puts itself at odds with the German government by insisting that central banks in the euro-zone should play a strong role in *banking supervision*. Germany plans to amalgamate three separate agencies responsible for regulating banking, securities and insurance markets under one roof. The ECB argues that EMU has changed the nature and scope of systemic risk. " ... A separate supervisory agency would most likely not be in a position to assess quickly and effectively the potential for a systemic crisis, since its pre-dominant micro-focus does not allow an evaluation of the consequences through payment and settlement systems", the ECB says. [194]

11 April

The Governing Council of the ECB decides that the minimum bid rate on the main refinancing operations and the *interest rates* on the marginal lending facility and the deposit facility will remain unchanged at 4.75%, 5.75% and 3.75% respectively. The ECB defends its decision on the grounds that the euro-zone should achieve solid economic growth this year, that some inflationary risks persist and that current monetary conditions are not restrictive.

20-21 April

At an informal meeting the EU Council of Ministers in Malmö, Sweden, reveals substantial support for the ECB's controversial decision to leave *interest rates* unchanged in the face of US economic downturn. But the meeting also shows how the EU, and more particularly the Eurogroup, are still far from presenting a confident and coherent front to the

[193] Christopher Brown-Humes. "Vladimir Putin's visit EIB to lend to Russia for the first time", *Financial Times*, 24 March 2001.
[194] T. Barber, "Banking supervision position at odds with German policy to create an independent regulator. ECB demands role for central banks", *Financial Times*, 23 March 2001.

outside world. Austria's Finance Minister Grasser told journalists, before entering the conference, that an ECB rate cut was 'long overdue'. The next day he went on further, announcing a majority of ministers wanted the ECB to take action. His comments prompted a rebuttal from Spain's Minister of Economic Affairs. R. Rato. In his view the euro-zone is divided over interest rate policy with Spain among countries supporting the ECB's approach. The German and French Finance Ministers are among those who avoid public comment, partly to uphold its institution's independence.

27 April     The ECB counters *mounting* criticism on its interest rate policy by saying it is wrong to expect the euro-zone to replace the US as the engine of world economic growth. *Bundesbank's* President Welteke says calls for an ECB rate cut are inappropriate because, unlike the US Fed, the ECB is not directly responsible for promoting economic growth and employment. Both economists give a clear warning that the ECB will not bow to political pressures to change its policies: "There can be no outside pressures from anyone whatsoever on the ECB Governing Council," Mr. Welteke says.[195]

28 April     During the G-7 meeting in Washington, the French Finance Minister Fabius indirectly raises *pressures on the ECB* to cut interest rates: "Vigilance will remain the order of the day in Europe. We have had the distinct feeling over the last several weeks that the balance of risks has altered. Our monetary stance will have to take these elements into account." With his comments, Mr. Fabius undermines a display of unity among the Finance Ministers and Central Bank Presidents not to discuss the issue. ECB President Duisenberg says the G-7 has accepted his explanation of why the bank had not cut interest rates. "Perhaps

---

[195] T. Barber and V. Mallet, "Issing hits back at critics of euro-zone rates policy", *Financial Times*, 28 April 2001.

we were not clear enough in our explanation. Now it is more widely understood that with inflation above the central goal, a move in interest rates in that context would not enhance the credibility of the ECB," Mr. Duisenberg says.[196]

The German Chancellor Schröder proposes an *overhaul of the EU's powers and institutions* in a bid to make the fifteen-nation group more democratic. His plan involves turning the Commission into a central government and creating a two-chamber parliament similar to the German model. His ideas feed the wide-ranging debate about the future of the EU's institutions in the run-up to the next Intergovernmental Conference in 2004. Under his plan, the Council of Ministers would become one chamber – similar to Germany's *Bundesrat* – and would protect national sovereignty. The European Parliament would become the second chamber and would be given more power over the EU budget, nearly half of which is accounted for now by farm subsidies. The Chancellor wants decision-making powers on EU aid for infrastructure projects to be shifted from the EU bureaucracy back to local and regional governments.

2 May

Belgium outlines an ambitious agenda for its six-month *EU presidency*, starting in July, putting particular stress on strengthening social protection for workers and promoting ideas for the future EU development. Prime Minister Verhofstadt discloses plans to widen the agenda of the December's Summit meeting at Laeken in Brussels to a "global project for Europe that would answer the fundamental question of how to structure political life in an enlarged EU".

ECB's chief economist Issing says there is no reason for pessimism about the *euro-zone economy* because,

---

[196] A. Beattle and S. Fidler, "France raises pressure on ECB to cut interest rates", *Financial Times*, 30 April 2001.

even if it is slowing, it is still expected to grow this year in line with, or even above, its long-term trend rate. The inflation rate which stood at 2.6% in March, "should not distract attention from the fact that the medium-term outlook for price stability has improved as indicated by monetary developments, and also owing to the moderation in economic activity".[197]

4 May

The National Bank of Hungary and the country's government agree to widen the forint's trading band. The currency will be allowed to trade in a range of 15% above and below a midpoint daily set, compared with 2.25% on either side of the midpoint previously. The new regime is the first step toward the EU's exchange rate mechanism, *ERM II.*

10 may

The Governing Council of the ECB decides to lower the minimum bid rate on the main refinancing operation and the *interest rates* on both the marginal lending facility and the deposit facility by a 0.25 percentage point to 4.5%, 5.5% and 3.5% respectively. The ECB justifies the decision by pointing to lower inflation pressures as growth slows, wages remain stable and recent spikes in inflation are deemed temporary. The rate reduction comes as a surprise. Earlier, ECB's Vice President Noyer, said, "We have kept and are keeping interest rates on hold." ECB President Duisenberg concedes that surprising markets is not something the bank strives for. "Sometimes it's unavoidable. That's a fact of life. New facts lead to new assessments. They sometimes lead to new conclusions. That is what happened."

*Dutch inflation* is expected to remain among Europe's highest. April consumer prices are expected to rise within a range of 4.4% to 4.8% year to year, more than double the euro-zone's price stability ceiling set at 2% by the ECB. Apart from that, four other countries in the euro-zone (Germany, France,

---

[197] T. Barber, "Euro-zone inflation outlook 'better' ", *Financial Times*, 4 May, 2001.

Spain and Ireland) report higher than expected inflation. Taken together average inflation in the euro-zone might have risen to as high as 2.9% in April from 2.6% in March.

17 May

The EU and Russia declare that they want to set up a high-level group forming a *"common European econ-omic area"* including Russia. They also agree to study ways of denominating more of their two-way trade in euros. The EU is Russia's largest trading partner, accounting for roughly a third of Russia's exports and imports. Commission President Prodi says the new group is necessary because, in the future, both economies will be more and more entwined.

23 May

The Governing Council of the ECB decides that the minimum bid rate on the main refinancing operations and the *interest rates* on the marginal lending facility and the deposit facility will remain unchanged at 4.5%, 5.5% and 3.5% respectively.[198]

28 May

French Prime Minister Jospin spells out a vision of the EU as a *"federation of nation states"* thereby rejecting the German Chancellor's idea of federalism and distancing himself from the French President Chirac's idea of a "pioneer group" to forge ahead with integration. "Europe is first and foremost a political undertaking and it is the 'content' that comes first and the framework afterwards," Mr. Jospin says.[199] The Prime Minister proposes to keep the existing balance between the Commission, the European Parliament and the Council of Ministers. But as part of his plans to make the EU's institutions work better, he suggests:

---

[198] On May 15, 2001, the *Federal Reserve* decided to cut short-term interest rates by a 0.50 percentage point reducing the federal funds rate to 4%, the lowest level since April 1994. With its fifth half-point cut since the beginning of the year, the move made it the most aggressive monetary policy easing since Alan Greenspan became chairman of the Fed in 1987.

[199] R. Graham, "Jospin rejects the German EU model", *Financial Times*, 29 May 2001.

1. The presidency of the Commission to be chosen by the largest group in the European Parliament, elected with additional regional representation.
2. The creation of a "Congress" formed from national parliaments which would meet and consult with EU institutions and hold an annual State of the Union debate.
3. The Council should have the right to dissolve the European Parliament.
4. The European Council of heads of state should meet every two months instead of twice a year and form a permanent ministerial council, to co-ordinate with the Commission.

Mr. Jospin explicitly rejects any model based on the German federal system or that of the US. "If, on the other hand, federation means a gradual controlled process of sharing competence's or transferring competencies to the nation level, then this refers to the federation of nation states coined by Jacques Delors, and is a concept I fully support". At the presentation of his vision, Mr. Jospin reinforces his previous suggestions that the EU enhance its social legislation with the adoption of a social treaty, the firming up of tax harmonisation, and a tighter legal framework to enshrine the role of public services in the EU. The German government has little to say about Mr. Jospin's ideas. In Britain, the Labour government says it welcomes the French intergovernmentalist vision.

31 May    The *euro* slides with $0.844 to a six-month low after ECB President Duisenberg's remark that the exchange rate "only becomes important if it no longer supports our inflation target in a serious way".

Governor Fazio of the *Banca d'Italia* delivers a sharp warning about the state of *Italy's public finances*, declaring that Rome will exceed "by a significant amount" the deficit target it has pledged to its European partners this year (0.8% of GDP). His stern warning comes at little surprise to international economists given the prevailing view that Italy's deficit target cannot be attained.

In a decisive move resolving internal differences ahead of the EU Summit in Gothenburg, Member States agree a common position for negotiations with applicant countries over their adoption of EU rules on *free movement of capital*. The day before, Sweden brokered a compromise on the free movement of workers that would enable EU countries to admit labour from new Member States after two years while permitting other Member States to delay the entry of workers for up to seven years. The EU will now be able to present a united front when negotiating the chapters on the free movement of capital and labour with deputy negotiators from the twelve candidate countries.

7 June

In the *Irish referendum* on the Treaty of Nice, 54% of the voters say "no" thereby refusing to incorporate the Nice Treaty into the Irish constitution. This implies that Ireland is in effect blocking its required ratification by all the member states. Adoption of the Treaty implies changes in the EU Treaty, changes which must be unanimously approved by the existing members. Ireland is the only country that held a referendum on the proposed changes. The vote causes consternation in the rest of the EU and dismay in eastern Europe.

In Great Britain the Blair Government wins the *elections* with a convincing majority. However, the current British press is curiously divided on whether or not Mr. Blair has the referendum on the euro in his sight. In the cabinet, the pro-euro R. Cook has been replaced as Foreign Secretary by a eurosceptic, J. Straw. Much is made of the five economic tests the government has said must be met before it calls a referendum.

15-16 June

At the *Gothenburg Summit* European leaders make the process of enlarging the EU "irreversible" by committing themselves to taking in members from the south and east of the continent in about three years. The decision has been made after France dropped its objections to tightening the enlargement table for entry and Germany which had resisted the idea of setting 2002 as the date for completing negotiations, caved in after being isolated among the other fourteen EU heads of state. The decision implies that the EU will open its doors to enlargement for the best prepared countries which should be able to complete negotiations by the end of 2002. The objective is that they should participate in the European Parliament elections in June 2004 as members. The Irish referendum rejecting the Treaty of Nice served as a catalyst to agreement on enlargement. A spur was also provided by the presence of all twelve candidates in negotiation with the EU as well as Turkey, which has not begun talks. But enlargement negotiations cannot be concluded until the EU has a common position on agriculture and regional policy including structural funds for the poorer regions.

21 June        In Dublin the Governing Council of the ECB decides to leave short term interest rates unchanged. According to ECB President Duisenberg the levels remain appropriate to ensure that the euro area economy will be able to maintain price stability in the medium term. He also says that, in spite of the significant uncertainty in the global economic outlook, the ECB believes the euro-zone will grow this year and in 2002 at a rate broadly in line with its long-term average of 2 to 2.5% a year.

27 June        The Commission warns four countries – Germany, France, Italy and Portugal – that they could have trouble meeting their EU *budget commitments* unless they take steps to restrain government spending. Among the biggest problems could occur in Germany and Italy which together represent 37% of EU's GDP. The Commission worries that poor budgetary management could limit the room governments have to manoeuvre in the event of a serious economic

downturn. As it is, only six euro-countries – Spain, Ireland, Luxembourg, the Netherlands, Austria and Finland – are in a position to let their budget deficits expand in the event of a downturn.

28 June

In Italy, Silvio Berlusconi's new centre-right government which won last month's elections unveils a package of *fiscal measures* aimed at boosting Italy's economic growth rate including the decision to extend the use of fixed-term labour contracts. The legislation aims to give tax breaks to companies that reinvest their profits, an amnesty for black market companies that enter the official sector and the abolition of inheritance tax. Expectations that the budget deficit will significantly exceed pledges made to the country's European partners have ruled out any chance of the new government making significant cuts in personal taxation to boost growth.

1 July

Belgium takes over the *presidency of the EU.*

The radical decentralisation introduced in Belgium since 1994 implies that all six of Belgian regional governments of Flanders, Wallonia and Brussels will have their turn at managing meetings of EU ministers. The Belgian government will chair meetings including foreign affairs, economy and finance and agriculture.

11 July

Italy's new government warns that reckless spending in the final months of the previous centre-left administration could expand the nation's *budget deficit* in 2001 to 2.6% of GDP, compared with the EU's target of 0.8% of GDP. The new Finance Minister G. Tremonti says he will introduce short-term measures aimed at containing spending between now and the end of the year by around €6.2 billion. These measures, to include the sale of government real estate, will not be sufficient to achieve the 0.8% deficit target.

22 July

In its report about employment, the Commission says

European Union is moving faster than expected towards its goal of an employment rate of 70% by 2010. In the year 2000, the employment rate rose above 63%. But the outlook seems to be much bleaker for the candidate countries of Central and Eastern Europe, where youth and female unemployment continues to rise. The report refers to the aim set out at the 1999 Lisbon Summit to lift the employment rate of the eligible population to 70% by the end of the decade, compared with 75% in Japan and the US.

26 July

The ECB plays down a sharp acceleration in the *euro-zone's money supply* which grew at an annual rate of 6.1% in June, its highest level since April 2000 and well above the May's rate of 5.1%. The ECB says the increase has been caused partly by a statistical effect, since a fall in M3 growth in June 2000 had dropped out of the calculation of the annual rate. Moreover, the latest M3 data include money market paper and short-term debt securities held by non-residents of the euro-zone, which the ECB says might have distorted the June figure upwards by a 0.75% percentage point. Once these factors are taken into account, M3 growth is closer to the ECB's loose target of 4.5%.

3 August

The Italian government expects a *budget deficit* of between 1.5% and 1.9% of GDP, far worse than repeatedly promised to the EU. The IMF, after a week of consultations in Italy, says the government's plan to have a deficit of 0.5% of GDP next year and balance the budget in 2003 is feasible, provided government spending remains very tight and is reduced by the equivalent of 1% of GDP in 2002.

16 August

The German Minister of Finance Eichel, advocates a more flexible approach to the German inspired Stability and Growth Pact agreed four years ago. He thinks it useful to focus more on *spending targets* than following rigid annual deficit reduction. At the Gothenburg Summit meeting in June, EU leaders already hinted at greater flexibility by saying that any analysis of Member States' budgetary position should be "cyclically adjusted" to take the economic situation into account.

17 August

The *exchange rate of the euro* rises to nearly $0.92. Since early July the euro has recovered by about 9% against the US dollar.

20 August

The Commission tries to close off a debate over whether limits on EU countries' budgets should be relaxed or reformed, despite signs of dissent from Member States. According to the Monetary Affairs Commissioner Solbes, the *Stability and Growth Pact* already provides some freedom of manoeuvre. Countries with "sustainable" fiscal positions would be allowed to let "automatic stabilisers" – such as a lower tax take and increased social spending – work fully during a time of economic slowdown. Referring to the German Finance Minister's suggestion of a greater flexibility, Mr Solbes says Mr. Eichel has reassured him that he has no intention of relaxing or redefining the terms of the Pact.

25-26 August

France and Italy begin the first stage of the massive *logistical operation* needed to distribute new euro notes and coins using heavily guarded trains and security trucks to move them to regional distribution centres.

4 September

Germany's Finance Minister Eichel says no EU country is likely to meet its *2001 budget objectives* and there is a debate about the degree to which governments can overshoot these goals. Speaking to fellow members of Germany's Social Democratic Party, Mr. Eichel again denies he has questioned the budgetary rules underpinning the euro when he recently suggested spending targets could be planned more easily than budget deficits.

9 September

Spain is setting five challenges to its European partners to modernise and make Europe more competitive when it takes over the rotating *presidency of the EU* in January 2002. These include strengthening transport infra-structures, liberalising the energy market, reinforcing the financial system, introducing greater labour mobility and flexibility, and strengthening education and training. Spanish Prime Minister Aznar, also warns his European partners he will vigorously resist any attempt to loosen the Stability and Growth Pact for the single European currency.

11 September

Expectations of further *rate cuts* from the ECB rise sharply as nervousness sweep through world financial markets caused by terrorist actions in the US.[200] The Bank of England and other central banks offer to supply whatever liquidity might be needed to enable financial institutions to cope with the closure of US financial markets.

Germany, France and Italy will probably have to pledge to cut their *budget deficits*[201] quickly once the economy starts to recover. Their governments missed the opportunity to do that in the previous years when economic growth was stronger. Germany's Finance

[200] On September 11, 2001, global financial markets reacted with horror to the terrorist attacks in New York and Washington with share prices plunging and investors rushing for save havens of gold and government bonds. In the US the Securities and Exchange Commission ordered stock markets to stay closed lasting until September 17.
[201] Euro-zone budget deficits* : 2001 targets versus
reality as % of GDP (surplus (+)/ deficit (-)

| Country | Target 2001 | Predicted |
|---|---|---|
| Belgium | 0.2 | 0.0 |
| Germany | -1.5 | -1.6 |
| Greece | 0.5 | 0.5 |
| Spain | 0.0 | 0.0 |
| France | -1.1 | -1.4 |
| Ireland | 4.3 | 4.2 |
| Italy | -0.8 | -1.5 |
| Netherlands | 0.7 | 0.6 |
| Austria | -1.1 | -1.1 |
| Portugal | -1.5 | -1.5 |
| Finland | 4.7 | 5.5 |

* source: EU Stability Programs, Fitch ratings agency

Minister Eichel admits that the government's 2.25% growth target for 2002 may not be met, having also acknowledged recently that this year the economy will grow at less than the 2% target envisaged. The French Finance Minister Fabius is still positive and repeats that growth in France is superior to that of many of her neighbours. However he has repeatedly been obliged to downgrade his predictions.

12 September

The terrorist strikes on the US threaten to drive the *global economy into recession*. Major central banks around the world pumped more than €88 billion into financial markets to prevent gridlock as financial markets gyrated, foreign airlines grounded flights to the US and Japanese auto makers idled some plants. "We are committed to ensuring that this tragedy will not be compounded by disruption to the global economy, the G-7 financial officials said in a joint statement. ECB President Duisenberg, for his part, cautions that it is far too early to judge what the consequence will be. He tells the European parliament's Economic and Monetary Affairs Committee "there will be no recession". The ECB interest rates are both "appropriate for the maintenance of price stability in the medium term" and "in no way a hindrance to economic growth resuming its potential path".

17 September

The Governing Council of the ECB decides to lower the minimum bid rate on the main refinancing operation and the *interest rates* on both the marginal lending facility and the deposit facility by a 0.50 percentage point to 3.75%, 4.75% and 2.75% respectively. The ECB's rate cut was announced three hours after the US Federal Reserve's decision to lower its target for the federal funds rate and the discount rate both by a 0.50 percentage point to 3% and 2.5% respectively.[202] This is the first time that the

---

[202] On the same day the World Bank and the IMF announced that they would cancel their annual meetings scheduled for Washington later that month.

ECB changes interest rates between scheduled sessions of its policy making Governing Council and that the Council itself has held an emergency meeting to discuss ECB's monetary policy. The central banks in Canada, Switzerland and Sweden follow the decisions of the Federal Reserve. Britain, Japan, Hong Kong, Denmark and Kuwait will follow one day later.

According to data released by Eurostat, *inflation rate* in the euro-zone slipped to 2.7% in August from 2.8% in July. It is the third successive monthly fall, but it still leaves the annual rate above the ECB's target ceiling of 2%.

21-23 September

The EU Council of Ministers produces a downward revision in *EU growth expectations* for 2001 but also documents considerable confidence that conditions are in place for recovery. EU Commissioner Solbes predicts that growth will be below 2%. A statement issued by the Ministers restates their commitment to the implementation of the Stability and Growth Pact.

Special EU Summit in Brussels issues a *communiqué* saying the attacks of September 11 in the US imply a "more pronounced" economic slowdown than had been predicted. According to the statement, it is possible for "automatic stabilisers" to play a role. That undercuts the EU's *Stability and Growth Pact*. The ECB accepts this slippage, saying it is within the Pact's rules, which allow for flexibility in times of economic downturn.

27 September

The ECB makes clear that it would not let rising *money supply growth* stand in the way of another rate cut. Annual M3 growth rose to 6.7% in August from 6.4% in July. At such levels, M3 growth is well above the ECB's reference value, or loose target, of 4.5% a year.

1 October

In Sweden an *opinion poll* shows that 44% of Swedes favour membership of the single currency, with 42%

against and 14% undecided. Sweden is one of the three countries, alongside Britain and Denmark, to be members of the EU but not of the single currency.

7 October

Informal meeting between the French Prime Minister Jospin and the German Chancellor Schröder. Both leaders agree that the EU needs a co-ordinated response if euro-zone governments feel the need to react to the sharply deteriorating economic climate. France is lobbying Germany to soften its opposition to making the *Stability and Growth Pact* more flexible to help offset the impact of an economic slowdown. However, an attempt to present a common front failed to conceal the different positions.

9 October

According to figures published by the BIS, London has retained its dominance as a *global financial centre* in spite of the introduction of the euro. The data drawing on research by 48 central banks show that more than 30% of spot foreign exchange turnover is dealt in London. This level is still the largest share of any centre in the world by far. The US take 16%, Japan and Singapore 9% and 6% respectively. Frankfurt, London's main rival in Europe, increased its share slightly to 5.4% of trading while the euro-zone collectively takes 13.5%.

11 October

The Governing Council of the ECB decides to leave short-term *interest rates* unchanged. ECB President Duisenberg says that a further move after the rate cut in September might not have encouraged stability. By holding back – the US reduced short term interest rates for the 9th time this year[203] – the ECB hopes to show a steady hand and a confidence in the future that would be transmitted to the markets and to consumers.

---

[203] On October 2, 2001, the Federal Reserve reduced the federal funds rate and the discount rate both by a 0.50 percentage point to 2.5 and 2% respectively. The Bank's action took short-term interest rates below the year on year core inflation rate – 2.7% in August – for the first time since 1993.

EU Commission President Prodi calls for an acceleration of *European integration* in response to the terrorist attacks on the United States. He says the EU needs now to turn to social issues, sustainable development, justice and security, after having almost completed economic and monetary integration. Greater convergence in foreign policy and closer relations in justice and home affairs could help to place differences among member states "in perspective" and ease solutions to EU institutional problems. A special convention, which is due to meet next year to prepare far reaching EU reforms in 2004, should focus on aims rather than on technical matters.

15 October

Speaking in Warsaw, ECB Vice President Noyer says Central and Eastern European countries should not try to qualify for euro-zone membership by suppressing inflation so quickly that they hinder the growth of people's real incomes. Referring to the Maastricht Treaty conditions he points out that the strict respect of the inflation criterion should be seen as a medium-term objective and not as an immediate goal, if progress towards achievement of this criterion would jeopardise the catching up process. His speech amounts to a signal from European policymakers that they want the *candidate states* to prove that they can achieve real convergence within the euro-zone economy rather than simply nominal convergence with the Maastricht criteria.

A group of EU leaders and Commissioners publishes the manifesto *"A wake up call for Europe"*. It reflects, among other things, contemporary thinking on the need to involve national parliaments more closely in debating revisions to constitutional arrangements, accession treaties and the financing of the EU. But variations between the English and French versions of the text show some confusion. Fearing that the rules negotiated at the Nice Summit, for "reinforced co-operation" on specific projects among a small group of Member States could prove too complex, the French text speaks of an *avant garde* group which should be prepared to power ahead with integration. The paper is sharply criticised by some EU diplomats as a pot-pourri of ideas most of which are old and some of which are inconsistent.

16 October

The German Chancellor Schröder underlines the growing impatience of euro-zone governments with the ECB's monetary policy by making clear he wants an early interest rate cut to help Europe out if its economic slowdown. He recognises that the ECB would be unable to pursue "a reasonable monetary policy" if governments fail to adhere to their Stability and Growth Pact. But he adds: "I won't comment on whether the peak of common sense has been reached at the ECB." Mr. Schröder follows the French Finance Minister who some days earlier declared: "I am convinced here are margins for manoeuvre in monetary policy."[204]

19 October

EU Summit in Ghent where the EU leaders agree to stick to *budgetary rigour and structural economic reforms*. Furthermore, they accept that the ECB will only have scope for a significant easing of monetary policy if inflation falls by more than already expected. At a press conference ECB President Duisenberg rebuts any idea that this means a policy change of the bank. The ECB was criticised by France, Germany and Belgium for its reluctance to cut interest rates. The leaders' statement mirrors little of the gloom about Europe's economic prospects expressed by forecasters. They acknowledge that the slowdown has been accentuated by the events of September 11 but express confidence that the "EU's sound economic fundamentals" and "fiscal consolidation already achieved" will help ensure the impact is limited and temporary. The Summit also says EU countries should allow the so-called

[204] T. Barber, P. Norman and R. Graham, "EU leaders show impatience with ECB", *Financial Times*, 17 October 2001.

automatic stabilisers to play their role in accordance with the Stability and Growth Pact. Apart from this, Belgian's Prime Minister Verhofstadt told his fellow leaders that he will present a first draft of the Laeken declaration on Europe's constitutional future at the end of next month. The convention will be chaired by a president to be decided at Laeken and steered by a presidium plus one representative of each of the Member States, national parliaments, the European Parliament and the Commission. The declaration should commit the EU to more integrated foreign defence and immigration policies.

29 October

In Copenhagen, *Bundesbank* President Welteke says there is definitely good news, with annual consumer price inflation having fallen between May and September. "If, in the Governing Council of the ECB, we see the possibility of reducing interest rates further without compromising price stability, we will do so." However, he underlines the ECB's view that those euro-zone governments running *budget deficits* even after last year's strong economic growth must not retreat from fiscal consolidation. "The appropriate stance for fiscal policy now is to make use of in-built stabilisers. There is no room for extra spending programmes in the euro area as these would compromise consolidation efforts."[205] *Bundesbank* Vice President J. Stark says the German economy will probably have the weakest growth in the euro-zone this year but it is not in recession. He refers to the Stability and Growth Pact that defines a "severe recession" as an annual fall in GDP of at least 0.75%.

6 November

Just nine months after criticising Ireland for policies fuelling an overheating economy, the Commission withdraws its complaints. Citing the dramatically slowing global economy, compounded by the foot-and-mouth crisis and the terrorist attacks in the US, the Commission concedes that the *Irish sanctions*

---

[205] T, Barber, "Bundsbank chief warns on spending", *Financial Times*, 30 October 2001.

have lost part of their force. The country grew by more than 11% last year, the fastest among European countries.

EU Council of Ministers meeting and informal gathering of the Eurogroup. Reporting on these meetings, EU Commissioner Solbes joins Germany's Finance Minister Eichel in expressing his "personal conviction" that Europe will escape *recession* despite a new round of increasingly gloomy euro-zone economic statistics. Hopes of an early cut in interest rates raise after the Euro Group meeting, when ECB President Duisenberg says he expects euro-zone inflation to fall "well below" the bank's 2% target ceiling early next year and stay there. Mr. Solbes cautiously upbeat appraisal of Europe's economic outlook comes in the late phase of preparing its next economic forecasts for 2001 and 2002 to be published on November 21.

8 November

The Governing Council of the ECB decides to lower the minimum bid rate on the main refinancing operation and the *interest rates* on the marginal lending facility and the deposit facility by 0.50 percentage point to 3.25%, 4.25% and 2.25% respectively.[206] It is the fourth move this year with a total reduction of 1.5 percentage points. The decision is followed by the Bank of England. The ECB will now make interest rate announcements only once a month, hoping to reduce the speculation from its previous fortnightly decisions. Mr. Duisenberg says financial markets should listen more to him when trying to understand the course of monetary policy and less to his often unruly chorus of 17 fellow governing council members.

12 November

Commission President Prodi calls on EU member states to agree a *code of conduct for budgetary and*

[206] On November 6, 2001, the Federal Reserve reduced the federal funds rate for the 10th time in 2001 by a 0.50 point reducing its benchmark rate target to 2% from 2.5% and its more symbolic discount rate to 1.5% from 2%.

2001

*economic policies* which would go beyond the Stability and Growth Pact. The code would need to set out the principles underlying the member states economic policies. It must also provide "criteria for deploying various economic policy instruments to increase capacity for growth and respond to unforeseen events that may affect the union as a whole, or individual countries". Mr. Prodi's call is reminiscent of past calls from France for an economic government for the euro-zone. It is also marked an attempt to inject momentum into ideas for strengthened economic policy co-ordination in the euro-zone, with increased Commission involvement. Without giving further details, Mr. Prodi says the Commission will present proposals for a code of conduct.

14 November

During a conference in Vienna, OPEC signals it intends to fight a price war, postponing a cut of 1.5 million barrels of oil a day until non-OPEC producers cut output by 500,000 barrels a day. Analysts say non-OPEC supply has grown by almost 3 million barrels a day since the first quarter of 1999. At the same time, OPEC supply has fallen by about 500,000 barrels a day, and the prospect of a loss of another 1.5 million barrels a day is widely seen as unacceptable. *Oil prices* fell sharply after the decision became known. On London's International Petroleum Exchange, North Sea benchmark Brent crude settled at $18.75 a barrel.

18 November

Italy's President Ciampi sends a blunt warning to Britain, France and Germany to abandon the idea of a return to *a Europe dominated by great powers*. Speaking in Berlin, the President makes clear that Italy expects to be in the front rank of EU countries. To this end, he calls for a "core group" of countries, large and small, that would move toward together on a path of closer integration. A future enlarged EU would divide two groups: the first would be a "broader" Europe anchored around the *acquis communautaire,* the rules and obligations related to membership and the single market, as well as the charter of fundamental rights. The second would be a "smaller, open-end group" at the forefront of progress. This idea of a two-speed Europe may draw fire from the candidate countries fearing that they could be relegated to second-class status as the present fiftien members seek to preserve their rights and privileges. Leading German politicians on the left and right are pressing for a radical *reorganisation of the EU* to deal with the likely "Big Bang" enlargement to Central and Eastern Europe.

Germany's Federal President J. Rau calls for a *European constitution* that would contain a charter of fundamental rights, a separation of powers between the member states and Brussels, and a two-chamber European legislature. The constitutional debate on the future of Europe is gaining momentum as negotiations with the twelve candidate countries reach a climax next year and the EU prepares to launch its own constitutional convention next spring. Experts believe that the EU will break with tradition and admit as many as ten new members at once.

23 November

In Birmingham, British Prime Minister Blair delivers his strongest signal that *joining the euro* could be in Britain's best interests by saying that the country has suffered from a "tragedy" of missed opportunities since the EU was founded: "The tragedy for British politics and for Britain is that too many politicians have consistently failed, not just in the 1950s but up to the present day, to appreciate the reality of European integration and in so doing they have failed Britain's interests." Mr. Blair goes through the history of Britain's post-war policy towards Europe, describing it as a history of opportunities missed in the name of illusions: "First we said it wouldn't happen, then we said it wouldn't work, then we said we wouldn't need it. But it did happen and Britain was left behind at every step of the way", he says.[207]

2001

27 November

Spanish Prime Minister Aznar warns of a return to *"eurosclerosis"* and issues a new call to European leaders to step up efforts to liberalise the European economy. Signalling his determination ahead of next March EU Summit in Barcelona, Mr. Aznar says it is time to tear down barriers to the creation of a single European market in energy, financial services and broadband telecommunications.

28 November

In a report published by the Commission, euro-zone countries are warned against allowing their budget deficits to exceed 3% of their national output, despite the effects of the economic slowdown. The Commission also says that the *Stability and Growth Pact* is working "reasonably well". But the current economic downturn underlines the need to get budgets into balance or surplus in the medium term, and an appropriate policy mix will involve "a cautious fiscal policy". The Commission repeats that inflation will fall below 2% at the beginning of 2002.

30 November

Belgian proposals to map out a radical agenda for the future of Europe at the EU Summit in Laeken runs into strong opposition from the other EU member states which feel they go too far towards a *federal European state*. The proposals, drawn up by Belgian Prime Minister Verhofstadt, an enthusiastic supporter of greater European integration, turn into a draft declaration on "the future of the European Union" outlining how the EU should reform its institutions and working methods by 2004 to be able to cope with an enlargement from fifteen to possibly twenty seven member states. Although Mr. Verhofstadt receives broad support for his ideas in Berlin, vital aspects of his plan struck raw nerves in London and

[207] B. Groom, "Blair set to deliver his strongest signal so far on joining euro", *Financial Times*, 23 November, 2001.

Paris. Britain and France object to the document's second part, the "challenges and reforms" to be considered by a special convention in 2002 which will prepare for the next round of negotiations among governments on changes to EU structures and operations.

US Federal Reserve's Chairman Greenspan speaks in Washington to the Euro 50 Group Roundtable about the introduction of the euro. He points out that, although the single currency will certainly bring efficiency gains to Euroland citizens and even to those outside, it is being curbed in its development by *sclerotic labour markets:* "Over the decades, Europe has sought to protect its workers from some of the presumed harsher aspects of free-market competition", but "the level of employment in the United States has turned out to be higher as firms find hiring less risky and, hence, are more willing to add employees to the roster".[208] This has been the "dividend" given off by America's ability to implement the new technological breakthroughs of the past decade. "Much, if not most, of the rate of return from the newer technologies result from cost reduction, which on a consolidated basis largely means the reduction of labour costs." As a result, the Fed Chairman continues to see large capital flows from Europe into dollar-denominated securities, keeping the dollar strong.

4 December            Commission President Prodi, responding to criticism that he has failed to show leadership, says he has been urged by fellow Commissioners to take a more visible role in driving forward *European integration.* He identifies three priorities for the rest of his term: the successful introduction of the euro notes and coins, enlargement of the EU to Central, Eastern and Southern Europe; and faster liberalisation of energy,

---

[208] "Greenspan on the euro. Either a social model or a strong currency – make a choice", *Wall Street Journal*, 4 December 2001.

financial services and other utility markets. In his view, the Commission has lost political power since the Maastricht Treaty a decade ago. Mr. Prodi is pushing for a convention of parliamentarians, national governments and diplomatic experts, to prepare options on Europe's constitutional future. He rejects any abandonment of the Commission's political role. "I think it is a battle we must win. The cost of a different outcome would be the end of a political Europe and instead a Europe of just a free trade area."[209]

6 December

The Governing Council of the ECB decides that for the year 2002, the reference value for the annual growth rate of the broad *monetary aggregate* M3 will remain at 4.5%.

11 December[210]

*Consumer prices* in France fell by 0.3% in November, pulling the annual rate down to 1.2%, the lowest level since the start of the year. Following 0.2% monthly declines in German and Dutch inflation, France's figures suggest a 2% euro-zone inflation in November, which is in line with the ECB's target ceiling.

14 December

The *euro* becomes tangible to millions of Europeans as the twelve euro-countries put coin sets on sale to the public. The Netherlands is the only member state whose citizens can cash in a free government coupon for a pack providing one each of the euro coins (the so called "Zalmkit"), which turns out to be a great success.

14-15 December

At the EU Summit in Laeken support is given to the *"Laeken Declaration"*, a hard-fought pledge to draft a new EU constitution in 2002. A special convention will be created on the future of Europe, chaired by

---

[209] P. Norman and L. Barber, "Prodi strikes back", *Financial Times*, 5 December 2001.
[210] On 11 December, 2001, the Federal Reserve lowered its target for the federal funds rate from 2% to 1.75% and the discount rate from 1.5 to 1.25%. It was the 11 th time in 2001 that the Fed had cut short term rates. For the first time in 40 years, the federal funds rate is lower than 2%.

ex-French President Giscard d'Estaing, to outline possible changes to the EU's treaties and working methods in 2004. While the declaration offers a chance to strengthen the Council of government heads, it also holds out the possibility of enhancing the Commission and the European Parliament. The review of powers can lead both to restoring tasks to the member states and to assigning new missions to the Union, or to the extension of existing powers. France and Italy reject a Belgian *compromise package* and Sweden expresses serious reservations about the proposed new agencies to be established throughout the EU.

31 December

The use of the *euro notes and coins* will begin on January 1, 2002 in the twelve euro countries.[211] Speaking about "A new future for Europe", ECB President Duisenberg pays tribute to Europe's leaders over the past decades. He remembers them as the true leaders because they had the foresight to take bold actions that would make Europe a place where people, ideas, and commerce would intermingle. They had the vision to see that a common currency would be an essential part of that, and would represent a formidable leap in the European integration process.

---

[211] In the Netherlands, the end-date of legal tender is 28 January, 2002, in Ireland 9 February, 2002, in Austria, Belgium, Finland, Greece, Italy, Luxembourg, Portugal and Spain 28 February, 2002. In Germany the end-date was 31 December, 2001, but in line with the "Joint Declaration" the use of DM banknotes and coins is allowed at least until 28 February, 2002.

# Appendix I

**Articles of the Treaty establishing the European Economic Community (Rome, 25 March 1957) [212]**

Article 3g (Treaty of 1957)

For the purposes set out in Article 2, the activities of the Community shall include, as provided in this Treaty and in accordance with the timetable set out therein:
(g) the application of procedures by which the economic policies of Member States can be coordinated and disequilibria in their balances of payments remedied.

Article 8 paragraphs 1,2,3,5,6 (Treaty of 1957)

1. The common market shall be progressively established during a transitional period of twelve years. This transitional period shall be divided into three stages of four years each; the length of each stage may be altered in accordance with the provisions set out below.
2. To each stage there shall be assigned a set of actions to be initiated and carried through concurrently.
3. Transition from the first to the second stage shall be conditional upon a finding that the objectives specifically laid down in this Treaty for the first stage have in effect been attained in substance and that, subject to the exceptions and procedures provided for in this Treaty the obligations have been fulfilled. This finding shall be made at the end of the fourth year by the Council, acting unanimously on a report from the Commission. A Member State may not, however, prevent unanimity by relying upon the non-fulfilment of its own obligations. Failing unanimity, the first stage shall automatically be extended for one year. At the end of the fifth year, the Council shall make its finding under the same conditions. Failing unanimity,

---

[212] Revised on 28 February 1986 as part of the *Single European Act* (which entered into force on 1 July 1987) and on 7 February 1992 as part of the *Treaty on European Union* which became effective on 1 November 1993.

the first stage shall automatically be extended for a further year. At the end of the sixth year, the Council shall make its finding, acting by a qualified majority on a report from the Commission.

5. The second and third stages may not be extended or curtailed except by a decision of the Council, acting unanimously on a proposal from the Commission.

6. Nothing in the preceding paragraphs shall cause the transitional period to last more than fifteen years after the entry into force of this Treaty.

## Article 67 (Treaty of 1957)

1. During the transitional period and to the extent necessary to ensure the proper functioning of the common market, Member States shall progressively abolish between themselves all restrictions on the movement of capital belonging to persons resident in Member States and any discrimination based on the nationality or on the place of residence of the parties or on the place where such capital is invested.

2. Current payments connected with the movement of capital between Member States shall be freed from all restrictions by the end of the first stage at the latest.

## Article 104 (Treaty of 1957)

Each Member State shall pursue the economic policy needed to ensure the equilibrium of its overall balance of payments and to maintain confidence in its currency, while taking care to ensure a high level of employment and a stable level of prices.

## Article 105[213] (Treaty of 1957)

1. In order to facilitate attainment of the objectives set out in Article 104 Member States shall coordinate their economic policies. They shall for this purpose provide for cooperation between appropriate administrative departments and between their central banks. The Commission shall submit to the Council recommendation on how to achieve such cooperation.

2. In order to promote coordination of the policies of Member States in the monetary field to the full extent needed for the functioning of the common market, a Monetary Committee with advisory status is hereby set up. It shall have the following tasks:

---

[213] In the revised *EC Treaty* of 1992 the obligation to establish the *Monetary Committee* is included in article 109c.

– to keep under review the monetary and financial situation of the Member States and of the Community and the general payments system of the Member States and to report regularly thereon to the Council and to the Commission:

– to deliver opinions at the request of the Council or of the Commission or on its own initiative, for submission to these institutions.

The Member States and the Commission shall each appoint two members of the Monetary Committee.

Article 108[214] (Treaty of 1957)

1. Where a Member State is in difficulties or is seriously threatened with difficulties as regards its balance of payments either as a result of an overall disequilibrium in its balance of payments, or as a result of the type of currency at its disposal, and where such difficulties are liable in particular to jeopardise the functioning of the common market or the progressive implementation of the common commercial policy, the Commission shall immediately investigate the position of the State in question and the action which, making use of all the means at its disposal, that State has taken or may take in accordance with the provisions of article 104. The Commission shall state what measures it recommends the State concerned to take. If the action taken by a Member State and the measures suggested by the Commission do not prove sufficient to overcome the difficulties which have arisen or which threaten, the Commission shall after consulting the Monetary Committee recommend to the Council the granting of mutual assistance and appropriate methods therefore. The Commission shall keep the Council regularly informed of the situation and of how it is developing.

2. The Council, acting by a qualified majority, shall grant such mutual assistance; it shall adopt directives or decisions laying down the conditions and details of such assistance, which may take such forms as:

(a) a concerted approach to or within other international organisations to which Member States may have recourse;

(b) measures needed to avoid deflection of trade where the State which is in difficulties maintains or reintroduces quantitative restrictions against third currencies;

(c) the granting of limited credits by other Member States, subject to their agreement.

During the transitional period, mutual assistance may also take the form of

---

[214] Article 109h in the *EC Treaty* of 1992. This Article has been extented by stipulation 4 which reads as follows: "Subject to Article 109(k), this Article shall cease to apply from the beginning of the third stage".

special reductions in customs duties or enlargements of quotas in order to facilitate and increase in imports from the State which is in difficulties, subject to the agreement of the States by which such measures would have to be taken.

3. If the mutual assistance recommended by the Commission is not granted by the Council or if the mutual assistance granted and the measure taken are insufficient, the Commission shall authorise the State which is in difficulties to take protective measures, the conditions and details of which the Commission shall determine.

Such authorisation may be revoked and such conditions and details may be changed by the Council acting by a qualified majority.

Article 109 (Treaty of 1957)

1. Where a sudden crisis in the balance of payments occurs and a decision within the meaning of Article 108(2) is not immediately taken, the Member State concerned may, as a precaution, take the necessary protective measures. Such measures must cause the least possible disturbance in the functioning of the common market and must not be wider in scope than is strictly necessary to remedy the sudden difficulties which have risen.

2. The Commission and the other Member States shall be informed of such protective measures not later than when they enter into force. The Commission may recommend to the Council the granting of mutual assistance under Article 108.

3. After the Commission has delivered an opinion and the Monetary Committee has been consulted, the Council may, acting by a qualified majority, decide that the State concerned shall amend, suspend or abolish the protective measures referred to above.

Article 235 (Treaty of 1957)

If action by the Community should prove necessary to attain, in the course of the operation of the common market, one of the objectives of the Commission and this Treaty has not provided the necessary powers, the Council shall, acting unanimously on a proposal from the Commission and after consulting the Assembly, take the appropriate measures.

Article 236 (Treaty of 1957)

The Government of any Member State or the Commission may submit to the Council proposals for the amendment of this Treaty.

If the Council, after consulting the Assembly and, where appropriate, the

Commission, delivers an opinion in favour of calling a conference of representatives of the Governors of the Member States, the conference shall be convened by the President of the Council for the purpose of determining by common accord the amendment to be made to this Treaty. The amendments shall enter into force after being ratified by all the Member States in accordance with their respective constitutional requirements.

Article 236 is replaced by the articles N and O in the EU Treaty of 1992 (Title VII Final provisions) which read as follows:

Article N

1. The Government of any Member State or the Commission may submit to the Council proposals for the amendment of the Treaties on which the Union is founded. If the Council, after consulting the European Parliament and, where appropriate, the Commission, delivers an opinion in favour of calling a conference of representatives of the governments of the Member States, the conference shall be convened by the President of the Council for the purpose of determining by common accord the amendments to be made by those Treaties. The European Central Bank shall also be consulted in the case of institutional changes in the monetary area. The amendments shall enter into force after being ratified by all the Member States in accordance with their respective constitutional requirements.
2. A conference of representatives of the governments of the Member States shall be convened in 1996 to examine those provisions of this Treaty for which revisions are provided, in accordance with the objectives set out in Articles A and B.

Article O

Any European State may apply to become a member of the Union. It shall address its application to the Council, which shall act unanimously after consulting the Commission and after receiving the assent of the European Parliament, which shall act by an absolute majority of its component members.
The conditions of admission and the adjustments to the Treaties on which the Union is founded which such admission entails shall be the subject of an agreement between the Member States and the applicant State. This agreement shall be submitted for ratification by all the contracting States in accordance with their respective constitutional requirements.

Article 109g (EC Treaty of 1992)

The currency composition of the ECU basket shall not be changed. From the start of the third stage, the value of the ECU shall be irrevocably fixed in accordance with Article 109l (4).

Article 109l (4) (EC Treaty of 1992)

At the starting date of the third stage, the Council shall, acting with the unanimity of the Member States without a derogation, on a proposal from the Commission and after consulting the ECB, adopt the conversion rates at which their currencies shall be irrevocably fixed and at which irrevocably fixed rate the ECU shall be substituted for these currencies, and the ECU will become a currency in its own right. This measure shall by itself not modify the external value of the ECU. The Council shall, acting according to the same procedure, also take the other measures necessary for the introduction of the ECU as the single currency of those Member States.

# Appendix II

**Redistribution of voting weights within the Council of Ministers**

| EU countries | Population | Current voting weights | Reviewed voting weights |
|---|---|---|---|
| Germany | 82.0 | 10 | 29 |
| United Kingdom | 59.2 | 10 | 29 |
| France | 59.0 | 10 | 29 |
| Italy | 57.6 | 10 | 29 |
| Spain | 39.4 | 8 | 27 |
| Netherlands | 15.8 | 5 | 13 |
| Belgium | 10.2 | 5 | 12 |
| Greece | 10.5 | 5 | 12 |
| Portugal | 10.0 | 5 | 12 |
| Sweden | 8.6 | 4 | 10 |
| Austria | 8.1 | 4 | 10 |
| Denmark | 5.3 | 3 | 7 |
| Finland | 5.2 | 3 | 7 |
| Ireland | 3.7 | 3 | 7 |
| Luxembourg | 0.4 | 2 | 4 |
| | | | |
| Poland | 38.7 | | 27 |
| Romania | 22.5 | | 14 |
| Czech Republic | 10.3 | | 12 |
| Hungary | 10.1 | | 12 |
| Bulgaria | 8.2 | | 10 |
| Slovakia | 5.4 | | 7 |
| Lithuania | 3.7 | | 7 |
| Latvia | 2.4 | | 4 |
| Slovenia | 2.0 | | 4 |
| Estonia | 1.4 | | 4 |
| Cyprus | 0.8 | | 4 |
| Malta | 0.4 | | 3 |

# Bibliography

"All Saints' Day Manifesto for European monetary union" (1975), *The Economist*, 1 November.

Bainbridge, T. with A. Teasdale (1995), *The Penguin Companion to European Union*, Harmondsworth.

Beaufort Wijnholds, J.O. de, S.C.W. Eijffinger and L.H. Hoogduin (1994), *A Framework for Monetary Stability, Financial and Monetary Policy Studies*, Dordrecht.

Beyen, J.W. (1957), *"Grondslagen voor het Nederlandse standpunt met betrekking tot het vraagstuk der Europese integratie"*. Archives of the Nederlandsche Bank, European Economic Community, History 1951-1957.

Bieckmann, F. (1998), "De EMU is 'second best'.", *Management Team*, 5 June.

Brandt, W. (1989), *Willy Brandt Erinnerungen*, Frankfurt am Main.

Cecchini, P. (1988), *The European Challenge 1992: The Benefits of a Single Market*, Aldershot.

Committee of Governors of the Central Banks of the Member States of the EC (1993), *The Implications and Lessons to be drawn from the Recent Exchange Crisis*, Basle.

Dankert, P. (1992), "Challenges and Priorities" in A. Pijpers. ed., *The European Community at the Crossroads*, Dordrecht.

Delors Report (1989), (Committee for the Study of Economic and Monetary Union), *Report on Economic and Monetary Union in the European Community* (with submitted collection of papers), Luxembourg: EC Official Publications.

Deutsche Bundesbank (1995), "Europa: Politische Union durch gemeinsames Geld?", *Auszüge aus Presseartikeln*, no. 50, Frankfurt am Main.

Deutsche Bundesbank (1996), "Die Wirtschafts- und Währungsunion als Stabilitäts-Gemeinschaft", *Auszüge aus Presseartikeln*, no. 10, Frankfurt am Main.

Deutsche Bundesbank (1997), "Right rate for Euro is fraught with difficulty", *Auszüge aus Presseartikeln*, no. 8, Frankfurt am Main.

Deutsche Bundesbank (1998), *Festakt Fünfzig Jahre Deutsche Mark*, Frankfurt am Main.

Directorate-General for Economic and Financial Affairs (1990), "One market, one money", *European Economy*, 44 (October), Belgium, Commission of the EC.

Duchêne, F. (1994), *Jean Monnet. The First Statesman of Interdependence*, New York/London.

EC Commission, *Bulletin van de Europese Gemeenschappen* 1960-1998, Brussels.

EC Commission (1962), *Memorandum of the Commission on the Action Programme of the Community for the Second Stage*, Brussels.

EC Commission (1985), *The Completion of the Internal Market, Commission White Paper for the European Council*, CCOM (85) 310 final, Brussels.

EC Commission (1990a), *Economic and Monetary Union* (Final Proposal), 21 August, Brussels.

EC Commission (1990b), *Economic and Monetary Union: the Economic Rationale and Design of the System* (Working Document), 20 March, Brussels.

EC Commission (1997a), *Action Plan for the Single Market*, Brussels.

EC Commission (1997b), *External Aspects of Economic and Monetary Union, Commission Staff Working Paper*, SEC(97) 803, Brussels.

EC Commission (1998*)*, *Convergence Report*, Brussels.

European Monetary Institute (1995), *Annual Report 1994*, Frankfurt am Main (Dutch version).

European Monetary Institute (1997), *The Single Monetary Policy in Stage Three: Elements of the Monetary Policy Strategy of the ECB*, Frankfurt am Main.

Hommes, P.M. (1980*)*, *Nederland en de Europese eenwording*, The Hague. Keesings Historisch Archief, 1990-1998, Amsterdam.

Issing, O. (2000), "Europe: common money-political union?", *Economic Affairs*, Volume 20, No.1, March.

Leerssen J. Th. and M. van Montfrans, (1993), *Yearbook of European Studies*, Amsterdam.

Lieshout, R.H. (1997), *De organisatie van de West-Europese samenwerking. Een voortdurende strijd om de macht*, Bussum.

*Maastricht Treaty (Treaty on European Union)* (1992), Council and Commission of the European Communities, Luxembourg.

Marjolin, R. (1989), *Architect of European Unity, Memoirs 1911-1986* (translated version), London.

Marsh, D. (1992), *The Bundesbank. The Bank that Rules Europe*, London.

Maystadt, P. (1994), "The Role of the European Monetary Institute" in A. Steinherr, ed. *30 Years of European Monetary Integration from the Werner Plan to EMU*, London/New York.

Monnet, J. (1972), *L'Europe unie: de l'utopie à la réalité*, Lausanne.

Monnet, J. (1978), *Memoirs* (translated version), London.

Ooijen, M. van, I.F. Dekker, R.H. Lieshout and J.M. van der Vleuten (eds.) (1996), *Bouwen aan Europa. Het Europese integratieproces in documenten*, Nijmegen.

Overturf, S.F. (1997*), Monetary and European Union*, New York.

Press articles taken from the Dutch newspapers *Het Financieele Dagblad, De Volkskrant, De Telegraaf.*

Pryce, R. (1973), "Historical development (of the EC)" in P.M. Hommes (1980), *Nederland en de Europese eenwording*, The Hague.

Report to the Council and the Commission on the Creation of Economic and Monetary Union by Stages in the Community, 8 October 1970, 16.956/II/70-N, Brussels.

*Rome Treaty (Treaty establishing the European Economic Community)* (1957), Brussels.

Szász, A. (1989), "Monetary policy in the European Community from the viewpoint of the Nederlandsche Bank", De Nederlandsche Bank, *Quarterly Bulletin* 89/1, pp. 21-27, Amsterdam.

Szász, A (1993), "Towards a single European currency: ECU, franc-fort, Question-Mark", in D.E. Fair and R.J. Raymond, eds., *The new Europe: evolving economic and financial systems in East and West*, Dordrecht, pp. 217-235.

Tsakaloyannis, P. (1992), "Risks and opportunities in the East and South" in A. Pijpers, ed., *The European Community at the Crossroads*, Dordrecht.

Vanthoor, W.F.V. (1996), "The Age of (Western) European Integration: A History of Trial and Error", *De Economist*, 144, no. 2, pp. 137-164.

Vanthoor, W.F.V. (1997), *European Monetary Union since 1848. A Political and Historical Analysis*, Cheltenham.

Vanthoor, W.F.V. (1998), "EMU: A Story of Success if the Rules of the Game are Followed", *Journal of Asian Economics*, vol. 9, no. 2, pp. 193-206.

Weimer, W. (1992), "Keine Währung ohne Staat", *Frankfurter Allgemeine Zeitung*, 18 August.

Wellink, A. (1994), "The economic and monetary relation between Germany and the Netherlands" in A. Bakker, H. Boot, O. Sleijpen and W. Vanthoor (eds.), *Monetary Stability through International Cooperation. Essays in Honour of André Szász*, Dordrecht.

Werner, P. (1971), "Floating and Monetary Union – Without Monetary Union there is no Political Integration", *Intereconomics*, 6 (8).

Werner Report (1970), (Werner Group), *Report to the Council and the Commission on the Realisation by Stages of Economic and Monetary Union in the Community*, special supplement to Bulletin 11-1970 of the European Communities, Luxembourg.

# Index